To Pamela
in appreci[ation of]
all you've done for
James & Josephine
& of course for the
pleasure of knowing
you

Jim Bullock

# THEM AND US

# THEM AND US

JIM BULLOCK O.B.E.

National President of the British
Association of Colliery Management
1956 – 1969

WITH A LAST WORD
BY
LORD ROBENS

SOUVENIR PRESS

Copyright © 1972 by Jim Bullock, O.B.E.
All rights reserved
First published in Great Britain 1972 by Souvenir Press Ltd.,
95 Mortimer Street, London, W.1, and simultaneously
in Canada by J. M. Dent & Sons (Canada) Ltd.,
Ontario, Canada

No part may be reproduced in any form
without permission in writing from the
publisher except by a reviewer who
wishes to quote brief passages for the
purposes of a review

ISBN 0 285 62024 X

Printed in Great Britain by
Clarke, Doble & Brendon Ltd.
Plymouth

To
"My Children"

# CONTENTS

| | | Page |
|---|---|---|
| 1 | In the Beginning | 9 |
| 2 | Bowers Row | 13 |
| 3 | Our Family | 15 |
| 4 | School Life and Early Recollections | 20 |
| 5 | Starting Work Underground | 35 |
| 6 | More About My Father | 45 |
| 7 | Teen Age | 52 |
| 8 | Early Manhood | 70 |
| 9 | Early Marriage | 83 |
| 10 | Early Management Experience | 93 |
| 11 | Colliery Manager | 105 |
| 12 | Managing Welfare and Labour Relations | 112 |
| 13 | Fryston Welfare Hall | 123 |
| 14 | Nationalization of the Coal Mines | 132 |
| 15 | The Birth of a Management Union | 145 |
| 16 | Courage and Humour | 158 |
| 17 | National President of Management Unions | 180 |
| 18 | Leaving Fryston | 203 |
| 19 | Then and Now | 209 |
| 20 | New Home: New Life | 218 |
| 21 | The Unions | 229 |
| 22 | Retirement | 237 |
| | The Last Word | 251 |

## ILLUSTRATIONS

|  | Facing page |
|---|---|
| My father, William Bullock | 64 |
| An early photograph | 64 |
| My maternal grandfather | 65 |
| Fryston Colliery, 1908 | 96 |
| Old road underground | 96 |
| During my days as an under-manager | 97 |
| As a young pugilist | 97 |
| Leaving by train for Buckingham Palace | 160 |
| Fryston Colliery Rescue Brigade | 160 |
| Speaking at the Opening of Fryston Sports Ground | 161 |
| Fryston Sports Arena in use | 161 |
| A lighthearted moment | 192 |
| The coal belt in a modern mine. Photo: N.C.B. | 192 |
| My wife and children. Photo: Sild | 193 |
| In retirement. Photo: *Yorkshire Post* | 193 |

CHAPTER ONE

# IN THE BEGINNING

In 1903, the little mining village of Bowers Row learned with unemotional enthusiasm that a sixth son and twelfth surviving member of the family of William and Naomi Bullock had been born.

There was no fanfare of trumpets, no gun salutes, no excitement, just another happening in this village where large families were the rule and not the exception. Some astonishment had been registered by the family for my mother was reckoned to be past child bearing age and my father was already old for this sort of activity. I understand that for a month or two the new arrival was suspected of being an ulcer and was treated as such.

When I did arrive in this very religious house, my mother said: "Surely this is a gift of God, what shall we call him? Jesus? No."

Father replied: "I don't care for Emmanuel"; so they settled on James Allen—the Allen being my mother's maiden name—which, as time passed, became Jim.

People have often asked, "What are your earliest recollections?" It's a long time ago now, but I distinctly remember the warmth of the house, the comforting presence of my mother, a certain awe of my father, but above all I remember the companionship of a large family.

Some were already married, but as the youngest and unexpected addition to the family, I never experienced any feeling of resentment about my arrival. I quickly learned that my father's health—already seriously undermined by years of mineworking in extremely bad conditions—was not good. Life was no bed of roses. Tragedy is never far from the great pulley

## Them and Us

wheels that haul coal and men from the depths. The pithead was always in view. Dirty black faces were as common in our village as they are in any big city today; but I was never conscious of any colour bar. These hardships never deterred the family too much, but acted more as a stimulant in knitting the family bonds tighter. We were compensated by our close family life. We enjoyed the friendship of our neighbours. Our home was always spick and span.

The importance of God was constantly being instilled into us. The complete faith my father had in the Almighty is something which never did and never has ceased to amaze me. He didn't talk to God with the reverence you expect or, indeed, receive from a pulpit, he talked to God as if he were his mate, his personal friend. But he taught us the basic truths of decent living: to be honest, trustworthy, hardworking and dependable.

Most of the hours I spent away from school were on the old disused tip about two miles from the village, and in the small scrublands that lay to the north of the village.

The first provided a battle area for our wars. Even in those days I was inclined to be a bit bossy; I wanted to be General and in my old faded blue shorts, wearing my brothers' old shirts, I would lead my troop against the enemy.

In the scrub—which was to us a forest—we went bird-nesting. I tried to climb higher than anybody else always hoping that I would not fall.

Naturally these activities left their scars, not only in eyes blackened by stones thrown by the opposing army and scratches from the tree branches but in the torn shirts and broken-toed shoes. Even at that age I quickly realized that the few pence necessary to repair the damage meant a further hardship for my mother. My first economic dream was how I could add something to the family exchequer to ease my mother's burdens.

We were taught independence, and were given tasks according to our age. Whilst small we ran errands, collected firewood, cleaned boots.

When we got a bit older we helped with the gardening, helped on the local farm, cleaned pigs out and sometimes, a

## In the Beginning

really great adventure, we were allowed to go on the muck stacks to pick coal from the waste for our own use.

Being made responsible for these things, however humble, instilled confidence. My father allotting jobs and seeing they were carried out—not only quickly, but cheerfully—taught me a lesson which I was going to turn to good effect later . . . though I didn't know that at the time. With self-confidence I acquired courage and faith in myself. The sort of courage needed in a mining village for, by the time I was eight, I was standing at the pithead with my mother, on that sight which is so heartbreaking, particularly to mining people, waiting for my eldest brother, her firstborn, to be brought up dead from the depths.

The sorrow and hardship his death caused made a lasting impression on me but, above all, the hours and hours we spent waiting at the pithead while the miners were digging to recover his body is something I shall never forget.

These scenes at the pithead after a tragedy sometimes involving many miners are harrowing indeed. There are the waiting relatives, mothers, brothers and sisters, old retired miners, wearing clothes that had just been thrown on in a hurry. The women with shawls round their heads. But it is the weary, worn and anxious look on all their faces that creates such a vivid impression.

A few years later my mother had another long wait at the pithead, this time—for me—though it didn't end as tragically.

One morning when I was about fifteen, and now a pony driver, orders came to each district for the pony drivers to go into the working places and tell all men and boys to go out of the pit at once.

We were working three miles from the pit bottom, nobody had told us why everybody had to go out of the pit. Two of us young pony drivers—not realizing the urgency—didn't hurry out, in fact we were having a game of noughts and crosses—with the result that we were the last two boys to get to the pit bottom.

When we did get there, the man in charge of the pit bottom gave us a real telling-off and told us that the upcast-shaft head-

## Them and Us

gear was on fire. This is the shaft where all the foul air is blown out of the pit by a huge fan.

When we reached the pit top a huge crowd had gathered round, each one watching with eagle eye, for their own relatives to come out. My mother was one of them. She knew that everybody wasn't out for as yet she had not seen me.

She did see me before I saw her, she broke through the crowd and got hold of me fiercely, folded me to her ample breasts and crooned over me as if I was a baby. Strong men gave way as she led me through the crowd and many had tears in their eyes for they were able to remember my mother's last vigil at the same pit with its awful consequence.

CHAPTER TWO

# BOWERS ROW

Bowers Row was the name of the village we were brought up in, it would certainly not have qualified for the National Trust. It had no beautiful stone-built cottages, no ancient church, no historic background; just three-hundred red-brick houses in long grubby rows. It had no paved roads, nor footpaths. The streets were largely bare earth, dusty in summer and muddy in winter. There were no gardens round the door and no trees growing in the street.

The houses themselves all followed the same pattern; one big living-room downstairs with a small kitchen, both with stone floors, and two bedrooms upstairs—you had to go through one room to get to the other. We had no hot or cold water; in fact, there was no water laid on to the houses at all when my parents first went to live there. They had no gas or electricity; just bare walls, not even a built-in cupboard.

Water was obtained from a tap situated in the middle of the long street and everybody shared it. Women and children used to carry water in jugs and buckets from this tap to their houses. Our lavatories were dry places known as closets and were built in groups of six at the top and bottom of the long rows of houses and five or six families shared each one.

In the big living-room downstairs there was a huge fireplace with an oven on one side and a sort of boiler on the other side. The fire was kept in day and night, firstly, because men were coming in at all hours and needed warmth and hot water, and secondly because the oven had to be kept hot for cooking meals at all hours. Pans and water were always on the fire heating water for washing.

## Them and Us

The women worked as hard and even longer hours than the men.

Why did we put up with this existence? The answer is: we had never known anything different. It was what we expected. But it was in my generation that discontent came to the surface and, what is more, we did something about it.

Between the rows of houses were open spaces where we played cricket, soccer and rugby. Street versus street, bitter bloody battles. Goalposts were our coats, our ball was a stuffed stocking or a pig's bladder blown up and stuffed into a yeast bag.

Cricket bats were made out of any old pieces of wood we could find and our wickets were cut from branches of trees.

Funny isn't it, how so many good footballers and cricketers develop from such homemade tackle and such poor playing conditions? There is an old saying among coal miners that we must have indiarubber pit bottoms, for every time anything drops down the pit shaft a sportsman bounces out.

Our homes, however, were always clean, tidy and well scrubbed. The women used to rub the doorsteps with donkey stones, either yellow or white, and these provided the only bit of colour in the village street.

We were all part of big families, every boy and girl seemed to have older brothers and sisters who, in their rough way, were our guides and very often protectors. We were launched into communal life at a very early age; literally thrown in at the deep end. Sink or swim was the motto and the fights for leadership were very tough. We had our own gangs who fought each other and among themselves. Brother fought brother; but immediately any personal quarrel was abandoned if outside trouble threatened. Then you had a really united front; the family would stand shoulder to shoulder against all comers.

## CHAPTER THREE

## OUR FAMILY

In our family we had a real mixture.

First, my father, a short thick-set man of fiery temper. A man, who in my time had a long white beard; before my time it had been ginger. He looked to me like an Old Testament prophet. His hands were gnarled and his knuckles out of shape. He used to sit with weights on his fingers to keep them straight. He suffered badly with rheumatism but tried never to let his joints become stiff. There was no doubt he was the undisputed king in his own house.

Intelligent, eloquent with his tongue and clever with his hands. A fine pitman, good at his job. He always finished an argument in the family circles by saying: "It *is* so, because I say so. That should be good enough for you."

A man who never knew any smooth times.

A man who at one time had to support eight children under fourteen years of age.

A man who never gave in, full of fight, particularly against the bosses, either at work or in chapel.

A man who claimed he had never ordered anything he could not pay for—"If you can't pay for it today do without it, because you certainly can't pay for it tomorrow." This was his favourite saying, boasting in his old age that he had never owed anybody a penny.

A man who taught us that it was not always what we wanted we should get, but rather what we needed we should strive for.

A man who worked hundreds of days when he was ill because he just could not have afforded to be off (there were no National Health Benefits then).

*Them and Us*

A man who worked for twenty-five shillings a week with no fringe benefits except coal.

A man who, as a result of working in such extremely bad conditions, had rheumatic fever which left him with heart disease.

A man who thought he would die at fifty-five and lived to be over eighty.

A man who had implicit faith in the Almighty, a faith which sustained him when all else failed.

A man who only worked a few years after I was born, but I remember seeing him lying down on the bedroom floor stretching his joints to enable him to get dressed and go to work.

A man who I never knew at his best. But I did know him as a man who gave wise counsel and quick correction.

Then, my mother.

How can I find words to describe her? To me she was beautiful, the kindest most sympathetic person I have ever known. A friend to everyone, very busy, but never too busy to listen to other people's troubles or ours.

Clean, tidy, hardworking, a veritable storehouse of knowledge about sickness, disease and accident. She had soothing hands, a quiet voice.

A complete contrast to my father—

He upset, she smoothed.

He hit, she talked.

He dictated, she persuaded.

He ordered, she asked.

He expected, she received.

He punished, she comforted.

He demanded, she encouraged.

You didn't do wrong things because you didn't want to hurt her. These were the differences, but together they made a splendid team. She told me as I grew older that never since her firstborn arrived could she remember when she was not either suckling a baby or expecting one.

My elder brothers and sisters seemed to understand my parents better than any of us. They had the same beliefs and the same faith.

# Our Family

It's a funny thing, but my father and mother were between five foot three and five foot four high but my eldest brother, John Willie, was five foot ten inches high. I was the youngest and I too was five foot ten, but in between us all the rest of my brothers and sisters were between five foot three and five foot four. It seems that the first and last efforts had the same result.

I only knew my eldest brother John Willie for a few years. He was killed when I was eight years old, but I knew him well enough to know, how kind he was, how gentle he was, what a good husband and father he was. He worked on the night shift but after he got married he would come back home each night to say good night to my parents. He always seemed to be so keen to please them. He would say a few well chosen words to stop family quarrels. He would pour oil on troubled waters. He was the organist at the chapel, a Sunday school teacher and a really devoted Christian. He had a wife and three children and lived about three houses away from us in the same long street.

My parents were heartbroken when he was killed. John Willie's eldest son was only a year younger than me; he was called William after my father. We two grew up more like brothers and he was one of my closest friends until he died a couple of years ago.

My other brothers and sisters had their talents and gifts. They could play the piano, violin, and had all fairly decent voices. We used to sing hymns every Sunday night after the chapel service, gathered round the family piano. I don't suppose that any of us had outstanding musical talents but we could amuse ourselves and all my brothers and sisters were intelligent and hardworking.

We were a close, tight-knit, family. All told there were twelve children: six daughters and six sons. As the youngest I learnt a great deal from each of them. And every one of my brothers and sisters contributed something to the moulding of the young Jim Bullock. Seven of them are still living.

The eldest of the girls was "Lizzie", who is now over ninety and in full possession of her faculties. Lizzie is a really religious woman, believing implicitly in the Bible and its teachings. Her youth was spent as a servant in the house of the colliery surface

*Them and Us*

manager. She didn't get married until she was well over thirty. She and her husband-to-be—a widower—did most of their courting over the backyard fence while she was cleaning our boots. We never had our boots cleaned so well or so often as during Lizzie's courtship.

At first, my father objected to their union because the widower went to the pub every Sunday lunchtime and drank two pints of beer. But Lizzie proved obstinate as she probably realized that this might be her last chance. So she listened to my father's words of warning as every dutiful daughter should do . . . and then went on with her own arrangements.

Most of my sisters seemed doomed to work as a servant on one of the managers' houses. Maybe my father had to agree or lose his livelihood, just as he was expected by the manager to deliver his sons to the pithead as soon as they were old enough to quit school.

The brother, whom I mention most often in this book, is Dick, the seventh child, who is now the eldest surviving son. Dick disgraced the family by marrying the boss's daughter. We forgave him in time; indeed, at the latter end of his working career he was overman for me at Fryston. Dick, now a widower, has seen over eighty years of life. His hobby in his retirement is baking and he's as good as any modern housewife, who generally seems to prefer the rather tasteless pre-packed article to the wholesome oven-baked variety.

The other brother who features prominently is Joseph, now seventy-six. Joseph's readiness to be converted year after year was a source of great amusement to me, once I had discovered the motives for his regularly "seeing the light".

I can't mention all of my brothers and sisters specifically but I had a deep affection for each one of them. They were all individuals with varying talents and vastly different characters. The next generation has also given me considerable pleasure for in them I see the continuation of the Bullock blood emanating from my mother and father. And again, the younger generation have provided their share of characters and non-conformists. There's young Fred who taught me how, with modern methods, Christmas trees can be planted *en bloc*, whereas I had until then laboured and sweated to plant a few. And Alan, the son of Lydia, who is a complete rebel: an artist, musician, poet and sailor.

This then is and was my family. All the nephews and nieces now have children of their own. And their children have children.

Many of them have won scholarships and are well established in academic or industrial careers. All are advancing slowly but surely.

I am very proud of them. How proud my parents would have been if they could have seen them all.

Once at Fryston, I decided to try and get all members of my family with their wives, husbands and children together for a party. What a gathering! An artist, parson, soldiers, sailors, airmen, builders, mechanics, electrician, union leader, accountant, miners, joiners, nurses, sisters, school teacher, chef, housewives, boxer, farmers, footballers, forester, horticulturist, mining engineer, insurance agent. You name it. We had it.

Beautiful girls and handsome men. All coming from one old man five foot three high. What an output per person employed. What productivity. What an example to the nation.

What a span of reproduction: from eighteen hundred and forty-eight—the birth of my father—to nineteen hundred and fifty-nine, the birth of my son.

And how they mixed! No snobbery, just a family. Why don't families get together more often, I wonder? We only seem to meet at funerals nowadays.

CHAPTER FOUR

## SCHOOL LIFE AND EARLY RECOLLECTIONS

My school life started in the village school built by the Lord of the Manor, Sir Charles Lowther. Catholics, Church of England, Baptists and Methodists, went to the same school. Scripture lessons were given in three separate classrooms—Catholics in one, members of the Church of England in another, and Non-Conformists, whatever their denomination, in a third. Friendships were formed during schooldays which lasted throughout life.

By 1911, even Sir Charles Lowther, a real aristocrat, realized that the days of democracy had arrived. A School Management Board was formed. My father was elected chairman. One year my sister and I had won the first prizes for the boys and girls at the school. It was a great day for the owner of the estate and founder of the school, Sir Charles Lowther himself, was due to present the prizes. All morning I had been taught to salute—and my sister to curtsy—when we received our prizes.

My father kept a few pigs and always carried with him that peculiar aroma associated with that useful animal. For this reason I sensed my father's presence in the school just when the presentation was about to begin. I was not mistaken for as I stepped up to receive my prize and make my salute, in a loud voice he shouted, "Stop." He walked through the crowded hall and stopped in front of Sir Charles and said, "When people like you command my admiration and respect then, and only then, will I allow my children to salute or curtsy to you." Then father turned to us and said, "Leave the prizes where they are. We have managed without their charity for quite a long time and we can still manage."

## School Life and Early Recollections

Even today I remember the disappointment because the prize I had won was a box kite and I had never had one.

Whilst I was at this little school, my elder sisters were all servants at the manager's and other officials' homes. We were constantly reminded of our position in society. We were allowed to gather crumbs from the rich man's table such as a drop of skimmed milk free from the colliery farm, an occasional rabbit shot by the boss in the harvest field, a few turnips for a day's weeding in the fields, permission to pick coal off the muck tips, chance of a job down the pit when you left school.

A great day in the village was the Chapel Anniversary and all the Sunday School scholars used to sing special hymns in a mass choir and give little recitations.

If the family could afford it, everybody had new suits or dresses.

When I was twelve I had a new sailor suit made of velvet and I was stood outside the chapel when the colliery manager and his party drove up in a carriage and pair.

The Anniversary was held in the month of June and the roads were very dusty and as the carriage was pulling up with a flourish dust settled on my new suit. This annoyed me tremendously and I remember grumbling to my father. His reply was: "Don't worry about a bit of dust, lad, it is easier for a camel to go through the eye of a needle than for a rich man to enter the kingdom of heaven." He explained very carefully that we had a closely knit family and that, although poor, we had great prospects of eternal life if we lived our present lives properly.

According to him the future of the colliery manager and the coal owners was bleak in the extreme. To me it was the bit in between now and eternity that was beginning to matter. Even then I asked myself was I doomed to spend all my working life at the coalface like my father and my brothers? Were these people really better than me, just because they had more money or were better dressed? I didn't think so, for when occasionally their children went to the same school they were no better at lessons than we were. When they played in our teams at soccer and cricket they were certainly no better. When we fought

## Them and Us

they were certainly not as good and the results of our contests quickly proved this.

Why shouldn't I get a bit of their heaven below? And so the idea was born. As I grew, it grew with me. As I developed, so the desire to be something different developed. I wanted to do something with my life and any talents I possessed for my family, for my people, and for myself.

I have mentioned briefly the fatal accident that happened to my eldest brother, John Willie, and the sort of courage that is instilled in mining families at a very early age to cope with situations like this.

The circumstances that surround his death happened when I was eight years old. At that time I never seen the sea, my greatest adventure had been a trip in a wagonette with the Sunday School scholars to Roundhay Park which was eight miles away. Now John Willie had promised to take my sister and I to Scarborough for the day. It was 29 July 1911.

We went to bed early on the 28th to make sure we were ready to set off by the 7.30 train the following morning. John Willie was working on night shift and came down to say good night to my parents as usual. He told us to be up in good time to be ready for the trip. We were so excited we could hardly sleep and were awake by five o'clock.

My father was already downstairs and was mixing pig food in the yard when a tap came on the front window. He thought it was us knocking from the bedroom window and just said, "Yes, I have heard you. It is time you were getting up now."

The tap came again, and he went through the house to the front window to see who it was. Facing him was the Trade Union Secretary, "I have some bad news for you, Bill. John Willie is in the pit." My father knew what this meant and he just said, "Is it bad?"

"It's as bad as it can be."

When I have talked about the faith my father had, we now saw a perfect example of it. He came up the stairs, breathing very heavily, went straight through our bedroom without speaking to us and knelt down at the side of my mother's bed

## School Life and Early Recollections

and told her, through prayer, what had happened. "If ever we needed God's help we need it this morning, lass." She didn't wait for the end of the prayer, for like any other miner's wife or mother would, she jumped out of bed, put on her coat over the top of her nightdress and literally ran across the common to the pithead. We followed her and stood close by her as she started that vigil which is so heartbreaking and so little understood, except by those who are born and bred into the mining industry.

She waited all through that day. Nothing could have dragged her away from the pit top. Kindly neighbours took her cups of tea and stayed with her. It was late on the night of the 29 July that other miners recovered my brother's body from under hundreds of tons of rock. This was my first real introduction to tragedy at the mine. It had happened to other lads' brothers and fathers. But now it had happened to *my* brother and it was *my* mother that was showing such grief. Even today I cannot forget the misery and distress this tragedy brought to my family, and John Willie's family; because he had three young children, the eldest being seven years old and the youngest only three months old. His widow only received two hundred pounds in compensation. John Willie was a well-loved son, highly respected in the village, and, I am told, his was the biggest funeral the village had ever seen.

Perhaps John Willie's death may have deprived me of my first view of the sea, but, three years later—just before the outbreak of the First World War—I did go to Blackpool with my mother, father and sister for a week's holiday.

This was the first time I had been away from home, but even on holiday my father maintained his continuing battle with the devil. We were not allowed to go on the sands on Sunday. We were not allowed to read anything except religious papers on Sunday.

My father, who was a Baptist, wanted to attend worship in a Baptist Chapel because in Bowers Row we had just a mission hall. In Adelaide Street in Blackpool there was a beautiful Baptist Chapel and he looked forward with sheer delight to us all going to the Sunday morning service.

## Them and Us

My mother was actually able to go with us as she had no dinner to cook, as we were staying in a lodging-house.

The service in this Baptist Chapel was most unusual. Being a holiday period the chapel was crowded, and so we sat right at the front. The first hymn was "Onward Christian Soldiers". In the Mission Hall at home, anybody who particularly enjoyed a hymn would strike up the last verse or the chorus again when the hymn was finished, and all the congregation would then join in.

Not so at this Baptist Chapel. My father struck up the chorus and we had to keep on our feet with him. I am afraid it was like a discordant quartet, for the rest of the congregation were sat down and took no part in it.

When the minister started praying he was accompanied by a constant encouragement of utterances from my father, such as, "Lord, answer prayer", "True Lord. True Lord", "Bless His Holy name", and so on.

The second hymn was "Oh for a thousand tongues to praise", and I whispered to my sister "That's done it, another quartet." And so it turned out to be. The stony silence with which our first efforts had been received did not deter my father one iota. He struck up the last verse again at the top of his voice. For our part we were just mumbling and very self conscious. But we had to stick it to the end of the verse.

The minister was a fairly old man. He put on his glasses, opened his bible, and looking over the top of his glasses he said to my father, "If the exuberance of my brother below will allow me, I will now read the fifty-third chapter of Isaiah." If he thought for one moment that this mild reproof would awe my father, he soon found he had made a big mistake. He just managed to get to: "Who hath believed our report, and to whom is the hand of the Lord revealed?" by the time my father had reached the bottom of the pulpit. In a voice shaking with anger my father shouted, "I came to this place of worship this morning to hear the word of the living God, not to be insulted by anybody like thee." He then turned round to us, saying, "Follow me. This is no place for us." He stalked out of the chapel, drawn up to his full height of five foot three, his white beard

## School Life and Early Recollections

just about stood on end with wrath and we all followed somewhat shamefacedly behind him. My sister and I felt rather pleased about this, we thought it might mean there would be no more going to chapel while we were on holiday. We went straight back to the lodging-house, into our bedroom and father had a word of prayer. To me, I'm afraid, his prayer sounded very much like the Pharisee of old: "Thanking God that we were not as other men were."

During the week we made friends with other children. We played on the sands and ran races. My father wanting to be a good sportsman and show his interest in children drew me to one side and asked if I thought if I could beat any of the other boys in a sixty yards sprint. "Yes," I replied. He said, "Right, I will give sixpence to the winner of a sixty yards race."

I didn't win and I felt the length of his tongue in no uncertain fashion. He hadn't enough sixpences to be giving them away to strangers he explained. We were taught as children to be seen and not heard, so I did not answer back. We were not expected to interrupt adult conversation. We must never contradict our parents. And we were not allowed to question their views.

What a difference today. We were brought up in a way totally alien to the methods of bringing up children nowadays.

During school life, the only real excitement was a fight. These usually took place after quarrels at school. Then we used to go and settle the matter in the woods, in a clearing known as "The Keeper's Walk". Many were the battles fought there. I enjoyed fighting. The headmaster did his best to stop this sort of paganism. When there had been a fight all the village and all the school knew. So did he. The next morning he would call the school together and his detective work was rather unique. He would say, "Come out, Bullock." When I got to the front of the school, he would ask, "Who were you fighting? At least I know you were one of them." Invariably he was right. By the time I was twelve I had the proud distinction of being the "cock of the school".

While I was at this school I was given a really first-class

example of human relations by a young schoolteacher. To me it was my first taste of psychology.

This young teacher started at the school straight from college. We, as mining lads, thought he was a bit of a cissy and treated him as such. We made his life sheer hell. We used to shout after him as he was going to catch his train at night. We used to lock his door so that he couldn't get out of his classroom. We used to write rude things on his blackboard. He quickly realized that I was the ringleader. One Friday he said to me, "Would you like to come with me on Saturday and watch Leeds City play?" This was before the days of Leeds United. I could not believe my ears. This was really a dream. I had read all about this great side but never thought I should be able to go and watch them play. I explained to him I hadn't any money, but he said he would pay my tramfare from Rothwell to Leeds and would meet me at the tram terminus there. What is more, if I wanted, I could take one of my elder brothers with me.

He met my brother and me as arranged and took us to the Elland Road Ground.

We could only gaze in wonder at this tremendous stadium. He had reserved us two places in the grandstand. He saw us to our seats, bought us some chocolates and told us he would have to leave us for a short while but we would be quite all right.

The greatest surprise I had ever had came when Leeds City trotted out from under the grandstand for my teacher was amongst them. When we looked at the programme we found he was playing inside left and what is more on this particular afternoon he played a "blinder", scoring two goals.

I could not wait to get back to the village to tell everybody what had happened and to let them all know what a wonderful player we had got as a teacher. Needless to say he hadn't any more trouble with any of the lads as long as he remained at the village school.

This taught me a lesson. Giving me the cane or inflicting punishment would have made me detest him. Doing what he did taught me a lesson I have never forgot and I don't think

## School Life and Early Recollections

I have ever made the mistake of underestimating people above, or below me, since.

People often ask how did we get on with girls in a mining village. Nature then, was the same as nature is now. Today there is a lot of talk about free love and the permissive society, and I agree that there is probably more open love making now than there was then; and probably better methods of "safeguarding" the lady. But we had one great advantage that the youth of today has never had: as soon as we went out of the house we were in pitch darkness. There was not a lamp to be seen for miles. As soon as you were out of the village you were in quiet country lanes or in deep thick woods. There were no motor car headlights lighting up dim corners. What we lacked in knowledge we made up for in ability and virility. Looking back I don't think there would be many people in that day and age who would die curious, for most of us had been in and out of love many times before we reached the age of sixteen. I was in love with a little rosy-cheeked girl who left our village to go and live in Bradford when I was eleven. I didn't eat for two days. I was mooning about like a sick cow. Time is a great healer and I soon realized there were plenty left. Older women were good teachers too, and there were always plenty of widows about. The atmosphere in a mining village was altogether different to what it is now. We had no means of transport and Castleford was three and a half miles away. If we wanted to get there we had to walk. As Castleford was the only place with a swimming pool in the locality, we used to swim in the scum covered ponds or the sluggish, dirty, river.

We used to delight in trespassing in pursuit of game. We were experts at snickling rabbits and stealing apples and pears from the colliery manager's orchards. We could be described as a set of roughnecks. But there was kindness when one was in trouble. There was sympathy when one got hurt. One touch of nature makes the whole world kin and all of us were very similar in the privations we had to endure. We had many things in common. We wore suits that were cast off by our elder brothers. We were very clannish and we all had a certain amount of inverted snobbery.

*Them and Us*

Once when a new boss came to the colliery, he sent his son—a boy about the same age as me—to our school. The lad turned up on the Monday morning, clean and tidy, his hair parted down the middle. He was wearing a velvet sailor's suit. He remained clean and tidy until playtime. It had been raining all morning and the playground was a quagmire. Nobody actually knocked him down, but everybody seemed to be running into him accidentally, and then tripping over him while he was on the floor. Of course, we helped him up very courteously. Just as he was nearly on his feet again, somebody else would run into us from the back, and down we would all go again. When our teacher saw him after playtime, he sent him straight home to change.

Later this boy, Arthur Booker became my friend and has been so all our lives. Indeed, he was best man at my first wedding.

He was a boss's son, but somehow his family were all different to the usual "boss family".

His father was firm; a man of high principles and a good local preacher.

His mother was kindly and gracious and after my mother's death her love and understanding meant a lot to me. Their home was my home for many years.

He had an elder brother, Percy—a first-class engineer—and two sisters, one of whom I was very fond through most of my teenage life.

We were all keen on cricket, tennis and soccer and we had our own sports facilities in their big field.

Arthur and I used to play any two of the others. Percy and my brother Dick, who lived nearby gave us tremendous battles.

Mr. Booker was a Derbyshire man and when Yorkshire beat them at cricket he was very quiet. If we wanted to please him, we used to let him bowl us out. He only bowled underhands but he was keen. But the real battles were fought as seriously as if we were playing for championships. We had no referees, so quite a few borderline decisions led to fierce arguments.

Arthur and I, by saving every penny, were able to go to Blackpool—on our own—when we were about seventeen. What

## School Life and Early Recollections

a time we had! By Thursday we had only a few shillings left. Arthur, always an optimist, decided to send a telegram to his father telling him of our plight, and to make doubly certain of money being telegraphed back he included in his telegram, "We have no money left to pay our fares back home." The eagerly awaited telegram came back promptly, containing only one word: "WALK." Of course we had return tickets but Mr. Booker didn't know that and it made no difference to his answer.

When Arthur was accompanying me in the taxi to my wedding he put his hand on my knee and said, "Jim, are you sure you want to go through with this? If you aren't we can tell the driver to take us back to the station."

I replied, "Of course, I'm going through with it."

Arthur, with mock solemnity, said, 'Father, forgive him, for he knows not what he does."

He and I took part in many teenage pranks. He was no more fond of the police than I was at that time. Our village constable was the victim of most of our mischievous actions.

As I've said, at this time we had no street lighting. We knew the constable's nightly route and a line of strong cord stretched tightly across the road, about a foot from the floor, caused many stout bobbies to trip and fall headlong into six inches of mud.

When the village constable was on night duty and peacefully sleeping in bed during the day, his family out at work, it was not a big job for two active young boys to climb up the fall pipe and place a grass sod over the chimney top and to fasten his door tightly from the outside. Then we'd retire to a safe distance and watch the house slowly fill with smoke while the bobby tried frantically to get out.

We were often spent up, and once at Holbeck Feast—this was an annual affair out at Leeds—Arthur and I were completely broke by 8 p.m. We decided I would go in to the boxing booth and challenge the boxer who was taking on all comers. He came from our own gym and I knew I could beat him, but the difficulty was, how could I challenge him? For he knew me as well as I knew him.

## Them and Us

So we decided that Arthur should make the challenge. This was a brave deed, for Arthur was no fighter. But we arranged that when he made the challenge and entered the stripping tent I would crawl under the tent, change, and go into the ring while he got out of the tent the way I had got in.

These arrangements went without a hitch but when the boxer saw me coming into the ring, there was a hurried conflab between him and the promoter.

The promoter knew that if he refused to let me fight his man the crowd would go mad. They were so used to seeing the challenger slaughtered that the crowd loved to see the boxer, who was on permanent duty in the boxing ring, get beaten.

So the promoter came over to my corner and told me he would give me two pounds just to box an exhibition. We made it look very real. The crowd didn't know anything about it, but I knew that it was the easiest two pounds I had ever received.

We spent it before we left the feast.

Yes! we shared everything; money, sorrows, joys and girls.

Arthur was a great cricketer and a first-class opening batsman. I was a stumper. In those days when a batsman got fifty runs or over, a collection was immediately taken from all the spectators on the ground. Arthur, got many fifties and was responsible for solving many of our boyhood financial difficulties.

Sometimes he would stay so long with his score at forty-nine waiting for the right ball to hit to get his fifty that I suffered from physical and mental exhaustion. For there was I, waiting like a greyhound on a leash, with my cap in my hand, to set off to help in his collection, for I realized that this collection was for me also.

We were both popular with the girls and had many good times together. Some of them are still living and if they ever read this book I hope their memories of our friendship will be as pleasant as mine are.

Different people came to the village but I can't remember anybody changing us, but a lot of people were changed by us.

## School Life and Early Recollections

Friday night was our great night. This was pay night at the colliery and the children were given one halfpenny each for pocket money, and we could do just as we liked with it. We stood for hours in front of the shop window studying the contents of the shelves and deciding how we were going to spend that halfpenny. The anticipation was better than the realization.

An event we looked forward to even more than Friday nights was, when my father decided to have a pig killed. This was a real village occasion.

Six strong miners were called to catch the pig and hold it on "the scratch". This was a strong wooden platform built on four stout legs with two handles at each end.

The village butcher was the local winding engineman from the colliery. He was the most important man—the star turn —on these occasions. He would arrive at the house at the appointed time wearing a butcher's smock and carrying his bag of knives. The six miners arrived at the same time and all the neighbours were boiling water in big pans on their coal fires. The chief personalities in the drama to be enacted, now set off to the pig sty followed by practically every man, woman and child in the village.

The condemned pig was captured, held on to the scratch by the miners and the butcher, speedily—and usually efficiently —killed the pig.

Then the economics of pig killing was brought home to us. The blood was caught in a bucket—this was used to make black puddings. The neighbours came carrying buckets of boiling water to throw over the pig's carcase and all the execution squad set about scraping all the hair off the pig.

It was then carried to the house and hung up in the kitchen. The butcher then opened the pig. The intestines were taken by the neighbours to clean, cook and then eat as chitterlings. The way the miners' wives cooked these they were really delicious.

My mother, now cut up the heart and the liver and sent a small portion to each neighbour who had sent potato peelings and scraps to help feed the pigs. The bladder was given in strict rotation to the boys of the family—this was blown up, put

## Them and Us

inside of a yeast bag or an adult's stocking, and made a good football until it was kicked to pieces.

We as children, had already been round the village booking orders for various joints of pork.

The next day the butcher came back to our house, and cut the pig up, we delivered the pork and collected the cash.

This cash was always placed in the "Pig's Money Box" and used to buy fresh pigs and provide food for the existing pigs.

Every part of the pig was used. There was literally no waste. The brains were fried and eaten with bacon. The head and trotters were made into brawn. The fat round the sides was rendered down into lard and the fried bits of fat were eaten and were known in the village as "scratchings".

Yes! for a few glorious days we lived like lords. We had a big joint, all the bits were fried up. Fortunate indeed were the families who managed to keep a few pigs.

Most of us tried to smoke before we left school and we used to make our cigarettes out of dried burdock or dock leaves rolled inside any sort of paper. It invariably made us sick and if this didn't cure us, we soon did get cured, when our parents found out. They used to tell us stories about smoking giving us lockjaw etc., and their warnings about what could happen made us very careful for a few days at least.

In mining villages there were diseases hardly met with today, such as rickets, tuberculosis, diphtheria, croup, whooping cough, to mention a few. These took a heavy toll of young boys and girls. Deaths among babies and schoolchildren were much more frequent than today.

While I was still at school the 1914–18 war started and miners flocked to the services in their thousands.

Conditions in the pits were very bad, miners were on short time and had very low wages. Misery and poverty was apparent everywhere. The posters began to appear at the street corners, "Kitchener wants you" with a photograph of Lord Kitchener with his finger pointing directly at you personally.

Did miners rush to the services, for patriotism?

For King or country?

Or did they join the services to escape the poverty stricken,

## School Life and Early Recollections

boring life in the pits? Up at four o'clock in the morning, down the pit for nine or ten hours. When they did come home from work they were very often too tired to do anything but sleep. No escape from the village. No transport. No theatres. No picture houses. Nothing.

Here was the opportunity to travel, to fight, to wear a smart uniform, all free, plus a shilling a day for doing it. It might even be possible to become a hero. Were these the reasons then, why my brothers and thousands like them were in the services by September, 1914?

I was the only son left at home. My brothers didn't come home on leave very often, they were soon packed off to France. But when they did come on leave I remember the pride when I saw them in bandoliers and spurs. I recall how I listened with awe and wonder when they talked of their travels and experiences; and how I longed to be old enough to join.

We soon found out that war was not all travel and glory; for after the battle of Ypres and Hill Sixty in which the miners' battalions were practically wiped out, the letters from the War Office began coming to nearly every house in the village, starting with the dreaded words: "We regret to inform you that...."

The grief of one household affected us all, for every boy and young man in the village was known to everybody in the village; and each loss was a personal loss.

I had now won a scholarship to the local grammar school but owing to my brothers being in the Army, and my father now permanently sick, there was no chance to go.

So like my brothers before me I had to go cap in hand to the boss: "Please can you find me work?" Where! To the pit of course.

There is a tremendous difference nowadays, young lads starting work are older than we were and are interviewed by a Training Officer, they have special training sessions, they are granted time off for education, but we were thrown in at the deep end. When I first went to see the manager we had to go down a long lane that connected his house with the pit. It was just a mile in length. He left his house about eight o'clock in

## Them and Us

the morning and walked the mile to the colliery. This stretch of roadway, was his interviewing office for each person that wished to see him, who stood fifty yards apart on this long lane. The first one to arrive stood fifty yards away from his house and the second person fifty yards away from him and so on. You walked at the side of him for fifty yards and then the next person took over. He never stopped walking. You walked by the side of him, bare-headed. It is the only conversation that I remember that was measured in yards and not in minutes.

When he knew they called me Bullock I had no difficulty in him giving me a job. I could start work the following night.

CHAPTER FIVE

## STARTING WORK UNDERGROUND

When I got home after seeing the manager and informed my mother that I could start work straight away there was a sort of subdued excitement on her part. There was nothing subdued about the excitement I felt, but I did feel that she had a tinge of regret that I was having to go down the pit. I think she had always hoped for something better for me.

She went out and bought me my first pair of long trousers; in mining we called them moleskins. They were made of very thick material to stand up to the wear and tear of pit life. She also bought me a new tin, known as a "snap tin", which was used to carry our food to keep it fresh, but chiefly to prevent mice eating it when we got down the pit. A new pair of clogs, too. Then she found an old coat belonging to one of my brothers, and one of their old caps, there were no safety helmets then.

I had to start on the night shift. I had to be down the pit at nine o'clock and spend the first week or two cleaning up coal dust and loading it into tubs.

I thought I knew just what to expect. I had lain for hundreds of nights in bed, between my brothers, listening to them reliving their days down the pit and talking of their ponies.

There were five or six brothers and a cousin who used to sleep in the back bedroom, where two large beds were packed close together and I, as the youngest, used to sleep in the crack between the two beds. The others kept me warm and I could hear all they were saying. By the time they went to bed they were tired out and sometimes their pit behaviour, being relived in their sleep, woke me up and kept me awake, hence I went to work fully prepared.

*Them and Us*

In addition to this, pits and pit work, were the chief conversation in the house, at the street corner, and the street corners were our chief community centres.

When the time came for me to go, my mother had packed me six slices of bread and fat in my tin. She came to the door with me and with tears in her eyes she said, "Be careful, lad, tha's the only one left." When I got to the top of the street I looked back and all the neighbours were out watching me. I arrived at the lamp cabin, and presented a note to the lamp-man from the manager authorizing me to have a safety lamp. The lamp cabin is situated near the shaft.

All the people I had seen in chapel and walking about in the village became important. The lamp-man, who didn't seem to command any particular attention in the village, was the boss in the lamp room. The banksman who was in charge of signals from the top of the shaft to the winding house on the pit bottom, lived in my street; he was just an ordinary neighbour, but here he was completely supreme in his own domain.

The pit I started at was only one hundred yards from the village. It was known as the Victoria Pit and worked the 'Beeston Seam'. Thirty yards away there was another pit and this was called the Albert Pit and the 'Silkstone Seam' was worked there. The miners, however, called them 'the Johnny' and 'the Star'—I started down 'the Johnny' pit.

When I got my lamp I had to take it to a deputy who tested it, that is he blew all round it to make sure there was no leakage, where the flame could get through to ignite outside gases. I stood with many other men and boys at the mouth of the shaft waiting for my turn to go down. It would be silly to say I was not nervous, but I certainly wasn't frightened. When it came to my turn to go down I was placed in the middle of the cage with men and boys in front and behind, so I certainly had company. The bells rang, the cage lifted a little and then plunged down into the depths. My heart and stomach seemed to be trying to escape from my body. We went down and down, faster and faster, nobody spoke and a silence came, sort of deadly silence and a queer, stuffy atmosphere filled the cage. Everyone seemed busy with his own thoughts. Our lamps were

## Starting Work Underground

held in our hands at about knee level, so by the time we reached the pit bottom we were in total darkness. It's difficult to describe the darkness of a pit, the blackest, thickest fog, is nothing like it. It's a darkness that can be felt. If you put your hand in front of your eyes you cannot see it. The darkness becomes oppressive. It seems to weigh you down and this horrible blackness, coupled with the awful silence, is enough to staunch the stoutest heart. The silence is only broken when you hear the creaking of the timbers and the slow settling of the strata on packs and roof supports.

Maybe, you would suddenly realize that there is over fifteen hundred feet of solid rock above you, and as a boy you think that all that terrific weight is supported on what looks to you as very flimsy props and bars. Later of course you realize that the strata is interlocked and one layer supports the other.

The atmosphere in the pit to an imaginative mind can be very terrifying. The only light is the dim flickering oil lamp, casting weird shadows which assume all sorts of fantastic shapes. Occasionally two tiny red stars are picked up in the glow of the lamp, you are frightened until you realize it is the reflected glow from the eyes of a mouse or a rat.

You are afraid to put your lamp down for fear it topples over, fearful of hanging it up in case it might drop and go out. You would like to turn your wick higher to get a bit more light but you dare not, for it might smoke the glass and then you couldn't see at all. You ask yourself what on earth will I do if it does go out? Later, you realize and indeed, are taught, that if you hold your pony's tail he will take you back to the pit bottom.

Pits in those days were largely "hand got", this means that there were no big machines cutting coal. The coal was cut and loaded by men using picks and shovels, they worked in small groups in separate places, each going down a separate tunnel to a place of work. So the pits were like a huge spider's web, some with over forty miles of roads going in all directions. You could walk for hours and think nobody had been there before you, except for horsedroppings and footprints in the dust. For-

## Them and Us

tunately, you get used to these things very quickly, more so, if you come from mining stock, but I shall never forget that first full night shift down the pit.

I have often wondered if I felt like this, one who had lived among miners all his life and been brought up in a miner's home, had listened to the vivid descriptions of the "hell hole" as they called it, what on earth must the Bevin Boys—those who volunteered for coal mines during the 1939–45 war—have felt when they encountered these conditions with no pre-conditioning whatsoever to prepare them.

This is one of the reasons why during the war, when I was manager, I understood their feelings and helped them accordingly. But on my first night down the pit, I was directed to a deputy called Wilkinson who told me to wait for him. He went into the office and I sat down until he came to collect me. All the other men set off, North, South, East and West, their lights growing dimmer and dimmer until I was on my own with one small flickering oil lamp. I don't suppose it was very long before the deputy came to collect me, but it seemed a long time to me. As he approached me he just said, "Come on" and we set off up a long, steep, low road, with tramlines at each side, with tubs being drawn along by steel ropes. Two miles from the pit bottom we stopped, "Leave your coat here and hang your food up out of the way of the mice." I proudly told him that the mice couldn't get my food as I had got a "snap tin".

He took me further in and showed me how to get tubs from the empty road across to the full road, and explained that I should be expected to fill at least four tubs. Seeing that each tub held ten hundredweights, and that all the dust had to be scraped up, and then loaded into the tubs, it was not a bad effort he needed, for a small boy to be asked to fill two tons on his first night down the pit. I thought all this at the time, but I didn't say anything. The deputy left me with the words: "I'll collect you about half past five in the morning." As he was going away he shouted back, "Jimmy, I forgot to tell you, but this is about the place where your John Willie got killed." And off he went. But he left the thought behind him. I shall never forget that night as long as I live. I saw my brother as

## Starting Work Underground

plain as day. In my imagination I heard the timbers cracking and breaking. It was sheer agony, I wasn't just nervous now, I was literally frightened to death.

It seemed miles back to where I had left my coat, I was afraid to put my lamp down for fear it toppled over, I could hardly see, it was so dusty and dim. I wondered if there was enough oil in the lamp to last until morning. The night seemed to go on and on, I thought it would never end. But eventually I saw a light approaching, hundreds of yards away. I watched it getting nearer and nearer until finally I could hear footsteps and the tapping of the deputy's stick, I knew the night shift was over. I had filled my four tubs and was now ready for home.

When we got to the pit bottom it was a busy scene, men and boys that had come down with me the previous night were all waiting to go home, but now all had dirty faces. As the cage came down men with clean faces were all getting off to start their day's work. But we were all jubilant, we were going home and they were just starting.

As I rode back up to the pit top for the first time, there was a real difference in the behaviour of the men and boys with me. Going down the pit nobody spoke but as we rode up everybody was laughing and joking. When we got off the cage I handed in my lamp and rushed home in the darkness.

My mother was already cooking my breakfast. Only the morning before I had had bread and jam, but now I could smell bacon and eggs. I was really a man and as she fussed over me I looked with pride at my black body and legs and no one could have persuaded me to get washed until I had been outside to let all my younger mates see me on their way to school. How superior I felt. They were school kids and I was a worker. I had arrived. I was important, a contributor to the family exchequor.

I wasn't on nights very long before the boss told me that I had to start on the day shift and I was given my first pony. They called him Windsor, he was a grey pony and was fairly old, set in his ways and inclined to be bossy. As a matter of fact on the first day he practically controlled me. Advice poured in. Some said, "Boss him", "Let him know who's gaffer."

## Them and Us

Others said, "Give him some bread and be kind to him." During the day he realized, I think, that he had a learner driving him, and he just deliberately refused to pull. I wanted to do well, I knew I wasn't doing very well and I pleaded with him, coaxed him and threatened him but I could not make him move. I saw a light approaching and I thought I was in for a real showing up, but it was one of my elder brothers. "What's matter?" "He won't go," I tearfully replied. "We'll soon see about that," and for some unaccountable reason as soon as he approached the pony, it set off and worked well for the rest of the shift.

But as thousands before me, I worked out my own methods and each day I grew more confident and handled him in my own way and we got on very well together.

I have always been annoyed when I have heard people who have never been down a pit talking of the way pit ponies are blind, hungry, badly stabled. Nothing could be further from the truth. They are well fed, they have good stables, nowadays they all have their own cap lamps, but above all there is the understanding that developed between the pony driver and his animal.

This understanding must develop because the pony driver's life depends on his pony's obedience, you have no reins, your commands must be obeyed.

Probably this is the first time you have been able to command anything. It is your first taste of power. You are a boss, you've got your own pony and in most cases the affection between the two is very real.

I had many ponies but the ones I liked best were those that were given to me to train. They came straight from the Welsh hills or the New Forest and, if only *you* handled them, you taught them in your own way. My favourite pony was called Tim. He would drink water out of my bottle, he'd nuzzle into my pockets and fetch out bits of carrot or sweets I had taken to work for him. He'd follow me like a dog. He would come when I whistled. He'd find me if I hid and he would let me ride on his back on the way to the pit bottom where the roads were high enough to ride.

When the ponies were brought to the surface during a strike,

## Starting Work Underground

nearly all the pony drivers used to go down to the field to see them. We hadn't much to eat at home during strikes but we took them potato peelings and anything else we could find, and each pony would come across the field to his own driver.

There was real friendship between pony drivers. We shared the same difficulties, we were dependent on each other. Though we might not share the same aspirations we ran the same dangers, the same risks. Accidents at this time were many and varied to boys that were pony driving. I had quite a few accidents.

One Saturday morning I was driving my pony and I thought everybody had gone. One of the tubs got stuck fast in the side and as I climbed over the tubs to liberate it, the tub began to move and fastened me in the side. If the pony had set off I would have been killed instantly. I was gripped so tightly between the tub and the rock side that I couldn't speak and the breath was slowly going out of my body. In my boyish mind I wondered if this was the end. Then to my relief I saw a light approaching, it was Jackie Moulding, who realizing I had not followed him down the road had come back to see if I was all right. He sensed immediately what was wrong and with superhuman strength for a young boy he eased the tub off and got me out. We realized that my pony had stood firmly and held the tubs with his back end and this is what saved me from being run over.

Just a simple little incident but one can imagine how well that pony was treated by me as long as I had him.

Pit ponies are wonderful animals. They work uncomplainingly and they have a sense of danger sometimes superior to the men who drive them. I have seen pit ponies give ample warning of impending falls of roof. I think their hearing is more acute than ours. They can open big wooden doors with their heads, they can spin round in their own length. Miners too have a reputation for courage and resourcefulness. Throughout the whole of my pit life simple little incidents like I have recorded were repeated many times by men who shout and curse, and still willingly risk their lives to help other men, sometimes men they do not even know.

## Them and Us

The Mines Rescue Brigades are a perfect example of this sort of thing. They have often risked, and indeed given, their lives to try and rescue men that they didn't even know, from pits they had never seen, in times of explosion and disasters. The courage I admire is the sort of courage shown when one knows the danger and still carries on in spite of it. It's not as courageous to do spectacular things when you are not aware of any danger as it is when you know you might lose your own life and still willingly risk it to help someone else. Colliery managers very often give examples of this for they do know the atmospheric, technological and geological dangers better than anybody in the pit and still they will carry out these personal rescue efforts without any hope of medals for valour.

When I was quite young I saw a miner trapped by a big stone, he was knocked flat on his back, with a big stone across his chest and body, he could hear the strata creaking and could see dust particles falling from the roof, and from his experience, he knew that a further fall was imminent. Then another big, burly miner came and stood astride the trapped man and carried the weight of the stone about to fall on his back, while his mates tried to release the man that was fast. When the man was released you could see the man who was holding the stone trembling and his knees shaking with the sheer weight that he was supporting, and then suddenly he released the weight and jumped for freedom, and the stone fell and stripped the soles from off his boots. Which just shows how near he was to being underneath the fall himself. When it was over he just looked at the injured man and said, "Have I done that for thee?"

This is real courage, but in coal mines it is an everyday occurrence.

The war was now over, my brothers had returned home and my mother became ill, far more seriously than any of us imagined. I had never visualized life without her, she had always been there. She had been so busy looking after my father and us that she never seemed to have the time to look after herself. I can't even remember ever having heard her complain, so when the doctor told us that she had no chance of recovery it was a terrible shock to all of us.

It was the custom in mining families that whenever any close relative was dying, particularly parents, all the family would gather round the bedside until death actually came. We had a big family and when my mother died we were all there. One of my elder sisters said, "Can you hear the angels singing?" My other sisters could. For my part I didn't hear anything. Hearing them talking my mother managed to open her eyes and with a weak gesture she motioned to me to go to the bedside. She feebly put her hand on my head and in a whisper murmured, "Tha seems to have got above thy share of brains. Make sure that whatever you do or whatever you become, never forget the pit from which you were dug or the rock from which you were hewn. Try and use the talents which God has given you to help other people." Shortly after that she died. My father knelt by the side of the bed saying to us, "There, she's landed. She's gone to her reward. There's no need to weep. Live your lives in such a way that when you die there is no doubt at all that you can go and join her." He then prayed for God's help, but I noticed he finished his prayer with the words: "We can't understand it, Lord, but Thy will, not ours, be done."

Their faith again seemed to sustain them, but after her death there was a gap in my life that I thought would never be filled and as each day passed I missed her more. Life at home was not the same. One of my elder sisters, Alice, who had never married, came to live at home to look after a very sadly diminished family. There were only two of the boys at home now and all the rest of the girls were married.

I had begun to enjoy my work. I was keen to learn and eager for knowledge. I took every opportunity of watching older men doing their very skilled tasks and I benefited from their great experience.

My brothers got fed up and impatient with my constant questioning. I forgave them. To them mining was a job both difficult and dangerous but one they put out of their minds

*Them and Us*

when at home, and to have me constantly questioning them was irritating to say the least.

They have told me since that they used to say to each other: "Ar young un, he'll go a long way." They didn't know quite how to say it to me, so they didn't say anything.

CHAPTER SIX

# MORE ABOUT MY FATHER

My father was a good organizer—today he would be a good Methods Man—he organized his sons, his sons-in-law and his grandsons.

When we came home from the pits he had all our jobs ready planned out for us. Some to clean the pigs out, some to dig the garden, others to wheel manure into the garden, tar to fetch from the gas house and other tasks, all shared out and measured off, according to what he felt we could manage to do.

There was one job that we didn't like, and that was fetching tar from the local gasworks, two miles away, and coming back with two two-gallon buckets full of tar, carried with a wooden square—for balance—all uphill. It was a dirty sticky job, one we all tried to avoid. During one period my father had asked and ordered us to fetch tar and we hadn't done so. He started a blazing row and gave his final ultimatum: "If you don't fetch it tomorrow I'll fetch it myself. And with my heart being in the state it is I shall certainly drop dead coming up the hill. Then how will you feel?"

We'd heard it all before and the next day after we came in from work and had our dinners, he renewed his ultimatum. There is a custom in mining families, and that is that the eldest will get washed first and the others will follow in order of seniority. When there is a job to do like fetching tar we used to do it before we got washed, so when my eldest brother prepared to get washed we knew he wasn't going to fetch it.

My father sat in his chair pretending to read but he was watching us all the time. The next brother pulled his shirt off, he wasn't going.

Eventually they all got washed but me, so now I was the

centre of attention, including his. I thought; if they aren't going why should I go? I took my shirt off. Father bounced out of his chair, threw his cap on and set off to the pig sty where the tar buckets were kept on the roof. He was in a real temper.

Unknown to all of us the night previous, one of my brothers-in-law, who was working on the night shift had heard the ultimatum, thought he would give us all a pleasant surprise and he fetched the tar when he came home at six o'clock in the morning.

My father snatched at the supposed empty buckets and down they came straight on top of his head. The tar ran right down his face, over his whiskers, shoulders, his shirt the lot. What a picture! He came back to the house worse mad than he was before. My mother saw him coming, met him at the door, "Oh, William, don't come in like that on my clean linoleum." "What have I to do, stand in the street like a scarecrow," he shouted.

"Stay there, William, I'll get some lard." A good recipe for removing stains.

He stayed all right stamping with anger. Mother rubbed and rubbed his whiskers with lard but it wouldn't come off, it only got worse. In desperation she took a can of paraffin and tried to get it off with that.

By now the usual crowd of advising neighbours had gathered, who had many comments and much advice to offer, but one of my brothers—the first to recover from our laughing spasm—went to the door and threw a box of matches. "Try a match, Dad." It was the last we saw of my brother for a long while.

My father was very fond of playing draughts, he used to play us quite often and we used to let him beat us. It put him in a real good temper for the rest of the night.

We were having a big revivalist campaign at the chapel and the evangelist in charge came to our house for tea. After the meal he pulled out a pack of cards and said, "Let's have a game of whist." My father was horrified. "No whist in this house. No child of mine is ever going to be able to say that he was taught the ways of the devil in my house." The parson was

## More About My Father

surprised. "Nay, Mr. Bullock, it's no worse than a game of draughts."

My father picked up the draughts and draughtboard off the cupboard top, threw them straight in the fire saying, "No more draughts then."

Oh yes, father was a character all right.

At chapel we boys used to go and sit on the back seats after we started work. During the singing of the first hymn the boss of the pit, who was also the boss at the chapel, came to fetch the new starters to the front. This was a ritual, rigidly upheld by both sides, until we were about fifteen when we could stay at the back.

One Sunday night one of my brothers who had just started work had gone to sit with the older boys at the back. I was sat at the front with my mother. My father was singing with the choir. When the manager went to fetch the young boys up to the front my brother resisted and the boss clouted him on the back of his head. My father who had been looking over the top of his glasses put his hymn book down, strode straight down the chapel, shouted the names of each of his sons, without any hesitation they came out. My father gave each one of them a sharp slap and sent them up to the front. Then without any warning my father swung a beautiful right hook to the manager's chin and shouted, "I want everyone in this place of worship to know, that when any corporal punishment has to be administered to any member of my family, I—and I alone—will do it." With this he turned, strode back through the now silent congregation, took his place back in the choir, picked up his hymn book and started singing. The service recommenced.

My eldest brother, John Willie, was working down the same colliery as my father, as a matter of fact he was pony driving to the coalface where my father was working. When the shift had finished and my father was going towards the pit bottom he came to a fall of roof and underneath it he could see two feet protruding. There was no one else about and father shifted the rock with his bare hands and realized that the man he had liberated was his son, John Willie. There were no telephones

## Them and Us

then and very little first aid. He picked my brother up and carried him a mile to the pit bottom. He rode up the shaft with him, put my brother in the lamp cabin in front of the fire and covered him with his own coat. He then went to see if he could get the horse and trap to have my brother taken to hospital, but the horse and trap had been taken to Woodlesford Station to fetch the coal owner who was a cripple. He went back to see if my brother was all right and realized he was very badly hurt, so he ran across the fields to intercept the groom on the coach road—which is now my road leading to my house—when he met them he stopped the horse and the groom struck father with his whip. Father reached up and pulled him from his seat, threw him on one side, unharnessed the horse, jumped on its back, and rode it at the gallop back to the pit. There he harnessed the horse to the cart and took my brother—who was really seriously injured to Leeds Infirmary—my father carried him in his arms to the first person he saw in a white coat and said, "Do something for my lad quick, Doctor."

We learned after that his action had certainly saved my brother's life.

There was an aftermath. The next morning when my father went to the pit he was told at the lamp cabin that he couldn't have his lamp and that he wouldn't be allowed to go down the pit again until he had seen the manager, and brought a note back from the manager, to say he could have his lamp again.

He came home and at 9 a.m. he went to see the colliery manager in his office. Before my father could speak the manager started giving him a real telling off. "Did you know it was the owner—a cripple—that you so cruelly left standing in the coach road?"—the coach road is a road a mile long leading through the Lowther estate, not a public road but one used by the coal owner. My father tried to explain what had happened but it didn't make any difference. No matter what my father said all the colliery manager could think about was that the coal owner had been inconvenienced, finally, the manager said, "You've finished, you'll never work at this pit again."

Just then a voice from the inner office said, "Who is that?"

"It's Bill Bullock, who left you in the coach road yesterday."

*More About My Father*

"Bring him in here."

My father went into his room, the owner looked at him: "Tell me all about it."

My father found him a kindly man and he was able to talk quite freely and after my father had finished his explanations the owner remarked, "I am really sorry, it's a terrible thing to have happened, what can I say to recompense you for all the trouble I've caused? But I'll tell you this as long as ever I or mine own this pit, there will be work for you and yours." The owner then gave my father half a sovereign and a cigar.

When my father came home he put the cigar and the half sovereign under a glass case on the sideboard and there they remained until he died.

No matter how short of money we were, that coin was not allowed to be touched.

When people were dying in the village, relatives used to send for my father to pray for the near departed, to administer the "last rites". He used to come back home and say, "A good Christian that man, he knows where he's going"; or he would say, "He's not much faith, he died very hard." Then my mother would go over to the house and lay-out the corpse ready for the undertaker to take over. There were no state nurses in those days, we all seemed to rely very much on each other and my mother brought practically every baby into the village during this period.

Families were big, we had literally scores of relations and family visits were the chief source of social activity.

I have talked a lot about my father, but only of my experiences with him, but there were many things I found out I didn't even know about him.

Years after my father died, an old uncle was talking to me about my parents, he was one of the elder brothers of my mother. I'd been saying that my father had set us all a great example, he never smoked or drank and I had never heard him swear or known him gamble.

My uncle asked if I would like to know the truth about my father.

"Of course."

## Them and Us

"Well! The first time I met your father he was twenty years old. He was stripped to the waist, stood outside the colliery offices at Popes and Pearsons, offering to fight any man for his wages. Miners could never resist a challenge and that day I saw him have three fights and he took three men's wages. We saw his possibilities and a few of us formed a syndicate to back him and arrange fights for him, not boxing as you know it, sheer all-in fighting. He never lost. But his greatest achievement," my uncle went on, "was a road race. Every competitor had to set off at the local pub, run or walk eighteen miles and drink a pint in every pub en route. There were over twenty pubs, your father—who you say never drank—was the only man who finished the course. A short time after this, your father came to our house to sign a contract for another fight and as we sat in the kitchen, your mother, then a bonny lass of sixteen, walked through the kitchen, your father looked at her and said, 'Is tha spokken for, lass?' Your mother replied, 'No, I'm not.' 'Then tha is now,' said your father.

"Your grand-dad who was listening to the conversation remarked, 'We're having no prize-fighters in our family, we are good living Baptists.'

"Your father jumped up saying, 'It seems I'm good enough to fight for the family but not good enough for the family. Right! Thee wait for me lass, I'll be back.' He then tore up the contract he was about to sign, within a day or two he went to the baptist chapel and in time he got baptized.

"Six months later he came back to the house, smart, clean and tidy and said to your grandfather: 'Can I walk out with the lass now?'

"'We are contractors, you are only a horse breaker. You cannot give her the standard of life she is accustomed to.'"

My mother was just a skivvy for a large family and yet he wasn't good enough for her.

My uncle continued: "Your father said, 'Wait for me lass I'll be back.' Then he left the local colliery and went to see the manager of Bowers Row Pit, about eight miles away and said to the manager: 'Do you want any contracting doing?'

"'What can you do?'

## More About My Father

" 'Anything,' your father replied."

Within six months my father was contracted to this pit making a new pit bottom and within twelve months my grandfather and my uncles were working for my father and a few months later my mother and father were married, living in a little miner's cottage, the same house as I have described previously, two bedrooms, one room and a kitchen downstairs, bare walls, no water, no lights, no sanitation. It was in a long row of thirty other houses just like it and in this house all of us were born and all of us grew up.

My father lived in this house for fifty-nine years, paying rent every week and when he died he didn't own a brick. A year or two ago all the old village was being demolished and I went and bought our old house from the contractor for five pounds. I didn't want to see it smashed to pieces by a bulldozer. I carefully took out the windows and the bedroom floors and I have used them in the reconstruction of the stables I have bought.

It may be sentimental, but I am reminded when I walk on the floor of one of my rooms that this is the floor of the bedroom where it started.

Yes, in this humble house all their sons and daughters grew slowly to be adults, brothers and sisters got married and lived in other cottages exactly like it.

CHAPTER SEVEN

## TEEN AGE

I was now growing fast, good at soccer, cricket and boxing. Life was exciting, I was now taller and bigger than my brothers. When they came back from the Army I was no longer the baby, but a worker, able to hold his own with them in games and fighting. I was attending night school regularly. Every night of my leisure was occupied. I was fond of girls, but didn't have a lot of time to spend with them.

I was beginning to realize that I should never get far in the mining industry if I stayed at the family pit. The bosses at this pit seemed to be here for ever, and their sons were waiting to take their places when they died.

Another thing set me back a bit. I had been brought up in the atmosphere of *Them* and *Us*; when suddenly my brother, Dick, who was now the eldest son in the family since John Willie got killed, had become engaged and had eventually married, the undermanager's daughter.

He had my father's temper.

He could scrap all night.

He taught me how to play cricket.

He was the captain of the cricket team.

He taught me how to swim—if taking me on the back of his bike and throwing me in at the deep end, can be described as teaching—and I knew when he did this, that he would fetch me out if I got into difficulties.

Now this hero of mine was selling the pass. He was going to marry the boss's daughter. This was going to be a real embarrassment. He had crossed over with a vengeance to the other side. His father-in-law made him a deputy, he was now one of *them*. He shaved with scented soap and his father-in-law—the boss—had begun to visit us socially. Dick built the first bridge between *them* and *us* because being a loyal Bullock, even though he had joined *them* he still had to come back to *us*.

Seeing the boss in our house was something I had never expected and something I thought I would never get used to. So I felt the time was now here when I ought to be seeking fresh fields to conquer.

My brothers were home again. The war was over. I had gone through several very important years without them. They had left me a kid and they came back to a young man bigger than them. But they came back with a new confidence and independence. They had done things, seen things and been to places that no one else in the family had. Some quickly got married and the family circle thinned down rapidly and drastically. I was now very good with horses, indeed, all my family were. My brothers had all passed on their knowledge to me, backed by hints and suggestions. I was determined to be a good pony driver and I was.

So much so that the boss asked me if I would take young ponies straight from the hills and train them. This was a real task, they had as many humours, habits and idiosyncracies as human beings. No two ponies were alike. Some were terrified, some quite composed. Some would work straight away, others had no intention of working. Once you had won their confidence, some were eager to learn; some were just obstinate. They are very similar to dogs. You have to be kind and firm, repeating lessons day after day, but not too long at any one of them. You must be patient to get good results. I succeeded to such an extent that I was asked to go to Fryston and break in their young ponies. Where we had forty ponies at this small family pit, Fryston had over three hundred.

Quite a while before I had this offer to go to break in ponies, I was playing for our village soccer team near Whitkirk and their right-half and myself were sent off for fighting. We continued the fight behind the goal posts. After it was over a man came to me and gave me a card saying, "Come to this address on Tuesday and it will be to your advantage." I went, very curious, and found I was in a gymnasium, dimly lit. The man

## Them and Us

who had met me at the football match came up and smacked me across my face. In a flash I let go back at him. "Stop," he rapped out, "I wanted to see if you had guts." Then he proceeded to tell me of my natural ability for fighting and how much money I could earn with my fists, I only had to place myself in his hands. I started training as a fighter. What a job, eight hours down a pit, travel to Leeds, two to three hours in the gym walking, running, skipping, boxing and then a tram to Rothwell and a six mile run home!

My father was bitterly opposed to anything like this, and if I'd a black eye I used to wait until he'd gone to bed, and then come in from work next day holding my eye and saying I'd been kicked by a pony. Now I was really living two lives. I adopted as my boxing name my middle name, which was my mother's maiden name, Allen, though I fought as an amateur in my own name and nobody seemed any wiser.

You couldn't do this today, communications are vastly improved.

At that time if you fought in Newcastle it was days before anyone heard about it. Radio and television have altered all this.

The training was really hard, particularly to me, for I had been working down the pit all day. Some nights were spent in the gym, other nights we went for a run through the centre of Leeds and round Temple Newsam Park, the trainer always went in front on a bicycle. He never seemed to look behind and he didn't stop, he didn't want any of us to catch cold. I realized if I was the last out of the gym, I could drop out of this long procession of boxers and the trainer didn't seem any the wiser. We always travelled under the dark arches which are really bridges over which the railway lines crossed. I looked on this as being very fortunate for me, if not for my training. Some months before, at a dance, I had danced with a beautiful, black-haired slim girl who had the merriest eyes I had ever seen. When I went home that night, I had her name written in my diary. To my delight I found she only lived two or three streets away from the dark arches. My training runs, therefore, took me close to where she lived. I arranged with her to be under the dark arches at seven-thirty, and as the boxers ran past in single file, I used to drop out and stay with her until the boxers came back an hour later. Then I would fall in behind them until we reached the gym. None of the boxers ever gave me away and I thought that the trainer didn't know. Training nights, instead of being dreaded became a pleasure.

However, the best things come to an end. At this particular time Kid Lewis, the famous middle-weight champion, was in training in Leeds for a fight in the north. All the boxers in our gym who were anywhere near his weight used to box one round with him in their turns. One particular night as we all trotted back into the gym the trainer watched us strip. All the lads but me were panting and steam was rising off their bodies. When the trainer saw me: "By God," he said, "what fitness. You haven't even turned a hair." He turned to the other boxers and told them they could get dressed and to me he said, "You can spar with the champ, you are fit enough." I quickly found out I wasn't and it is a lesson I didn't forget.

It was about this time that our sex education began in earnest. Crude was our introduction, brutal and earthy were our sex lessons. Elder boys told us a lot about sex but our trainer used to give dire warnings as to the outcome of sex or masturbation. He used to tell us we would go blind, weak, daft and God knows what else.

It was all exciting, sex lessons were freely given by the most unexpected ladies in the most unexpected places.

Our trainer told us that sex dreams must be avoided, he advised going to sleep with an old bobbin, tied with a big bandage, in the centre of our backs, then we couldn't lay on our backs and so should not dream. Very telling arguments to young men who knew nothing different.

Our trainer always claimed that he could tell by our performance in the gym how we had behaved since he saw us last. So here again the old crude psychology succeeded: If you can't love 'em into it, frighten 'em into it. That was his theory, he was very successful and trained many champions.

His methods were all his own. When you were fighting and getting a real hiding he would calmly say when you returned

*Them and Us*

to your corner: "Good lad, you've got him going, one more round and he's yours."

Being good at sports made you popular with the boys and girls. Your relationship with boys was distinguished with a certain amount of respect.

It was through boxing that I first came into real contact with the police. One night in Leeds a chap had his coat half off and was shouting, "I'll fight anybody in Leeds for a pound."

As I passed, I dropped him one on his chin and I was summoned for disturbing the peace.

During this period I seemed to be in constant trouble with the police and I got summoned for causing a disturbance outside the Technical School. When we appeared at court the Chairman of the Bench, a man who knew me very well, asked me if I had anything to say. Very cockily I replied, "Yes. I would like to meet the policeman who brought me here in his own gymnasium. There I'll teach him a thing or two."

The police inspector stood up in the well of the court and said, "That can easily be arranged, your worship." Thereupon he invited me to the police headquarters a week later. My pal went with me but he was told at the door that he hadn't been invited and asked if he had any grudge against the police. When he assured them that he hadn't he was not allowed in, I went in alone. Never again.

The policeman whom I'd had trouble with, was conspicuous by his absence, but waiting for me, ready stripped, was the Police Heavyweight Champion and more to back him up. They told me: "Your grudge isn't against one policeman, it's against all police, right?"

"It is."

"Come on then, you can work it all off."

Needless to say this was just one more lesson I learned—Don't threaten anything you are not sure you can carry out.

If we had been fighting in a proper ring, I could have kept away from this big fellow a lot longer than I did in that gymnasium. The policemen, gathered all around, kept closing in until I couldn't use my feet to carry me out of danger.

One of our local police inspectors saw me fighting at Keighley. He told my father, "You must be proud of your youngest son, Mr. Bullock."

"Yes I am," said Dad. "He is doing very well at night school."

"Night school? I mean boxing," said the inspector. "I saw him fighting last week-end and I was very impressed."

Previously I had told my father that I had been staying with my married sister and, unfortunate for me, when he arrived home my sister was visiting the family.

"How long since you saw the lad?" he asked

"Oh weeks and weeks," she replied.

"Right, wait until he comes in. Stripped to the waist in front of crowds of people like a barbarian, making a spectacle of himself and worst of all, I fear, fighting under his mother's maiden name, dragging it in the dust."

He had evidently forgotten that Allen was also my middle name.

When I got home father went raving mad:

"Had I paid my board out of boxing money? If so, how often?"

Then he proceeded to give me an ultimatum:

"Give it up, or get out of this house and never come back..." and so on and so on.

I asked him if I could clear the contracts I had already signed. He agreed to this as he respected the written promise as much as the spoken one.

During this time I had the opportunity of meeting for the first time, young men and women of a different faith and a different race. Nearly everybody in the gym were Jews except myself. I found them good sportsmen and exceptionally fine fighters. Some of them took me to their homes and introduced me to their families. This was a new experience for me—all I had known about Jews was what I had been told and what I had read. I liked them very much, they had a real sense of humour and some of the friends I made then are my best friends today.

Eventually I couldn't pretend I had any more contracts to fight, to honour. My father's word was law. I had also started going out with a girl seriously and she didn't like fighting so I hung up my gloves ... at least officially.

I would have missed boxing, the clamour of the crowd and the challenge of the man in the opposite corner, had I not accepted the offer to train unbroken ponies at Fryston.

I didn't realize quite how this offer would change my life in linking me to a pit where I was one day to step over the fence and become a "gaffer", one of "them".

But as I saw it the offer was a good one, Fryston was only six miles away, the job meant an increase of sixpence a day, which would bring my wage up to five shillings and eightpence a day. Because it was a much bigger pit than our family pit it was far more modern, there would be more opportunities, a fresh environment, different people, but above all, away from the family influence and all the local bosses.

I would be on my own feet. I would be able to do more what I wanted to do. But what a difference.

I had left a pit where there were forty ponies and a shaft which was two hundred yards deep, where men worked with their trousers and shirts on. The pit was cool and had plenty of ventilation.

Fryston had over three hundred ponies. The shaft was nearly six hundred yards deep, the cages were nearly three times bigger and there were five times as many men. It was certainly the hottest pit in Yorkshire and the wildest set of men and lads I had ever met. The atmosphere underground was stifling. When you went on some of the working faces it was like going inside a Lancashire boiler. Everyone underground worked practically naked. I had heard swearing before but had never heard swearing with such venom and accompanied by such foul oaths as I heard here. The conditions down the pit were inhuman and the men had made themselves fit their environment. I couldn't believe such conditions could exist. Accidents to pony drivers and ponies were an everyday occurrence. More ponies were killed in a month at this pit than had been killed at the family pit that I had just left.

For the first year I cycled or walked to Bowers Row, six miles each way, but I eventually left home and went to live with a

*Teen Age*

well-known Fryston family called Astbury. I thought my family was a large one until I met theirs. We had a basic dozen, plus in-laws, but the Astburys had a score plus, in-laws. On my first visit to the village—I was going to be interviewed for my new job—there was a funeral. As I was passing, the coffin was just being taken into the church. As I cycled past it the last mourner had still not left the house, and the house was over a hundred and fifty yards away from the church! All of the funeral train were descendants or in-laws of the old man Astbury, who had died.

They tell you in the village that the old man Astbury—the founder of the flock—used all the names of the disciples, with the exception of Judas, plus Shadrak, Meeshak and Abednigo to name his sons.

When I eventually went to live in Fryston I lived with one of his sons and he told me a lot about the Astbury family.

The Astburys had an Auntie Jennie who had thirteen children of her own, and during the First World War some of the Astbury daughters and some of the Astbury's son's wives wished to work at the local ammunition factory. The problem was what to do with their children. Aunt Jennie solved this for them. She had a young baby of her own at the time and every day for months she took over five other young suckling babies belonging to various Astburys and suckled the lot. This was considered to be her war effort.

The more I got to know this family and one or two more large families like them I realized that if they were with me in my pit life, who could be against me?

I took an active part in the life of Fryston village. I was doing a bit of preaching and I formed physical culture classes for young men and women in the local chapel. The village curate had started boxing classes in the local church hut and I used to go there to help him. My boxing ability stood me in good stead and I think they respected me more for this than they would have done otherwise.

So my life in a new environment with total strangers started. In a couple of years I left pony driving and started my apprenticeship for a coalminer, with a family of six brothers, called

## Them and Us

Kelsy, who lived at Fairburn. This was another important part of my development. Before I proceed to describe my actual coalface training, I ought to describe Fryston as a village and its history. It is a village of great antiquity and it was destined to play a very important part in my whole life because I remained there for thirty-four years.

Its name is a derivative of Friga, the Saxon God after whom Friday was named. In the year 1240 it was a small but important hamlet and was known as Friston upon Aire. The parish priest at that time being William De Fengars. Records of this period are scarce but one of the earliest written accounts mentions one Alice Haght who "Oaned mutch property of value and valuable land in Friston" and who, among other details was taxed for "Ten score of lands at sixpence per acre". In 1332 a vicar of Friston was appointed and given eighteen acres of land in Queldale Town (Wheldale). From such information one can assume that Fryston land has always had a high value placed on it.

It was long known that the land around this village was rich in minerals:

"Earth burns ryte well with much useful warmth and littel smoake," wrote an old chronicler. The importance of which will be better understood by adding that it was two hundred and three years later in 1535 that at nearby Glasshoughton it was recorded: "The people burne much yearth cole by cawse it is plentiful and sold good chape."

England in those days was a far different land from the one we know today. It was a land steeped in ignorance and controlled by fear. A very unequal distribution of the good things of life created dirt, poverty, for the peasant classes and it can be here added, without offence to the religious or political beliefs of anyone, that life was little more than a burden to many and that everyday existence was without happiness, as the future was without hope.

In the fifteenth century, Fryston Hall, set in the rich beauty of the Park, was owned by the Rotherfields. Together with the great houses Temple Newsam, Swillington, Ledsham, Methley and Oulton, Fryston Hall in its original state served as a slant on an age of elegant living for the few, and an evolutionary phase in English history.

In 1604, James I was on the throne and the Hollings family lived at Fryston Hall. At this time Fryston was a "place of rare beauty—and had goodly air". But also in 1604, one hundred and sixteen persons, young and old, were "Buryed in Fryston, all of whom had dyed of the plague." It was more than a hundred years later that one George Crowle, M.P. for Hull from 1722 to 1741, during the reigns of George I and George II, settled in Fryston and if the Crowles left a mark on Fryston history it is now of no consequence.

Fryston's more important history seems to have started in the eighteenth century when the estate was handed over to a family called Milnes. Originally Derbyshire folk, the Milnes had entered the woollen trade in Wakefield and earned a great deal of respect for their domestic and industrial integrity. They also earned a vast fortune in business and did good work in and around Fryston. The Milnes family "found much comfort and interest in the lovely surrounds of Fryston". It was the respected Robert Pemberton Milnes who was offered one of two important government posts, either the Chancellor of the Exchequer or Secretary of State for War. He declined the offer of a peerage with the same firmness he declined the offer of the important position.

History tells us that after Edward II captured Pontefract Castle, the Earl of Lancaster was made prisoner, taken before the King, and sentenced to be beheaded.

Five hundred years later his remains were found, carried to Fryston Hall and there buried in a great stone coffin made from the same sort of stone, taken from Fryston by the monks who built Selby Abbey. Soon afterwards the age of elegance drew to its close. Richard Milnes' son became the Earl of Crewe and a sweeping change came over the face of Fryston.

The time had come when industry had assumed more importance than ancestry. Men were badly needed, men who, without claiming an equal share from life, would put their time, skill and labour, at the disposal of the country.

It was an important phase, both in history and industrial

## Them and Us

development. It was the period when England was first making great strides in international trade. It was the first step in a march that has resulted to a large extent in ancient lands and properties being invested for the use of the many rather than the few.

Man was, in fact, slowly coming into his own.

It is with this knowledge and history on our side that we realize how much man has achieved from such poor beginnings.

I have always felt proud of Britain's coalminers in general and proud of my great team at Fryston in particular.

What are the men of Fryston like? Their conversation is spattered by dialects that will not fade, even if they live in Yorkshire for another thirty years. They are neat and tidy; or they are slipshod and untidy.

They believe in God because they have been taught to do so; or are agnostics and believe only what they wish to believe.

They are strong.

They are noisy or they are quiet with the quietness of men whose lives are in constant peril.

Argue with them and you're met with a torrent of invectives that would make a stranger gasp. Two minutes later you can have a drink with them and wonder whether the argument ever really happened.

The men of Fryston are like that.

They are afraid, yes; but only afraid of a future that may be less secure than the present. And some of them fear neither God nor Devil, and to hell with the future.

They have great talents and equally great skills for their daily tasks.

They curse the pit, curse the manager and show deep contempt for all authority; especially if authority wears a collar and tie.

But they have a deep respect for competent authority; collar and tie or not.

Their tastes are simple and they organize their lives to have the least complication.

They are completely selfish, yet will perform noble deeds when danger threatens.

Their voices are like their hands, rough and hard, but they will assure those who are afraid and their hands can be very gentle on injured limbs or flesh.

They are the cussedest, kindest, loudest voiced, clean-minded, biggoted, good mannered lot of men you could ever wish to meet.

Such are the men of Fryston. Such are the people who have inhabited the village ever since the pit was sunk.

I know them. I respect them.

These then were the men that I was to spend thirty-four years of my life with. I had to work alongside them, and what is more important as things transpired, they had to work with and for me.

When I eventually went to the coalface the Kelsy brothers were in charge of me. Men worked in groups of six and they were to give me my coalface training. There were five brothers and me working on a district where the coal was only two foot thick. All the coal had to be got by picks, hammers and wedges and filled by shovels.

The seam was so low that we had to throw all our coal back by shovel for a distance of fifteen feet. I had been brought up in a family who worked hard and I had worked hard myself ever since I could remember.

Training was hard in the gymnasium. In the local football team I had played football until my muscles ached.

Now, however, for the first time I realized what physical effort was. My back, arms and legs were so stiff that I felt I would never straighten them again. The brothers laughed at me when I complained. "If you feel you can't straighten them, don't try to, until the end of the shift."

This aching and stiffness was followed by violent cramp and by the end of my first shift I had blisters on my hands and sores on my knees.

The Kelsy brothers had been through all this in their early days and they just laughed and told me in their rough, kindly way—not in the words I shall use—to wee on my hands! To rub tobacco juice in my cuts until I toughened up and grew hooves instead of blisters.

All my previous physical training counted for nothing by the side of this toughening up process.

We also had to contend with the overpowering heat. It was absolutely stifling.

Everybody seemed to have a nasty itching rash known as the "Fryston heat rash".

Everyone of us carried six pints of water, and in addition to this water was sent down the pit in barrels. Even then we hadn't enough to drink.

I can understand now far better than I could before the reason for the swearing and the oaths. They cursed the conditions. They cursed the management and they cursed each other.

No matter how hard we worked and no matter what hardships we endured, at the end of the day, we were paid two shillings and three farthings for each ton of coal we filled.

At this price miners had to work eight or nine hours, shovelling non-stop, to try and get enough money to pay for the bare essentials of living. He couldn't afford to be off work so absenteeism was no problem.

Every miner was in the trade union. I never met anybody working in or about a coalmine who was not a member of the National Union of Mineworkers. Then, as now, union meetings were not very well attended unless there was trouble. A few leading characters had the official positions and the others more or less left it to them to make decisions.

I attended union meetings but I never became a union official in the miners' union. About this time I was spending more time at chapel. I had begun preaching. My father had always said I had got "the gift of the gab".

Preaching I enjoyed for usually the colliery manager and his officials attended chapel and when you were in the pulpit you knew there was no debate following the sermon. What a good way to get your message across.

There were several texts in the Bible which lend themselves to the subjects that one wished to preach about in this company:

"Who is my neighbour?"

My father, William Bullock.

I'm standing next to my mother on the extreme left of the group.

My maternal grandfather: the man that told my father he was not good enough.

"Ye stiff necked, venomous, and vipers."

In these two texts alone they had ample outlet for the venom of generations.

The religious atmosphere was changing now. Even today some people who don't know the working man believe trade unions to be the tool of the devil.

This is odd, because the early unions were often led by deeply religious men who saw nothing strange in fighting for justice for six days and then kneeling humbly before God on the seventh.

Indeed, even as I began to take an interest in the union I was also beginning to make my name as a preacher. Some of these old union leaders were what is known as Primitive Methodist ranters.

They preached hell-fire, and damnation.

If they couldn't love you into the kingdom of heaven they swore they would frighten you into it.

The prayer meetings that followed divine service were as good as any of the near hysterical rallies of negroes sometimes seen on television.

Chapel prayer meetings were really inspiring and to many people were a great comfort.

Enthusiasm ran wild. Usually the colliery officials prayed publicly first, but then came the turn of the miners.

This was their finest hour.

This is what they had waited all week for. God was no longer an omnipotent being in heaven.

He was in this chapel. He was their mate.

These are the phrases I have actually heard my father use in a prayer meeting in front of colliery managers and other officials—

"We know, Lord, there is no need to tell Thee anything. Tha knows it all."

"Tha knows our difficulties, but *they* don't."

"Tha knows what we have to put up with at work, and Tha knows *their* tactics."

"We thank Thee tonight, Lord, that Tha canst see through *them* and has promised that Tha'll punish the wicked."

*Them and Us*

"When the rich young ruler asked Thy son what he had to do to be saved, Jesus replied, 'Go sell all thou hast and give it to the poor.' We are poor, Lord. Tha knows that but do *they*? If *they* do *they* keep awfully quiet about it and *they* give us nothing."

"We be thankful tonight, Lord, if Thou in Thy wisdom would point out to *them* the error of *their* ways."

These religious gatherings and prayer meetings were to miners a way of letting off steam, a safety valve, a temporary escape from reality.

What a really marvellous thing their faith was. Their lives were a living example of "The faith that moves mountains".

It kept them going through really bad times. Indeed, sometimes their faith was the only thing they had.

When attendances at the chapel were beginning to fall the Chapel Committee would arrange an evangelistic campaign.

They would appoint a well-known saviour of souls for a fortnight. A sort of miniature Billy Graham. The evangelist had all Billy Graham's fervour and enthusiasm if not his education.

Before the revival was due to start, prayer meetings were held nightly in the chapel, in the miners' homes, and in the open air. Before the missioner arrived the spadework had been done. The faithful had reached "concert pitch".

They were in good voice and they were in good heart. As children, while not understanding all it meant, we were very excited and thoroughly enjoyed these fortnightly campaigns.

The preacher was welcomed into our midst, he usually dined first with the boss, and then he would try to have meals in as many different houses as he could manage during the two weeks he stayed in the village.

We all turned up to hear his first sermon. This was his first test. When he preached it was usually a torrent of eloquence. "Open thy mouth and I will fill it," said the Lord, and in the case of the evangelist he fulfilled his promise. He would talk about the evils of the world and the people who inhabited the world, about the goodness of God, the sacrifice of God in allowing—and Christ in enduring—the agonies of the cross.

We had the vision of the crucifixion so skilfully and vividly described that we became living witnesses of this great tragedy. We were taken into the very presence of the Last Supper. We were there in the Garden of Gethsemane. We were present at Jesus's trial by Pontius Pilate. Then came the most glorious of all, the evangelist's description of the Resurrection.

All this, however, was only the hors d'oeuvres, the main course came with the preacher's clarion call to everybody present to come to the penitent form. After he had made his appeal the choir would softly sing:

> Sinner, how thy heart is troubled,
> God is coming very near.
> Do not hide thy deep emotion,
> Do not check that falling tear.

Then the minister would cry out:

> Oh be saved his grace is free,
> Oh be saved he died for thee.

Then the choir:

> Art thou waiting till tomorrow,
> Thou may never see its light.
> Come at once, accept His mercy,
> He is waiting, come tonight.

Now the minister again:
"You are miners, brothers, think of the dangers of your calling," and you would begin to hear the breaking of the timber, the falling of the rock, and you would sit there, waiting. Again the preacher would talk about the agonies of the cross until you could literally see and feel that people were getting the message he wanted to convey. There was a feeling, of fear, of hell-fire everlasting. Sorrow for the man who had suffered for *them* on the cross.

Then a feeling of gratitude that without this sacrifice they could never have had the chance to avoid eternal damnation.

Then the evangelist would tell them how they could repay this debt. "There is more joy in heaven over one sinner that repenteth, repent now."

## Them and Us

People used to shout, moan, laugh, pray and sing all at the same time until you couldn't tell whether they were carried away with real joy, or whether they were suffering intense mental anguish.

Despite all the evangelist's efforts there was a shyness about going to the penitent form.

Someone was needed to go out to the front and kneel and pray, "God be merciful to me a sinner."

If the minister could get a single sinner out there, to break the ice, others would follow and he was on the way to winning the fight.

One of my brothers seemed always to be the one to go out first.

Joseph didn't just get converted once but practically every time there was a mission. We used to wonder why he felt this divine call to forgiveness so often. He was not a bad lad, he'd no more than his share of wickedness. But there he was, first out every time.

What a fuss my father made of him, each time he was converted. He stayed up for supper telling the neighbours of his joy that coming back into the fold had given him.

A fold, that none of his other brothers ever realized he had left. The evangelist called him by his first name, the boss chatted him up at work, and all the elders of the chapel pointed my brother out to people as a shining example of what we ought to be.

What I do know is that he was allowed to stay up for his supper with the evangelist and my parents, having ham and eggs, while we were sent to bed with a slice of bread and dripping.

We used to chide him when he came to bed about his attitude but he used to quite calmly reply: "I forgive you, I forgive you."

The people that were converted at these missions were really enthusiastic. Some used to stick it and remain chapel-goers for the rest of their lives and with others it soon used to wear off.

I've seen converts on their feet at these prayer meetings

crying, "We are all sinners, Lord," and immediately being told by another convert:

"Thee speak for thisen. Thou might be a sinner but it doesn't mean we all are."

Looking back on these gatherings I have never seen the colliery manager overcome by this sort of emotion. Although he always looked a bit kinder, a little more tolerant during this period.

My father's belief in the Bible has always amazed me. He believed it to be literally true. He could quote scripture by the yard to prove his points.

He had quotations for every occasion.

When I was studying for one of my important examinations I had to write a treatise "On the formation of the Coal Measures".

I worked six months on this and in the article I wrote all I knew about the different theories of how the coal measures came to be formed. "THE DRIFT THEORY, THE IN SITU THEORY AND THE COSMIC ICE THEORY." In my opinion it was a really good article, but alas it never went to the examiners.

For one night while I was out my father picked up the treatise and read for the first time the story of evolution. My sister informs me, that to say he was annoyed was putting it mildly, he made a scene about blasphemy being written in his house, and that he never thought he would live to see the day when his son would be writing atheist propaganda.

Then he threw the whole lot in the fire with the exception of the first page. Right across this he scrawled in his scraggy handwriting, "Read Genesis, Chapter I 'In the beginning God', and may he forgive you."

## CHAPTER EIGHT

## EARLY MANHOOD

One week-end I had been fighting, I received a nasty black eye, so I decided I would go and stay with my sister instead of having to answer a lot of questions from my father. My sister didn't know I was coming and when I got to her house I found they had gone to a dance at the local Adult School.

I went across to join them at the dance. As soon as I got in the building I saw a beautiful girl dancing. I went up to my sister and said, "Who's that?"

"She's staying with us."

"Oh good, so am I; will you introduce me?"

"I certainly shan't. She's far too good for you to play around with."

"My fame has gone before me." I murmured sadly and went up to the girl, who was called Anne, and introduced myself.

She had evidently heard about me and not much to my credit —as far as girls were concerned—from my sister. Not surprisingly, therefore, she showed little interest in me, if any.

This was a real setback and—I suppose—roused my fighting spirit. Where before I had been interested I was now determined, "And the villain he pursued her to the end."

It wasn't an easy matter to get her to meet me for my sister had not been very charitable in her description of me. But during the evening I found out that Anne lived at Skipton, in North Yorkshire, that her father was one of the founders of the Labour Party and her mother was a keen party member.

They were all members of the Adult School Movement.

I met her once or twice, largely by accident, but I wrote to her regularly and I was fully determined, that this was the girl, who was going to be my wife.

## Early Manhood

Perseverance pays and we reached the stage of going to each others homes. There was a marked difference in her first visit to Bowers Row and my first visit to Skipton. Anne's first visit to us in the mining village must have been a real ordeal. Anne came from a family of four; now she was with a family of fourteen, plus in-laws.

Her family were refined; we were rough.

They came from a lovely market town steeped in history and surrounded by lovely hills and moors.

We existed in a drab colliery village surrounded by dirt stacks instead of mountains, and by mines instead of moorland.

When she first came to the village the first person she met coming down the street was a very old woman, our next door neighbour, who was the mother of our only international Rugby League footballer. Her son had just come back from a tour of Australia. I introduced her to my young lady. She placed her big rough, work calloused hands on Anne's shoulders and said, "Thee be good to him, or tha'll eh me to reckon with." She had deep-set eyes and her eyelids were bright red, a terrifying sight for one's first introduction.

The family welcomed Anne with the usual playful warnings as to what she was letting herself in for. We went to chapel on the Sunday and after evening service there was the usual family get-together for singing and prayers. She'd never experienced ought quite like this for in the Adult School they were very similar to Quakers and they had silent prayer.

What a difference!

As we sat on the sofa one of my brothers said, "Look at General Booth yonder," meaning my father with his long white beard. Anne laughed and my father saw her, "Don't make fun of us," he shouted. "These hymns are being sung to the glory of God and it would please me much better if you would join in."

I stood up, "Don't you speak to her like that."

Father looked flabbergasted, he picked up the poker, shouting he would split me down the middle if I dare talk to him like that in his own house. He gave me a violent shove that deposited

## Them and Us

me on top of Anne and ended my rebellion almost before it started.

My sisters started telling her about my childhood days. They told her that when I was very young I was short-tongued and used to pronounce 'G' as 'D'. On my birthday I had asked for something as a birthday present but hadn't received it and I came downstairs saying, "I wouldn't be dood today not even for dod." Then they told how I prayed all year for a football at Christmas, hadn't got one, and then was so offended with God that I refused to pray for weeks.

How I said at last that I would give God one more chance next Christmas and if I didn't get one, he—God—had had it.

As I walked with Anne through the village to attend chapel I was very proud of her, she was really good looking, full of a quiet dignity and looked—somehow—different.

A week later I went to Skipton to her home to receive my baptism of fire.

But it wasn't difficult. They were so different from people I had known before. They were kindly and intelligent and in their little humble home at Skipton, I began to learn a new way of life. Was taught a new philosophy, but above all, I saw examples of people doing something about the very problems that we in our village spent so much time praying about.

Anne's father was a kind man, persuasive and gentle. He had a wonderful flow of quiet eloquence. He could hold an audience enraptured. He could also talk a long time about nothing at all if he was filling-in time for a main speaker to arrive.

Anne introduced me to her friends. Again there was a vast difference. It was the quietness of their voices that was so difficult for me to understand.

At our house there always seemed to be so many of us, talking over the heads of each other, several conversations and different subjects, being carried on simultaneously. All of us having to shout to be heard at all.

Here, however, at Skipton conversation seemed to have some point, some objective, altogether more friendly.

It seemed strange to me to hear an argument quietly pursued

## Early Manhood

to its logical conclusion without anybody losing their temper and either stalking off to bed, dashing out of the house or finishing the argument by saying, "It is so, because I say so."

They were "pacificists", they didn't believe in war, they didn't believe in fighting physically amongst themselves. Their fights were of a different sort. They banded together and by propaganda fought—what was to them—the common enemy CAPITALISM.

How would a quick tempered young prize-fighter fit in with a family like this?

It was not difficult, they made it easy. Not a word of reproach about my activities, they just quietly set an example.

The time came when I could not go there for a week or two because all my spare time was spent training for a boxing contest. I had promised to send a telegram as soon as the fight was over to let them know how I had got on.

Next time I went to their house Anne's father asked, "I wonder if you really think it's worth it, Jim?"

"Why?"

"Well, all through the evening you were fighting there was a quietness. Anne hardly spoke. She spent a lot of time watching the clock and I am sure she was imagining that you were being slaughtered. I believe she suffered more than you did, Jim."

I hadn't suffered at all, I had gone in the ring at 8.15 p.m. and was out again fifteen minutes later having won quite easily, but I took the point.

I weighed things up carefully, took into consideration the row there had been with my father, the trouble it was causing at home. So after talking it over with her we decided it was not worth the anxiety it caused her or the trouble it was causing me.

So, as I have said before, I hung the gloves up, but giving up boxing did not mean that I gave up the desire to fight or the skill to fight.

My intention to become something different now became very real and for the first time in my life I was given real encouragement. I started studying both at night school and through correspondence courses. All my spare time was now

## Them and Us

spent at Skipton and I was introduced to many leading members of the Labour party and got to know them very well.

Under her father's influence and guidance I began to take a really keen interest in Labour party politics, my conversion was different to that of my brother. He was converted to religion many times, I was converted to Socialism once.

Later I began to speak on Labour platforms and to take part in their study groups.

In that little house in Skipton I met men like Philip Snowden, Sir Stafford Cripps, Herbert Morrison, O. G. Willy, Maurice Webb and many more.

Anne's, and my, friendship changed to courtship and we arranged to be married in May, 1926.

Unfortunately, for us, the great Strike started three weeks before we were due to be married, but we were young, we were enthusiastic, we were full of hope and courage. How could a little thing like a National Strike affect us?

It didn't.

Arrangements went smoothly ahead and we were married at Skipton Baptist Church on 22 May 1926.

However, the Strike did interfere drastically with our plans for the future.

Before our marriage we had applied for, and obtained, a new council house in the new village of Airedale which was being built near to Fryston colliery. We greeted the news with great joy but we little knew that we should have to pay fourteen shillings and twopence for twenty-eight weeks before we could go and live in it. All through the strike I lived at Skipton with Anne's people and Anne kept on working in Dewhurst's Cotton Mill.

It was awful to see our savings slowly disappearing. We hadn't a lot of money but what we had soon went and along with it went our hopes of a nicely furnished home.

The Strike dragged on and on. Poverty with its hardships and hunger grew in the mining villages. Living at Skipton, I was out of the real hardships caused by the strike but the suffering of my fellow miners and my family were never far out of my mind.

*Early Manhood*

To try and relieve some of the hardships in the mining villages we formed the Miners' Concert Party and Dance Band, conducted by my old friend Jack Woolford. Here I felt I could be a real help for I was now fairly well known, living with a family far better known in the Skipton division. A locality not affected by the strike but inhabited by a lot of people who I felt sure would support me. So there began what proved to be the best possible training I could have for my future speaking career. John the Baptist had nothing on me, for I also went "On ahead to prepare the way for them".

Wherever we went we were met with real kindness and sympathy.

We worked to a programme, well planned. We arranged with the local Labour Party to book the biggest hall in their locality. The miners then gave a concert and I made a speech to let the audience know what the Strike was about. We then took a collection and appealed for hospitality for the miners. The remainder of the evening was spent with our orchestra playing for dancing.

Never once did we lack a bed or food until we were ready to go to the next town or village.

On one occasion we were being chaired by a local Communist Party leader and the miners band played with far more gusto than skill "The Caliph of Baghdad". The chairman jumped to his feet and said very enthusiastically, "People who think that miners go about wearing red handkerchieves round their necks and spend all their spare time training whippet dogs ought to have been here tonight and heard these miners play 'Poet and Peasant' as beautifully as it has been played by our friends!"

Another time we were giving a concert in the old market town of Settle. It was a very wet day and the violin strings had got very damp, and all through the concert, strings kept breaking.

Our drummer was an old miner who stuttered very badly and had no knowledge of music whatever. The reason he was in the band at all was that he was very friendly with the conductor and did just what the conductor told him. We had no bass fiddle or cello so that bass music had to be supplied by a

## Them and Us

vigorous beating of the drum. The arrangements between the drummer and the conductor were marvellous. Every time the conductor moved his left hand the drummer hit the drum, and the wider the conductor moved his left arm, the harder the drummer hit the drum. We were playing a piece of music this particular afternoon, a piece that needed bass instruments that we hadn't got. The conductor got rather excited and threw his left arm wider and wider demanding more and more and heavier and heavier hits from the drummer.

The drummer tried his best. He was wet through with sweat and finally he stood up, turned round to me and stammered "WWwwwwwwwhat the h—— does he want?" And he let go with a mighty swipe at his drum but he missed it completely, he was striking with such force that his own impetus spun him round completely and he fell off the platform straight into the audience. If this concert had taken place in the Royal Albert Hall this episode might have ruined it, but it didn't ruin our concert, it made it. For everybody agreed that it was one of the best turns of the evening.

Our next engagement was at Silsden. Then, as now, the Skipton Conservative Party had a branch of the Young Imps. The Young Imps didn't like the miners and they didn't hesitate to let us know their opinion.

Neither did they like our methods of raising money. Therefore, when we went to Silsden we were surprised to see them attending our dance in strength. I knew they hadn't come to support us and I suspected trouble from the beginning.

Our orchestra was a big one and there wasn't room for all of them on the stage. The same old drummer had to have a chair on the floor near the band and every time the Young Imps were dancing past him, they pulled his drumsticks out of his hand, pushed him off his chair and made a real nuisance of themselves.

After watching this for a while I went on the stage, told the piano player to make a loud chord to get the attention of the dancers and I gave this ultimatum to the Young Imps: "You are here in force and it is quite evident you are here to make trouble, but there are many people enjoying the dance

## Early Manhood

who have come to support us, but you are determined to break it up. Now I've a simple suggestion. You people who want to dance please go to the back of the hall. We miners are now leaving the stage. We are going to stand back to back in the middle of the hall and we are going to give the Young Imps five minutes to come to us and we'll guarantee to give them all the trouble they want. If they don't come to us at the end of five minutes and if they haven't left the dance hall we shall go for them." Our band left the platform and stood back to back.

My brother, Fred, who had never been a fighting man was one of our violin players in the orchestra. He whispered to me, "Make sure I stand behind you, Jim." We waited about three minutes but we had no trouble and they quietly left the dance hall.

At that dance was one of the founders of the Socialist Party in the Skipton Division, they called him Wesley Jennings. He went back to our house and said to my father-in-law, "You know, Will, for forty or fifty years we've been preaching socialism and pacificism. We've been pelted with tomatoes and rotten eggs. We've turned the other cheek, we've never raised a finger in retaliation or self-defence and wherever we go these people follow us to heckle and annoy us. Will! We've been wrong. Your son-in-law didn't stand for it last night, he cleared them out in five minutes!"

My father-in-law then told him what had happened a week or two before in the Skipton town hall. The Conservative Party were having a meeting, and after the meeting the chairman asked if there were any questions.

"Oh! I see my friend Tillotson is in the audience so no doubt there will be some questions."

My father-in-law stood up and said, "I've just one question and if that's answered satisfactorily I haven't any more."

"What's your question?"

"Is this Bill that the Conservative Party are bringing in, to purify the Labour Party funds?"

"Yes."

"Oh! It's not answered satisfactorily. I'd like to know what you are going to do to purify the Conservative Party funds."

*Them and Us*

"Our funds don't need purifying."

"Well, I think they do." My father-in-law then went on to give the names of a long list of people, who he alleged, had been giving vast sums of money in exchange for a title. The chairman didn't pursue this at all and announced the "National Anthem".

At that particular time in the development of the Labour Party a lot of the old socialists either sat down when they were singing the "National Anthem" or put on their hats and walked out. Not because they were opposed to royalty, but rather as a protest against society.

My father-in-law put his hat on and walked out. I followed him. I had my hat in my hand, he had his on his head. As we got to the door one or two of the Young Imps were stood there and they knocked his hat off, in so doing they knocked his glasses off and he bent down, fumbling on the floor trying to find his glasses and his hat. I picked them both up and gave them to him.

Now I had got to where the Young Imps were standing. I stood in front of them put my hat on, and said, "Knock that off." One of them lifted up his hand to do it. I hit one in the belly, another on the chin, I kicked one on the kneecap and in seconds there were three of them on the floor.

My father-in-law turned round and said, "Who on earth's done that, Jim?"

"Yes."

He was disappointed but he didn't shout and bawl at me like my father would have done if I had displeased him. He spoke more in sorrow than in anger. He told me about preaching pacificism for forty years, he would never be able to hold his head up in the town again and when he got home he told the story with such anguish that I began to think I had ruined the Labour Party's chance at the next general election.

When Wesley Jennings told him what had happened at Silsden I like to believe he had a sneaking respect for my attitude.

Later, he got me out of one or two awkward situations. I remember taking the chair at one of the big public schools in

*Early Manhood*

Sedburgh, for Philip Snowden, and he gave a very learned discourse on the financial situation, being Chancellor of the Exchequer at the time. At this public school there was a mathematics master who considered himself to be an authority on finance and he jumped up and asked a question and Philip answered it. Then the master asked another and he answered that. My father-in-law nudged me and said, "You must tell that man that there are a lot more people here tonight who want to ask questions." So I did and this particular chap jumped up again and said, "There you go, that is a typical Socialist trick. Here I am, the only man who can really tackle the Chancellor on his own subject and you stifle discussion. Before I sit down I would like to challenge Philip Snowden to open debate on any subject at all connected with finance and the winner of that debate shall agree with the loser that the fifty pounds the loser pays shall go to any charity . . . so long as it isn't a charity of the Labour Party." I didn't know what to do because I was only about twenty-two, but Philip Snowden touched me and said, "Leave him to me." I can see him now, with his two sticks, leaning forward and looking straight at this bright boy from the public school. Then speaking quietly he said, "I'm deeply touched by the honour you have done me but I wonder if you would be very kind and look around and find a foeman more worthy of your steel."

This was a smashing answer from the Chancellor of the Exchequer to a schoolteacher, but these are the sort of experiences you get when you are knocking about with people like this.

I remember a story I was told about one of the first constituencies that Philip Snowden ever stood for. It had got to within three or four days of the election and nobody had held a meeting, Philip Snowden kept saying, "Wait, wait." His Labour Agent was really getting worried but finally his opponent, who was a Brigadier General, held a meeting. For about an hour and a half of the two hours he spent vilifying Snowden and all his ancestors. Telling his audience that Philip was the son of a farm labourer. He finished his speech by saying, "How dare a man like this insult an intelligent elec-

## Them and Us

torate by asking for its votes? Why! He can't even run a fish shop."

Next morning Philip Snowden went into his headquarters and said, "The Lord hath delivered him into my hands. Book the biggest hall in the town, and arrange for overflow meetings."

The Labour Agent did as instructed. He got all his committee round him and placarded the whole town with bills to make sure that everybody knew of the meeting.

Philip Snowden stood on the platform and said, "I understand that last night, my opponent talked to you for over two hours and at least eighty per cent of that time was spent in talking about me. I understand that none of it was very complimentary. I'm not going to spend much time replying to what he said because it's either factual or it isn't. My father was a farm labourer, that is true, so it isn't difficult to imagine that I am the son of a farm labourer. You know all about me. You know the things that are true and the things that are not true.

"There is one thing, he said, however, that I must reply to."

The reporters all sharpened their pencils.

"He said *I* couldn't run a fish shop. Well, *he* can."

The election was practically won on that one little episode. Next morning the newspapers had glaring headlines: "Philip Snowden gives Brigadier General So-and-So permission to run a fish shop."

It's surprising what little things can turn the tide in an election campaign.

There was a Tory Party speaker, who was talking on behalf of his candidate, who was a baron and the speaker said:

"My candidate is a baron, his father was a baron, his grandfather was a baron, his great-grandfather was a baron."

A wit from the audience shouted:

"It's a pity his mother wasn't barren and then we shouldn't have been bothered with him."

Through all the difficulties and experiences during the 1926 Strike we were instrumental in raising over seven thousand, five hundred pounds from people who had no more money than we had, but who were working when we were on strike.

Simple people, humble people, working class people, who

## Early Manhood

really understood what we were fighting for and tried to make our lives a little bit easier, not knowing when they might be in the same position.

Many people talk about strikes, and more people, read about strikes, but to really understand the hardship a real strike brings, one has to live through one, as long and bitter as the strike of 1926. This lasted for twenty-eight weeks and it is an experience which leaves its mark. The first week is all right. At the end of it you have last week's wages to draw. For another two or three weeks you can live on the bit you have saved, in our case in 1926 we got a small amount of strike money—about one pound per week. But when nearly one million men are drawing this amount of money and so much for each dependent the union funds are soon exhausted.

Then, the ignominy of having to go to the Relieving Officer, as he was known, for public assistance. Soup kitchens were started for the children and miners and their families began to really know what hardship meant. Clothes could not be replaced. Shoes became worn out. The only thing on our side, was the thing that defeated us, and that was the glorious weather. It was a marvellous summer. Nobody wanted coal and we could practically live outside.

If ever I was leading a miners' strike I would try to arrange for it to happen in the middle of winter.

In 1926 the owners were determined to teach the miners a lesson. They were determined to win. The miners were determined they would not.

When the strike had lasted twenty weeks or more, the Notts. and Derbyshire miners broke away from the strike and under a man called Spencer they went to work under new agreements.

This was the first real weakening of what had been a solid front of the miners.

We were disappointed of course before, for the railwaymen and the transport men left us, but we were determined to fight.

When the Notts and Derbyshire miners went back to work, however, it certainly weakened us. Men started drifting back to work but they were very, very few in number.

Occasionally you got a man of tremendous character who

## Them and Us

was probably not a Labour man at all and was courageous enough to say so. There was one such man living in the village of Airedale called Albert Saunders, who put a notice in the daily paper to tell everybody that he would be presenting himself for work at 6 a.m. on Monday morning at Glasshoughton colliery. As far as I know this was the first sign of anybody going back to work in the whole of Yorkshire.

On that Monday morning practically every miner in the locality turned out to see if this man kept his promise.

He did.

When he came out of the pit at the end of the day the colliery band was waiting to welcome him and they marched in front of him all the way to his house playing a funeral march. He had to follow the band and keep to their pace because all the miners and their families were stood on each side of the roads, bareheaded, with their heads bowed as if it was a funeral procession.

I've got to hand it to him. He showed great courage for he did more than go back to work, he entitled himself to the term "Blackleg"; which means a man who has gone to work when he should have been on strike. In mining circles "Blackleg" is the most hateful, odious name that can be given to anybody connected with the mining industry and the name lasts for generation after generation.

CHAPTER NINE

## EARLY MARRIAGE

So the Strike eventually ended and we collected our meagre belongings on one little horse-drawn flat cart to go to the council house, we had had for twenty-eight weeks. What's more the driver only charged us thirty shillings for the long journey and he allowed us to pay him one and sixpence per week until we had straightened it off. So we set up house with an armchair that my father-in-law and mother-in-law gave us, an old bed from my father, two or three good packing cases, one table, a few knives and forks, blankets and towels—all wedding presents—and that was just about the lot. But it was home and what a wonderful feeling it was to be in our own house. No matter how kind the in-laws had been, it was a wonderful feeling to get away from them and to feel that we were on our own.

I started back at the coalface with the brothers called Kelsy, that I have mentioned before. But then our difficulties started. After twenty-eight weeks without using a shovel and without using picks, our hands had got soft, our limbs slackened off from the rawhide toughness that we'd had just before the strike and within a week I'd got what we call a "beat hand". That's a kind of carbuncle in the middle of the hand. Then I slipped coming out of the working place and threw my knee out of joint and we were face to face with the problem of all this back rent we'd got to pay, plus working a week before we got any money at all.

When we worked a week, we had only three pounds five shillings, this wasn't much to keep us and also pay off something towards our debts. I couldn't be off work so I carried on

## Them and Us

with thick poultices on my hand, and my knee strapped so tight that it just about stopped the circulation.

Day after day I went down the pit as early as possible so that I could limp down the long roadway and be at our working place by the time my mates arrived. I filled coal with my back leaning against a prop. I did what I could but I couldn't do as much as the Kelsy brothers. They never complained, which just proves how decent men can be towards each other, for we all worked and were paid as a team and, if one man was not doing his full share all the team suffered.

For days when I got home I had to bathe my knee and my hands for hours. It was imperative to keep going if we were to keep our heads above water.

These were very, very difficult days but in time our hands got hardened again and things settled down. I had now passed the qualifying examination for a colliery deputy's certificate—an examination which certifies that one is able to test for gas accurately, capable of measuring the quantity of air flowing and do a certain amount of simple mensuration.

I was longing for the day when I would be appointed to take charge of a district as a deputy. I came out of the pit one day and there was a note left on my check telling me that I had to go across to the manager's office. I went across rather excited. The manager didn't send for you unless it was something good or something bad. I thought of all the things I might have done but when I arrived at his office he didn't waste much time in telling me why he had sent for me.

"How old are you?"

"Twenty-five."

"I have been watching your progress for a long time now, Jim. I have just received a report from the Technical School. You have done well in your examinations. Your lecturer speaks very highly of you and I wonder if you would like to try your hand at being a deputy?"

"My word, I would."

The manager then gave me a lot of useful advice telling me that I now belonged to *them* and that I had to have the interests of the company at heart at all times. I had to treat men fairly

## Early Marriage

but firmly. He then gave me a note entitling me to carry a deputy's safety lamp and to carry a deputy's yardstick, which is the deputy's badge of office. This yardstick is used to measure distances and is also used to sound the roof to see whether it is safe. It is also used for inserting powder into shot holes and ramming in the stemming before you fire a shot.

I couldn't get home quick enough. I was bursting to tell my wife that I was on the first rung of the ladder. "I've got a stick," I cried, but she didn't understand what on earth I meant. If she had lived in a mining district she would have known, because "I've got a stick" means "I am now an official". "This is the beginning, I'll never go back to being a miner again," I promised.

It *was* the beginning.

I never did go back to the coalface as a miner again.

My wife and I had now begun to take a very active part in the life of the village. There was no village hall or institute. There had never been a dramatic society or choral society in the village. We started getting the young people together, at the local chapel, and formed a very amateur dramatic society.

We had no money at all so we couldn't pay any royalties, to give plays as other dramatic societies could, so I decided that I would carefully read Dickens' "Christmas Carol". Then I would re-write it to suit our village actors. In short I would write our own script and then my wife and I would try and produce it. I spent hours writing this script and at the first meeting the snags started.

Nobody wanted to play Scrooge. I have never seen a production quite like this. As things developed I became the prompter, producer, author and practically the stage manager. But we tried our best and we decided to have a full dress rehearsal in the chapel and let the old people of the village come and see it free.

My wife was playing the part of Bob Cratchett, she did it extremely well, she had done quite a lot of acting while she lived at Skipton. After the ordinary dialogue in the first scene she approached my desk very nervously wanting to know if she could have the day off tomorrow—Christmas Day. The

## Them and Us

dialogue that takes place in this scene went very well. Then she went to blow out the candles on her desk. As she blew the left-hand candle out, the right-hand light went out. When she went to blow the right-hand candle out the left-hand light went out. We carried on, she left the stage and when I turned round to the fire to await the visit of Jacob Marley the fire had gone out and I was left there in total darkness.

The audience didn't seem to know that anything had gone drastically wrong, they had never seen it before, so I carried on with the dialogue.

"Seven years ago this very night Jacob Marley died"—and with a loud whisper—"There's no fire, Roland"—Roland was the stage manager.

No response from Roland so I carried on.

"He didn't talk nonsense about Merry Christmas, not Jacob" —"Roland, there's no fire"—"Stocks and shares, markets and prices, mortgages and foreclosures, these were the staple of Jacob's conversation and I wouldn't wish to hear better."

Then suddenly the stage manager called out:

"No need to shout at me, Mr. Bullock, somat's gone wrong with the lights. We shall have to start again."

Fortunately, the colliery electrician was present and he found out that the lights had fused but we had to start again.

The play went on all right. Various people forgot their parts but I had done it so often and knew it off by heart that I was able to prompt them. The audience thought that my promptings were the mumblings of old man Scrooge so we got away with it.

But when the ghost of "Christmas past" was on the stage showing me the humble home of Bob Cratchett, Tiny Tim was present. Tiny Tim was being played by my little daughter, Marie, who was only five years old. I had had her a special pair of crutches made at the pit. Her speaking part was not very difficult, she had only to say:

"God bless us, every one."

But instead of limping on to the stage on her little crutches as she had done so well at rehearsals she now dropped her crutches and came straight across to Scrooge—who she knew despite the make-up was her Daddy—and calmly said:

## Early Marriage

"I've 'cided not to be in it."

On another occasion, after I had become the manager at the colliery, we were producing "Christmas Carol" and again we hadn't been able to find anybody to play the part of Scrooge so I had to act the part. We had a packed chapel because we had sold tickets to miners at the colliery. The whole play went off exceptionally well on this occasion and in the last act I was giving all I'd got as the reformed Scrooge, delighted that I had the chance to be a different man. I had just got to the lines where Scrooge was saying:

"Peace, mercy, forbearance and benevolence, shall be my aim," and a miner shouted right from the back of the chapel:

"Benevolence will do for us, mate. Thee keep it going until tomorrow."

Tomorrow was pay day.

Scrooge, to them, was a fitting part for the colliery manager to play.

Airedale, the neighbouring village to Fryston, had a zinc hut for a church and it was called The Holy Cross. A new vicar came called John Daly.

What a wonderful character. Forceful, upright, a real man's man. Tall, good looking. A man who commanded tremendous respect throughout the whole of the villages.

He decided there was going to be a new church in Airedale. He had plans drawn up and they were really marvellous. He talked about his new church until I am sure he convinced himself first, and later everybody else that it would be built. Very few of us believed it possible. He was a man after my own heart. He had very little money, but he determined he would have voluntary labour, that he would beg every piece of stone or steel that could be built into the new church.

He was a great friend of the Reverend "Tubby" Clayton, in fact he worked with him in London. The Reverend "Tubby" Clayton was the founder of Toc H and Vicar Daly decided he would form a branch of Toc H in Airedale. I joined and I was given the post of "Job Master". This was not an easy position to fulfil for everybody had to work for nothing. We did all sorts of jobs. We ran classes for young people in various subjects.

## Them and Us

We worked for the hospitals. We took old people out on trips. We did gardening and interior decorating for the old people. All this was organized by the Job Master and done by the miners after a full shift down the pit. But then the vicar came to the meeting one night and said he wanted Toc H to do the digging out for the foundations of his new church. What a job that was.

We arranged teams of miners to follow on one after the other digging the foundations out.

The vicar went round all the pits and building yards begging old girders, borrowing cement mixers and lorries. I understand he even sacrificed six months of his own salary in advance to pay for materials we needed—a truly wonderful character—he really did know how to get the best out of people.

When we actually started putting the foundations in, I had got six of the roughest miners we had at Fryston pit—and the strongest—mixing cement in a cement mixer.

It was a real windy day and the Bishop of Ripon came with the vicar to encourage the men who were working for nothing. The clerics were not in their dog collars, they were just dressed ordinarily. As they stood watching the work the wind was blowing the cement dust right into their faces. One of the colliers looked up and shouted:

"Haven't you enough bloody sense to get out of the dust?"

Turning to me the miner said:

"Who the bloody hell are they?"

The Bishop looked at him very kindly. "I'll remember you in my prayers, young man." That was all he said.

John Daly didn't mind my miners swearing, what he wanted was to get some work out of them—and he did.

He managed to beg the ruins of Fryston Hall. The entrance to Fryston Hall was still intact and it had some beautiful, big, round stone pillars. The vicar wanted these taken down in such a way that no damage was done to the pillars. He came down to see me and I took a team of men with blasting material from the pit and blew the whole place up, but we protected the pillars.

The vicar was still not satisfied. He persuaded all of us to

## Early Marriage

load them and cart them up to his new church. Now the church is completed and these beautiful pillars are at the entrance to the new church.

John Daly has gone to a much bigger job—he is now a bishop—but as long as ever Holy Cross church in Airedale stands it will be a testimony to John Daly, for without his vision and his drive it would never have been built.

It is also a testimony to hundreds of miners, to some colliery managers and to many other people who did what they could to help him in this wonderful project. Wherever John Daly is I am sure he will never forget the days he spent at Airedale or the friends he made while he was there.

During all these activities I was studying harder than ever and got to be the Undermanager at the pit, having already passed my examination, I was a very proud man because I was the first man from Bowers Row ever to do this. But now I was told, as good as promised, if I could get my First Class Certificate, which was more difficult, there was the chance of becoming the manager at Fryston Colliery. This was really something to aim for. I started swotting at nights, went to night school four nights a week. I had a man working for me as Overman called Ernest Mason, who was a Bachelor of Science, and he came up at week-ends and during the evenings when I was free to give me private tuition. He was a tremendous help to me. The biggest help of all was my wife, she used to be making me coffee in the middle of the night. I've even seen her sat with cold cloths on my head while I was trying to prepare for this examination, because I had only about a year in which to take a three-year course and I had to cram it all in. Remember that all this time, I was up at four-thirty in the morning, looking after a big pit, and was doing all this studying in addition to this work and by the time I sat for the examination I was practically a nervous wreck. But, my goodness, I knew my stuff and I can say that I literally blinded the First Class Certificate and within six months of having got it I'd become the manager of Fryston Colliery.

When I was actually made manager of the colliery I think it was the proudest day I've ever experienced because you can

## Them and Us

never go through this twice and although I occupied much higher positions than this as time went on, I always remember the day when we moved into the "house on the hill". In every truth I'd landed "the house on the hill", I'd got, and become, everything I had set out to be.

While these activities were going on in the village chapel and the pit, we had not been altogether idle in our home. My wife gave me the wonderful news that we were going to have a baby. We were both very excited and rushed up to Bowers Row to tell my father, elder sister, who kept house for him, and my older brother, Fred, who was still a bachelor. Fred was about fifty years old, but when we told my father, he said softly:

"Sh! Sh! Fred's in the kitchen, he'll hear you. He's still not married you know."

We were still very short of money and I was not well so it was decided that I should go and spend Easter at Skipton, walking with my father-in-law. We had three pounds altogether and train and bus fares were about twenty-two shillings and sixpence, so we couldn't both go.

I was walking down Aire Street in Castleford on my way to the bus when I stopped to look in Jacksons Furnishers' shop window. For three pounds down and five shillings a week there was a lovely little bedroom suite and a carpet. I hesitated a bit and then went in to see the manager.

I told him: "If you can deliver the furniture straight away I'll have them."

He promised to do this and I hung about until I saw the van set off.

When I arrived home, what excitement, the furniture arrived and now I wasn't going away. Anne switched on the light many times that night to make sure she wasn't dreaming.

These sort of things wouldn't give thrills now, but they did then. This was the first real new furniture we had had and every stick, every penny had to be really earned. It was ours.

When our first baby was born she was one of the most beautiful little girls we had ever seen and she was *ours*. We had spent hours through the long months of waiting looking at

## Early Marriage

the picture of "Bubbles" hoping in some way our baby would be like the picture, and she was. She was a real joy and pleasure to us and we felt we had really achieved something. We decided to have a family while we were still young . . . but it was not to be.

During the next pregnancy, while spending Christmas at Skipton, tragedy struck. At a party, while Anne's sister and I were fooling about, my wife started laughing and twisted her inside somewhere. We had to rush her to hospital and she was there four months. I had to go back to work and Marie, our little girl, had to stay with her grandparents.

The emptiness of our house when I got back home, the silence was something I'll never forget. Little shoes and toys around, dresses, scarves, all reminded me so much of what I was now missing. My wife was really seriously ill, they found she had gangrene and I was asked to make an awful choice. The baby had to be taken away or my wife's life was in real danger.

These are life's tragedies for young people to face, but the other bad news was we hadn't to have any more children. We didn't want Marie to be an only child, we knew we should spoil her, so after a lot of serious thought we decided to adopt a baby boy. We did this through the auspices of the N.S.P.C.C. and brought our new baby back with us when he was six weeks old.

I could now write a chapter on the advantages and disadvantages of adoption, on the difficulties one meets, whether it is better to tell the child the truth from the beginning, but that is not the purpose of this book. Suffice it to say that years after we found that the doctor's statement about us not having any more children was not correct and fourteen years later we did have another beautiful baby girl. We called her Diane.

My wife's religion was like mine, originally Baptist. I say "originally" because we had not followed the Baptist faith insomuch that neither of us had been baptized. We weren't christened because our parents' views were, that we should, of our own free will, be immersed when we felt the call.

These principles were still with us at the time of Marie's birth, but we decided to christen Diane and we've never regretted it.

## Them and Us

By this time we had made a lot of new friends, including doctors, dentists, schoolmasters, ministers and solicitors, but we'd still kept our old friends as well. We were largely forming a circle of friends similar to the Skipton types, though not necessarily of the same political faith.

CHAPTER TEN

# EARLY MANAGEMENT EXPERIENCE

The 1939–45 War was now being fought and I was busier than ever. I was helping to organize something for the village every night, dances, whist drives, discussions and plays. Also, I was captain of the local Home Guard.

I quickly realized that although I could recruit and organize the strongest platoon (numerically in the Castleford district), due to my position as Manager, I'd never make a really good junior member of a body like the Army, I wasn't too fond of discipline. To me the protocol and red tape seemed ridiculous. Too much time was spent showing people how to salute, slope arms. My idea was, we should train to fight in the way that Hitler was proving successful.

A good example of this was that during some of our exercises it was decided that the Home Guard—that is all the various platoons in Castleford—would unite and attack Castleford. Castleford would be defended by the Regular Army. As a sort of tribute to me and because I'd the biggest platoon in the area they gave me full charge of the attack on Castleford and I was told I could attack just as I liked. We had taken match-boxes as token hand grenades and whenever we dropped a match-box into a machine-gun post, defended by the Regular Army, that machine-gun post was supposed to be wiped out.

Before the attack started we got all our platoons over at Allerton Bywater, which is about two miles away from Castleford, and I sent two of my men down to the Drill Hall in Castleford, where the Regular Army were parading. There they heard the officers and sergeants telling them just which points they had to defend. My men immediately got on the telephone to me at Allerton Bywater and told me exactly where the

## Them and Us

Regular Army was stationed. So when the time came for me to attack at ten o'clock, we walked straight into Castleford and wiped out every machine-gun post by about half past ten!

The trouble was that this exercise should have lasted all day. We should have broken off for lunch at one o'clock, continued the attack in the afternoon, had tea, then at five o'clock there was a General coming from the Northern Command to hold an inquest on what had taken place.

Things had not gone according to plan, however, for by half past ten the battle was over and Castleford was ours. We went home for lunch and then came back for the inquest at five o'clock.

Now I had my first real taste of Army methods. I'd never seen anything quite like this before.

The general asked for the officer who had been in charge of the attack to come out to the front and tell him how it had been done. I went out, saluted him and described our morning's efforts as follows:

"Hitler has captured Holland, France and Belgium in a short time. He has been able to do this by practising the policy of infiltration, that is, he got men behind the enemy's lines and sabotaged their war efforts.

"Hitler has been so successful that I felt it would be a good idea if in our attack on Castleford, I, as the officer in charge, adopted similar tactics. So I placed men where they could hear what the Regular Army officers were saying when they detailed their men.

"This information was then telephoned to me at my headquarters so I knew just where to attack, wiped out the defending forces and captured Castleford in less than an hour."

"Damn it, man," he said, "you can't do that it's not playing the game."

"Well," I replied, "I've never thought that war was a game."

He flushed with anger. "Well, we know you've done it, but we don't admire your methods. Seeing you are so clever let me ask you a few questions."

"How should you have attacked according to the book?"

"I should have probed the centre."

"Say your men were wiped out?"
"I should probe the left flank."
"Say they were wiped out?"
"I should probe the right flank."
"Wiped out?"
"Then I'd send for tanks."
"Say the tanks were destroyed?"
"Then I'd send for aircraft."
"They were brought down. What would you do then?"

I was fed up by this time and I replied: "I'd take a team of men down Allerton Pit and start driving a drift to Glassboughton colliery, which is behind Castleford. I'd then come up the Glasshoughton shaft and attack Castleford from the rear."

"And how long would that take?" he asked.

"About three and a half years, I should think. We'd do about eight yards a week."

The general got really angry now and started shouting:

"You're just being bloody silly. This isn't a foolish game. We are not here to make fun. Let's have a bit of common sense."

I looked at him.

"Can I ask you a question, Sir?"

"Yes."

"If your tonnage was down and your costs were up and you were losing money, what would you do?"

"What the hell are you talking about?" the general said.

"I'm talking about my job and I know how to do it. I wasn't educated at Sandhurst. You are very clever when you are talking about your own job. You expect me to know all about your job also but you evidently don't know the first thing about mine. But I believe in results, and the results are that the Regular Army have lost Castleford in less than an hour to amateur soldiers."

He said, "I don't admire your methods and I don't want any more questions from you at all."

"If this is the spirit and method that you are using," I replied, "it's no wonder Hitler is winning. If he can play the game as he thinks fit and you insist on playing the game as it ought to be played you'll lose. So surely it's time to change your tactics."

*Them and Us*

I never saw him again.

Sometimes when I watch the television programme "Dad's Army", I am reminded of my experiences in the Home Guard.

People who had no experience of the Home Guard think the programme is fantastic but it is not. It's a very real programme and is true to life. These are the sort of things that did happen.

In my experience a barrage balloon broke loose from Sheffield and as its anchoring rope fell into Fryston Wood an alarm went out and we were all told that German parachute troops were dropping in the wood. We surrounded the wood and our only weapons were picks, hammers and pitchforks.

Later, I was ordered to attack Ferrybridge Power Station with my platoon and the Power Station was going to be defended by the Ferrybridge platoon.

This time I did study the manual and attacked according to the book.

It was a bitter cold, foggy night, raining like hell. My platoon approached Ferrybridge through Fryston woods and Fryston park. There was about a thousand yards of open country to travel before we got to the hill that was representing the power station.

We literally, crawled on our bellies, through wet grass and sludge right across Fryston park, we got to the foot of the hill without being detected. I thought this was marvellous.

I passed the word down the line: "Are you ready?"

"Yes."

"Right, charge."

We got to our feet, ran up the hill, yelling like mad. When we got to the top there was no opposition whatever, just one private, sat, covered by his macintosh. He looked up at me:

"Mr. Bullock?"

"It is."

"Oh! Our captain sends his compliments, and, says it is far too wet to turn out tonight but he would be very pleased if you would all come and join us in the Red Lion. [This was a well-known pub in Ferrybridge.] We are all playing darts."

This episode made me realize that everybody wasn't taking the Home Guard as seriously as I was. The Home Guard was

Fryston Colliery, 1908.

Old road underground with breaking wooden props.

During my days as under-manager at Fryston Colliery. Here I'm waiting for my lamp and stick to be brought to me before going down the pit.

As a young pugilist.

not without its red tape and "bull", particularly if Regular Army officers were going to be present.

One Sunday morning a really big parade of all the district had been arranged to take place on the Castleford Rugby Ground. There was another general coming to review our troops and our commanding officers really wanted a good show. They were sending me urgent messages all week, would I make sure that everybody was on parade on this great day.

I notified all my lads that they must be there on Sunday morning.

On Sunday morning I went down to the office at 9 a.m. One of our Home Guard members was a young lad called Fletcher, who was a famous Rugby League footballer, he played half-back for Wakefield Trinity and Yorkshire County. He came across to my office and said:

"I got your note, Mr. Bullock. I'd like to go on parade but I can't find my gaiters anywhere."

I immediately answered, "It isn't your gaiters we want, it's you. I'm not bothered as long as you come."

"If you're not bothered I'll be there then."

The parade met in Fryston pit yard at half past nine.

Because I didn't know much about the Army and its methods a young second lieutenant, called Ted Ablett, a very keen soldier, was loaned to me. I explained to him that Fletcher couldn't find his gaiters and that I'd told him it didn't matter.

When Ablett walked through the ranks he came to Fletcher and—despite what I had said—said, "You are improperly dressed on parade."

Fletcher replied, "I know, but I've had a word with Mr. Bullock and he says it is all right."

Lieutenant Ablett turned smartly round, marched across the pit yard, saluted me and reported:

"The platoon is ready for inspection, sir, but Fletcher has no gaiters."

"I know Fletcher hasn't any gaiters, I've just told you so. What the hell does it matter anyhow, he doesn't fight with his gaiters."

*Them and Us*

Lieutenant Ablett didn't like this, he straightened himself up:

"I've reported it, sir, and now the troop is ready for inspection."

As we walked across the pit yard to carry out the inspection of my platoon I said to the lieutenant:

"When we get opposite Fletcher, don't tell me any more that he hasn't any gaiters. He's told me so himself. I've told you. You've told me so there's no need to tell me again. He's going on this parade."

"I shall have to tell you again, its protocol, sir," and he told me again.

The inspection over, the lads set off marching to Castleford Rugby Ground, Lieutenant Ablett in the lead, and I followed on in the car.

When all the platoons were lined up on the football field the general from the Regular Army and the commanding officers of the Home Guard were all in the grandstand. Each junior officer marched out again and inspected his own platoon and reported back to his senior officer. Then the senior officers went out to inspect and they in turn reported back to their seniors until finally it got to the general and we all went round together.

I took the trouble to have a quiet word with my major and my colonel to inform them about the serious situation that had arisen regarding Fletcher's lack of gaiters and I warned them, quite plainly, that if anybody mentioned Fletcher's gaiters again I should tell Fletcher to go home, and it wouldn't take him two minutes to do it.

My senior officers said, "That's all right. It's just a question of protocol."

Despite all this the colonel who knew all about it stopped when he got to Fletcher, looked him over from head to foot as if he had never seen anything quite like him before. Screwed up his nostrils and turned round to me and very haughtily said:

"Do you realize that this man is improperly dressed on parade?"

## Early Management Experience

I turned to the ranks and said:

"That's done it. I've had as much of this as I can take! Fletcher, bugger off, off tha goes."

Fletcher ran across the rugby ground he knew so well as fast as he had even run when scoring a try.

"Where's he going?" the colonel shouted.

"He's going home," I replied.

"What for?"

"Because he's improperly dressed and he's going to find his gaiters."

"But he can't do that."

"But he's done it, and if there's much more the whole platoon will go with him including me, I'm about fed up with this."

This is the sort of thing I mean. What do gaiters really matter? I could understand it, if we had been parading in London in front of foreign dignitaries, but here we were a set of miners who were giving up their time voluntarily, giving it free and didn't get a penny. They were trying to form themselves into some sort of a force, that had no weapons hardly, and here we had all this row, all this stink, all this time wasting, on a fellow that had turned up without his gaiters—this is the sort of thing that sickened me with the Home Guard.

Another time, we went down to the Drill Hall and were being shown by Regular Army officers and sergeants, a new drill called the 'Montgomery Battle Drill'. I'd only just joined and was keen to learn. I was enthusiastic. I sat at the front with the other officers. There were four or five hundred miners and people from all walks of life in the Drill Hall. An officer came and with a very disdainful sort of attitude talked down to us. He made me feel a bit sick to start with. Then he said:

"I want six officers to come out and we'll demonstrate this new drill, six of you go to the armoury. I want six volunteers, you, you, you, you, you and you. Come back with six rifles."

He said it as quickly as that, and I was one of the "yous" and I'd never handled an Army rifle at all. I'd done no sloping

*Them and Us*

arms, no rifle drill, no parading, no anything. I could shoot, but mostly because I went poaching with a ·22 rifle. I could knock a pheasant's eyes out at fifty yards but I'd never used an Army rifle in this way.

We came back with the rifles and he said:

"Now we'll go through the ordinary loosening up drill. Squad!"

Everybody's hands slipped down the rifle barrel to where the belt fastened and I did the same. I was watching them to see what they did. We stood with our legs apart. I suppose that's "Stand at ease" and then he said:

"Wait for it. Attention!"

I didn't know whether to bring my left leg up to my right or take right leg up to my left, but I took the wrong leg anyway because I bumped into the man next to me. However, we quickly righted ourselves and he said:

"Now we'll have the ordinary slope arms. Slo . . . . . . . ope arms!"

When this command came I had no idea what to do but I tried clumsily to follow what the other chaps were doing, my rifle barrel hit the bloke next to me at the side of his neck. The officer bawled out at me:

"I've never yet had a squad without a clumsy b—— in it. Come on out, you. Take three paces forward."

I took three paces forward, and was feeling a bit of a mug now because a lot of my miners were watching. Then he said:

"Throw me your gun," and he came and got my rifle, he threw it about.

I've got to give him credit, I'd never seen anybody do this so easily. I've never seen anyone quite so smart. He threw it on his left shoulder, his right shoulder, he did it with one arm, he did it with two arms, he sloped arms, and everything was perfect, but, suddenly he threw the rifle at me and said:

"Now do it like that."

Of course I wasn't prepared for him throwing the rifle back and it clattered to the floor. By this time I was completely fed up and said:

## Early Management Experience

"Listen, mate, if you want to give orders, and you want them carrying out, just pick somebody else to give them to because I've had it and I'm not picking that gun up. Tha's thrown it theer and if tha doesn't pick it up it can stop theer."

The dialogue that followed was so silly that it reminded me of one of Stanley Holloway's monologues entitled: "Sam, pick up thy musket and let the battle commence."

The officer was determined I was going to pick it up and I was just as determined that I wasn't going to pick it up. This silly little affair developed into an argument that assumed mountainous proportions and it just about stopped the whole of the exercise. The officer was really angry and shouted at me:

"You are wearing the King's uniform and you carry out my instructions, or...."

I interrupted:

"Or what? I can soon get rid of the uniform."

I took the coat off, put it on the floor and said:

"I'm not wearing the King's uniform now, but I'd like you to understand that for the next months and probably for the next few years, I have to control these men who are watching and listening to what is going on up here, and I'm not going to be shown up by a chap like you. If you want any orders carrying out give them to somebody else because I'm off." And I went.

But what I didn't realize, was, that all my platoon would follow me.

There was no real discipline in the Home Guard, they couldn't confine us to barracks.

The whole affair was so tactless, here we had got a body of men who were volunteers, they were giving up their own leisure freely. The officer should have known that I was learning, that I was giving the talents I'd got in a different way. I had brought all my men there and now I had to listen to insults, thrown out right, left and centre by a fellow, who after the war was over, would probably be working for me.

It wasn't just that, however, I knew he had his job to do but Regular Army officers should realize that we were not paid

## Them and Us

soldiers, and if they treated us like this, how must they be treating Regular Army men.

This fellow gave me the impression that he felt he was God Almighty but I think he was made to realize that there were other people who had opinions and weren't afraid to express them.

This thing annoyed me so much that I left the Home Guard but I did other things instead with our own pit men. We formed an official Colliery Guard and this became very efficient as time went by.

During the first air raids we used to place firewatchers on the top of the pit head baths. In one of the air raids what we thought was a bomb dropped right in the pit yard, but it didn't explode. I was on the roof of the pit head baths with the men on this particular occasion. Everybody except me fell flat on their faces. I was too petrified to move. I just stood there like a graven image, but I quickly recovered and said:

"Come on, you've no need to be laying down there, it's nothing."

They looked at each other and said:

"What a bloody nerve."

The old mining agent, who was my boss, came down after the raid and walked round what we thought was a bomb and suddenly he said:

"It's ticking."

I said, "Well, if it's ticking it's a bomb."

Suddenly my boss bent down and picked this thing up and put in under his arm.

"Where are you going?" I asked.

"I'm going to throw it in the river," and he set off at speed.

Everybody thought the thing would blow up at any minute. He called out:

"Don't come near me, walk ten yards behind me."

So I walked ten yards behind him, practically on tip toe. I could see the thing under his arm shining like aluminium. I thought there is something funny here, I didn't think you could lift a bomb as easy as that, and he isn't the sort of fellow who would take unnecessary risks.

## Early Management Experience

When the procession got near to the river I went up to him and said:

"Let's have a look at this thing."

It was only the casing that contained incendiary bombs, that had evidently been thrown out of an aircraft when it was empty.

I didn't make anyone in the colliery yard any wiser and the agent was treated as a hero for the rest of the war.

At street corners and in the public houses they talked in whispers of how he walked away with a live bomb under his arm and threw it in the river to save the pit and the lives of the people who were there at the time.

This was a real build-up for him. He was the type of man that might have done something similar if it had been a bomb.

The war was a bad time but probably better for miners than for some. Everybody was short of food but we in the mining industry had extra food rations and we served meals in the canteen.

We started a co-operative effort of breeding a few pigs so we could get home-fed pork in the canteen.

One Christmas an old miner came to me and said:

"Would you like a leg of pork for Christmas?"

This was before we had started breeding pigs at the colliery. We hadn't had any pork for a long time.

I asked, "Can you get some?"

"Yes. I've killed two pigs but keep it to yourself and I'll see you get a leg of pork."

When I went home that evening I told my wife with great pleasure that we should be having a leg of pork for Christmas dinner. But on Christmas Eve he came to see me looking very sad.

"Have you brought that pork?" said I.

"No." He looked very rueful.

"I'm sorry, Mr. Bullock. I hadn't told anyone that I had killed the pigs, I had to keep it quiet. So when I had them killed I hung them up in my little outhouse. I went out this morning to cut them up and found somebody had been before me and

## Them and Us

stolen them. I am in a real mess. I daren't report it to the police because I wouldn't have been allowed to kill them."

We didn't get our pork for Christmas. He didn't get his. But we consoled ourselves with the thought that some people would have pork, even though they hadn't paid for it.

CHAPTER ELEVEN

## COLLIERY MANAGER

There were several things of which I was justly proud. One, I was the first man from the village of Bowers Row to have successfully passed all his examinations and obtained the necessary certificate to manage a coalmine. Second, I was the first local man to have become the manager of a coalmine.

This itself was a great honour and privilege, but it was also a great responsibility. More so in my case than many other colliery managers.

"Why!" you may ask did I think I was different to the countless other colliery managers? There were varied reasons.

I was an active member of the Labour Party. I was locally well known as a propagandist on their platforms.

I had been a leader and a speaker for a miners' orchestra which had toured through the Yorkshire Dales during the 1926 Strike to raise money for the Miners' Relief Fund.

I had given scores of speeches on the wickedness of the coal owners and the righteousness of the miners.

I had lived among miners, worked with them as a miner, been a pony driver, a shotfirer, a deputy, an undermanager and now I was a manager.

I knew their hardships and their worries. I had lectured them on what they ought to do as miners and what I felt the coal owners ought to do.

I had advocated nationalization of mines constantly all over the countryside.

I had made constant pleas for further safety in the mines, for more consultation, for less exploitation, and had repeatedly stressed that there was a real need for a much more human approach to labour relations by management particularly.

## Them and Us

Why did I leave all these activities to become one of *them*?

While this question is easy for me to answer it might be more difficult for other people to understand.

While studying I had had a greater opportunity of watching and comparing the standard of living of the boss class with ours.

I was envious. I wanted a bit of heaven down here. I was not content as my father was, to wait for my eternal reward in heaven. I wanted security of tenure. I wanted a carriage and pair. I wanted holidays with pay, a pension, education for my children and more than anything I wanted the "house on the hill".

That, was the envious side, but I knew full well how much hard work this would require if I was to achieve my ambition but I was fully prepared to work for it.

Work I did. For six years I attended Technical School four nights a week, I took private correspondence courses. I had private tuition by a very wise friend, Ernest Mason, B.Sc., who finally became my undermanager and later left me to become a professor of mining at a Midland technical college.

There was another side, however, that had nothing to do with envy. I felt I could do more for my own people as a colliery manager. I believed in the old saying "Example is better than precept".

There were plenty of aspiring trade union leaders and politicians but few I've met who were prepared to sacrifice practically all their leisure, to work like mad day and night, and if they were successful in qualifying, the chance of getting a position, that he was qualified for, was practically nil.

Many people will work to get the necessary qualification hoping that they will then get an easy, clean, pleasant and well-paid job. Anyone who thinks so, should never go in for being a colliery manager or he will soon be disillusioned.

The colliery manager's job is one of the hardest and most exacting in British industry. I know of no job so arduous, carrying such responsibility, with such dire penalties if things go wrong, with such little reward—materially—when things go right.

A manager is on call day and night seven days a week.

## Colliery Manager

He carries the responsibility for his undertaking whether he is there or not.

'The Coal Mines Act' firmly places responsibility on his shoulders, both for his own or for his subordinates' mistakes.

The outcome of any slackness on his part or by his staff can have truly disastrous results.

If an explosion or other disaster occurs at, or in, his pit the manager stands in the dock, like a criminal, a lonely figure, with his critics gathering like vultures to destroy him.

Overnight he finds he has become headlines on all our means of communication. But when he does well, you never hear his name mentioned.

So, therefore, choosing the career of a colliery manager I knew was no sinecure. It was no bed of roses.

But if one of *us* got a job as colliery manager, what an opportunity to prove that what he had preached for so long could be put into practice. So the first step was to qualify.

At that time, the second step, was to work so hard and so well at your daily task that even a reluctant employer would be bound to notice you.

My opportunity to fulfil the second step came when we had a disastrous underground fire at Fryston. I was one of the fire-fighters and later I was put in charge, for a short while, of not only fire fighting at the colliery, but in charge of fire prevention.

I often speak of THEM and THEY.

THEM and THEY are very real in the mining community. The expression is spoken with awe, sometimes with respect, sometimes in anger and sometimes even in fun.

Sooner or later, however, we always get back to *Them, They* and *Us*.

*They* usually means the boss, the government, or in some cases it could mean the trade union leaders.

*Us* means the workers.

*They* are blamed for so much and *They* are credited with so little. Weak managers will say to discontented men:

"I agree, I would pay you but *they* won't let me."

The trades union leader will say to the manager:

"I agree, but *they* won't do it."

## Them and Us

*They* in this case could mean the miners.

When you had fulfilled the necessary steps to become a colliery manager, that is to obtain the qualification and the job, there were several essential things you needed to enable you to carry out a manager's job successfully.

You had to be determined, level headed, tactful, sometimes eloquent, persuasive, and never to work with one eye on the clock.

I was very fortunate that when I was made manager the old man who had been manager before me was made colliery agent. He took me under his wing and he gave me the full benefit of his many many years of mining experience.

He also introduced me to the other side of those techniques that I had always hated.

His attitude was different to mine, particularly his attitude to workpeople. He was a good pitman, he was a hard taskmaster, he was loyal to his owners and always maintained that that was where his only loyalty lay.

His approach would not, and could not, be tolerated today but one of my greatest causes of satisfaction is that by the time he retired, and I took his place, he had changed his attitude and his outlook tremendously.

So I took over the management of a colliery where I had always belonged to *Us* and now I belonged to *Them*.

Cheap and cheaper coal was the order of the day in 1930 to 1938. It was a world of fierce competition, every penny spent had to be proved to be a wise investment, but apart from these difficulties there was a psychology abroad that I was determined to alter.

Kidding, lying, giving wrong impressions, deliberately deceiving men, cheating men, all done by professing Christians was something I just could not understand.

Why couldn't men and management be straight with each other and say what they mean, and mean what they say?

What a battle had to be fought then for ordinary decent standards.

Let me give a few examples. It can't harm anyone now but it can serve to fill in the background as to why there was so

## Colliery Manager

much bitterness in our coalmines right up to the advent of Nationalization.

Fryston was one of the hottest pits in Britain, men were collapsing with cramp, carrying six pints of water to drink in addition to water that was sent down the mine.

When my boss and I were visiting the really hot parts of the mine he'd stop just outside the working face, wipe all the sweat off his face, put on a big thick scarf, button up his jacket and sally forth.

"My word, it's cool today, Mr. Bullock. You really have improved this ventilation. What have you done? Don't you think it's cool chaps? Quite a breeze, I really must congratulate you on this improvement, my boy."

I'd done nothing, the place was red hot; not a breath of air, But by the time he left the men were agreeing it was cooler, but they were still working naked and wet through. I still think he was wrong and I thought so then and when we got out of earshot I told him so.

When we got to the next place the procedure was the same.

The men explained to him about the hard work in shoving tubs up a steep hill.

He asked, "Where is it steep? This steep? Good God, when I did your job I used to shove so hard I went up to the knees in solid rock. No, no, no. This isn't steep. Come on, Mr. Bullock, no allowance for this."

Next place the men asked:

"Can we have some allowance for the extra dirt coming down?"

"Extra dirt! I don't want it, put it back," he replied. "If I ask for margarine and you insist on giving me best butter that's your fault. But I'll only pay for margarine. Come on, Mr. Bullock, we haven't time to listen to such nonsense!"

Another place there had been complaints about the men working in water and for which they were due to an extra ninepence per day. The boss looked round in surprise:

"Now. Where's this water?"

Then he'd sit straight down in water a foot deep and say: "I can't see any water. Can you, Mr. Bullock?"

*Them and Us*

A collier would venture:

"This, here. That you're sat in."

The boss went on: "This! I thought this bit of damp was sweat." Then he looked at the complainant.

"But I say, aren't you a leader of the Sunday School?"

"Yes."

"Didn't you take the children to the seaside last week?"

"Yes."

"What did you do all day?"

"Played on the sands and paddled." By now the collier was feeling pleased at the interest the boss was taking in him.

"Paddled!" The boss seized on the word. "Stop there lad. You paid seven shillings and sixpence a head for the privilege didn't you? Say no more, you can paddle here for nothing. It's free. Come on, Mr. Bullock, not worth discussing."

Now I ask, and I asked then, what did he save? What did he achieve?

He saved three shillings and achieved the satisfaction that he had won.

But he hadn't. He'd lost their trust. He'd increased their dislike and made them look on him still more as an enemy.

What did I think ought to be done and what did I do later?

If I had signed an agreement agreeing to payment, I paid it and tried to avoid making agreements, that you could drive a horse and cart through the clauses for either side.

But these are small things, what about big things?

The settling of price lists on which a miner's whole economic future depended. These are indeed major negotiations.

In the past, there was more trickery, more deliberate lying, more deceiving during this period than at any other.

What I am trying to prove is that there is a history behind the bitterness that existed in mining right up to the time when the pits were taken over by the nation under the Nationalization Act. These negotiations very often proved to younger miners how right their fathers were when they used to say:

"If the boss is nice, watch him! For if he hasn't twisted you he's just going to do it"; and, "The only good boss is a dead one."

## Colliery Manager

These feelings existed at the time when I entered higher management. And my story tells, how I tried to overcome them and bring a new understanding, and a new trust into the relationship between management and men.

History has proved I did it. Men can be trusted. Men will respond to fair play and they will respond to good leadership.

You *can* have friends among workmen, you *can* be firm and still command respect.

CHAPTER TWELVE

## MANAGING WELFARE AND LABOUR RELATIONS

Being a colliery manager is not just planning and organizing a coalmine. It's much more than that. You must be interested in your men and boys, in their families. You have to listen to their troubles, share their joys, take part in their social activities and organize events in the village.

Some people have different ways of dealing with human relations. One manager may be a keen sportsman and spend his leisure organizing sports events in his village.

Another may be a studious type who arranges discussion groups and other cultural activities.

But to be successful you must be interested. You must convince them that you do understand; that you are willing to listen and willing to help. There's an old Yorkshire saying that: "Sympathy without relief, is like mustard without beef."

I've found that loyalty is never one sided, that loyalty begets loyalty and, my word, it pays to have the men on your side.

I'm trying to explain how I tackled the job. I was fortunate in many ways. I was interested in all sports. I could talk, and if what you have to say is interesting, there are no better listeners than miners and their families.

At Fryston we had a really good football team which won every possible trophy, captained by a young man named Fred Astbury, a member of the big family of Astburys that I have spoken about earlier. Fred Astbury is still with me. He was an ex-professional footballer who knew his job. As colliery manager and keen supporter of the team I travelled everywhere with them and at half time I would go to the dressing-room.

## Managing Welfare and Labour Relations

They knew I was interested and they knew I expected them to win.

During the war, like every other village, our village was "blacked out" but unlike most villages we had only one way in and one way out, a dead end, no transport. It could have been a dead village but it was not. It was alive, teeming with activities every night.

I was very pleased during the war to welcome to our colliery the Bevin Boys. These were young men who had the option of either going into the forces or going into the pit. Some were not even given the choice. They were drafted into the pits.

We were particularly fortunate that fifteen of our Bevin Boys were professional footballers. Eight of whom were internationals. To name a few: Len Shackleton (Sunderland), Geoff. Walker (Middlesbrough), Johnny Downey (Manchester United), Stephens (Portsmouth), Farrell (Bradford Park Avenue), and many others.

These players coached my boys into one of the finest junior sides in the country. We had over twenty Rugby League players, many of them internationals, and we turned a full professional Rugby League side out to play Castleford Rugby League in a charity match to raise money for our injured comrades.

We had many professional boxers, referees and a boxing promoter all working at the colliery.

Some of the famous local boxers at that time were Chick Duggan, George Hinchcliffe, Jimmy Lumb, young Bull, and many others.

Chick Duggan had over three hundred contests. He was a tear-away fighter, cast in the same mould as the famous 'Yiddle' Kid Berg and Ted Kid Lewis. He fought fifteen rounds for me many times for nothing. Him and all the other boxers fought any opponent I picked for them, never asking for reward if they knew the proceeds were for our Injured Miners' Fund.

We opened our canteen for whist drives, for dances, we held "Brains Trusts" there with famous guest visitors. We had

*Them and Us*

Sportsmen's Nights when stars of every sport came and answered questions from the platform.

I then arranged a new innovation. Once a week I arranged with my committee to close our pit head baths for four hours so that the village women and children could come in and bathe.

We staged all-in wrestling shows. We held beauty contests, in fact anything that would take the minds of our people off the tragic happenings if only for a brief period.

One of the results of all this was we had no strikes during the war.

The older men of Fryston would say even now: "When Bullock asked us to do a job, no matter how difficult or dangerous, we never even asked him how much he was going to pay. We knew he would be fair."

That's a tribute for you.

"We knew he'd be fair." It also gave me a standard I had to try and live up to.

Eventually the war ended and great was the rejoicing in the coalfield. At Fryston we had many displaced persons from Europe working down the pit. It's worth recording how we managed to get them accepted by our people to such an extent that, by now, most of them have married miners' daughters. Good husbands and fathers they have proved to be.

When they first came to be interviewed by me in my office they were accompanied by an interpreter. The first questions I asked were:

"Can you sing? Can you play an instrument? Are you any good at sport. If so, which?"

If they were singers or musicians we put them in our concert party, orchestra or colliery band. If they were good at sport we tried them out in our colliery teams.

Our people loved to hear them sing and play in our concerts.

It's very difficult to appreciate their talents at night in the pubs and give them the cold shoulder at work the next day. I found this to be the best way of getting them settled in at the colliery without any objections from our own men.

## Managing Welfare and Labour Relations

Fortunately, we didn't have a lot of serious accidents at Fryston but suddenly, in one year, we had four different accidents all resulting in fractured spines to the men involved.

They spent a long time in hospital but when they finally came home, I used to see them being carried to the top of the streets to take part in the usual street corner parliaments and my heart ached when I saw their complete helplessness.

Young, strong, vigorous men, in the prime of life, suddenly finding themselves paralyzed from the waist down and I decided that something must be done for them and their families.

In the days when I was a boy, a miner with a broken back was doomed to spend the rest of his brief life on a water-bed. They usually lived about two years after the accident, then they developed bowel infections, they were covered with bed sores, and their last days were spent in misery and pain.

But now modern surgery was changing this and in Pinderfields Hospital in Wakefield there was a lady surgeon, called Miss Pearson, who made a special study of these seriously disabled men. Bed sores disappeared. Some degree of activity was encouraged and a different attitude slowly developed towards this very serious disablement.

I felt that if she and her team could work so hard and do so much at the hospital, we, at the colliery ought to help also. But how to do it? How had we to raise the money? That was the problem. Time and money was scarce.

So the concert parties that we had already formed went round every pub and hall within a ten mile radius of Fryston and gave concerts. The landlords of pubs and the committees in clubs were very helpful. Our activities started at a little pub in Berwick-in-Elmet called "The Fox and Grapes". The pub was managed by a young couple, Jerry and Jennie Oddy, they helped to get us started, they were keen to help but they hadn't even a piano.

This didn't deter us. We took a piano with us and gave good concerts to a public house full of customers who didn't work in a mining area at all. Jennie made us sandwiches, Jerry ran raffles and they never charged us a penny.

## Them and Us

Other landlords came to hear us at "The Fox" and soon we were in great demand.

A very talented London lad married one of our Fryston girls during the war. He could play seven instruments at dance band standard and he started writing songs about our injured miners, about our rescue team. He used to sing them. They called him Les Aplin, and his songs are still sung in the village.

In less than twelve months after these activities started we had raised sufficient money to buy our injured miners a motor propelled chair and a leather jerkin. We kept on working. invitations poured in for our parties and in a short time we were able to buy our paraplegics a television set each.

Local tradesmen let me have these at just over cost price and they maintained them free.

Enthusiasm continued and eventually we were able to buy the unfortunate wives, electric washing machines. It was very hard work for all of us but the gratitude of the injured men and their families was ample reward.

Other pits saw the good work we were doing and responded in such a way that the Yorkshire Section of Miners' Welfare made it a county responsibility.

The Miners' leaders were very helpful. Indeed, their president, Mr. Alwyn Machin, became chairman of the first County Paraplegic Committee in Yorkshire and Miss Pearson, the surgeon, Miss Barstow, the coalfield's medical social worker—now my wife—and myself were founder members of this committee.

After the nationalization of coalmines a National Paraplegic Committee was formed of which I was again a founder member. Later this Committee broadened its activities to help all the seriously disabled in the mining industry.

The things we had done and started at Fryston as an exception now became the rule throughout the whole of the mining industry. This was a development that has been rich in its rewards. The way the disabled are looked after now in the mining industry, compared to how they were previously neglected, is one of the most satisfactory things in my whole career.

## Managing Welfare and Labour Relations

Most men, after obtaining a position as colliery manager, seemed to keep themselves apart; they lived in a big house, an ivory tower of isolation. I didn't.

My house was open to our miners.

There were several reasons for this. I wanted them to come. It enabled them and me to talk over their problems in privacy. My relatives worked at the pit and they visited me as always. I have never wanted to be anything different to what I had always been. We had a big garden attached to the manager's house and we used it to hold garden parties to raise money for various charities.

I never had any temptation to move away from the class from which I had sprung.

My inclinations and desires were different to most middle-class people.

I loved breeding and training dogs. I liked shooting, but where could I shoot? A mining area has usually been poached to death. I bought a ·22 rifle and practised in an old quarry whenever I had a spare moment. I started taking the gun in the car with me and shooting an occasional rabbit.

It was only a short step from here to having a silencer fitted.

Now I felt really equipped to develop the finer art of poaching adventures. Finesse was added to the crude methods of my boyhood.

People ask how did these activities affect the opinion of the miners about their boss. It appeals to them. Anything like this fills any gap and there was nothing they liked better than when they came with me and shared these adventures.

A lot of miners are really good poachers, and them and I worked out various methods of outwitting gamekeepers and policemen, we developed it to a fine art.

We trained dogs to watch from the back of a car for things worthy of shooting. A small whimper; a quick look from us to where the dog was looking; a silent shot; a quick leap by a good dog from a moving car; a marvellous retrieve and back to a moving car. We timed this operation and we reduced it from minutes to a matter of seconds.

I am not pretending that these are good traits in one's

## Them and Us

character but all of these things, good or bad, were part of me, and I survived.

Later, when I had become the National President of the British Association of Colliery Management I kept up these activities; I had more opportunities now not less. Doing my job as president took me further and further afield, and so my scope for these nefarious activities widened.

My game reserves began to expand from a local pond or wood to national and even international fields, by-ways, ponds and woods. My shooting grounds stretched from Land's End to John o' Groats. No landowner had bigger or better shooting rights than I.

Is it wise? Of course not. When do we grow up?

I do know, however, that Fryston old people ate pheasants from England, Scotland and Wales.

Shooting without permission gave me the same sort of excitement I used to get out of colliery managers' orchards.

Nobody need bother to get in touch with me to tell me this is all wrong. Of course it is. I knew it then. I know it now. But I enjoyed it then. I wouldn't now, but the reason for that is simple. Physically I couldn't stand the excitement.

Let me give an example of poaching.

I had to lead many deputations on behalf of higher colliery management to the National Coal Board whose headquarters are in Hobart House in London. Our National Joint Council met at 10.30 a.m. Many times I left home at 4 a.m., by car to try and arrange to get to Stamford by dawn. I had the time of my life in those quiet country lanes while ordinary decent people were still in bed.

Often I had to go into the cloakrooms at Hobart House to wash the blood from my hands and try to remove ugly stains from my clothes.

It was then a great thrill to proceed to the conference room, to lead our side of the N.J.C. and talk about law and order with the most law abiding citizens of the land for the next two hours.

It was a greater thrill when I arrived back at Fryston and distributed the results of my activities to the old people of the village. It was marvellous to feel that so many old people were now tasting delicacies they had never tasted before.

Once when I was leading a deputation to the South Yorkshire area there was an old general manager in charge who was a real relic of a bygone age. He still thought that he could rule the officials and the men as if it were his own private empire.

His headquarters was housed in a country mansion surrounded by beautiful grounds, teeming with game and hundreds of rabbits.

When I met him on this deputation I quickly realized that I was meeting a character who had made up his mind that he was right and nothing that the management union representatives could say could make him change his mind. If ever I had met a pocket Hitler, here there was one.

It wasn't very difficult to make him lose his temper, which would give me an excuse to *pretend* to lose mine. I said to him:

"You sit up here in isolated splendour, kidding yourself that you not only run this place but that you own it." Pointing to the rabbits running about on the lawn, I said:

"These grounds, these offices, and even those rabbits belong to everybody in this nation just as much as they belong to you."

That did it. He jumped up and shouted:

"It does all belong to me even those b—— rabbits."

The question of rabbits rang a bell, and I conceived a wonderful idea. I would teach him a lesson. The idea filled me with such exhilaration that I brought the meeting to a close as quickly as I could. Had a cup of tea with him and got back to Fryston.

On arriving at my office I sent for the pit chauffeur and one or two old experienced pitmen—all good poachers—and told them of my scheme. They were delighted and immediately went home to get all their nets, lines and other equipment necessary for a massive rabbit drive.

It was a beautiful moonlight night when we set off. We borrowed a Coal Board van to take us to poach Coal Board property. We left the van in a little by-lane a short distance away from the Area Coal Board offices. We travelled stealthily among the hedgerows and with the wind in our favour we approached the rabbit warren and my miner assistants netted the whole warren. We then went back to the end of the grounds and let out our long line, right to the other side of the big field where we knew the rabbits would be feeding.

When one of the miners had got to the far side of the field he gave a sharp tug on the line, this was a quiet signal to move slowly forward dragging the line all along the field towards the warren.

The noise made by the line rustling in the grass was sufficient to startle every rabbit feeding and they all dashed back to their warren and straight into our waiting nets. What a catch we had! I've never seen so many rabbits. Now for the first time I saw real poachers in action. They killed the rabbits quickly, quietly, humanely, efficiently and what is more enthusiastically.

Even during this exciting adventure, my managerial instinct took over for a brief moment and I couldn't help thinking that if only they would work as enthusiastically at the pit as they were working here we should have much better results at the colliery than what we were getting.

We gathered the rabbits into sacks, collected our nets and lines, packed everything in the van and went quietly back home. We had never seen or heard a soul.

This was private enterprise versus nationalization in a different way and private enterprise won, hands down.

On the journey home I was quietly thinking when one of the miners, chuckling with glee said:

"Don't worry, boss, it says in't Act that all the pits and all connected with them belong to the nation. That's us isn't it?"

We sent rabbits to every needy family in the village. We sold and raffled others and the proceeds went to the Injured Miners' Fund.

A week later the postponed deputation in the same general office was resumed. When it was over I casually remarked to the old Area General Manager:

"I haven't noticed many rabbits about today."

The old man looked up and said, "It's a funny thing we haven't seen a rabbit since you were here last week."

Jumping up with assumed indignation I was going to reply but he was on his feet saying:

"Nay, Mr. Bullock, you don't think for one moment, as bad as you think I am, and as bad as I may think you are, that I'd accuse you of coming all the way from Fryston to here in the middle of the night and doing anything so wicked as poaching rabbits on a Coal Board estate, do you?"

What is more he meant it.

Once I was out for a little motor run on my own and going past Harewood House I saw pheasants to the left and pheasants to the right. I pulled into a little by-lane, walked into a small plantation and in front of me were beautifully-kept lawns with many pheasants quietly feeding. My favourite gun dog was with me. She was specially trained for these sort of activities. I looked carefully all round, shot what I wanted but before doing any recovery work I looked back to where I had left my car and there beside the door stood a gamekeeper. This I thought would be a real test for my skill.

I buried my rifle in bracken and impressed on the dog very urgently that she had to lay down, guard the rifle and stay there. Then I went boldly to the car fastening up my trousers. The gamekeeper glanced down and said:

"I wondered what the car was doing here, but now I know." He paused, "But you are still trespassing."

"Yes," I replied, "but when nature makes its call as urgently as it has just done I've not much choice."

He was quite nice and we chatted for a while. I asked him if he was troubled much with poachers.

"Good Lord, no," he said. "We watch them far too well for poachers to come and get them in broad daylight."

He then gave me a lot of very useful tips on how to deal with poachers, we got on so well together, that I asked him if would get in my car. Then I took him up to the local pub—Harewood Arms—and bought him a pint. While he was drinking it I told him that nature was calling again, I nipped out through the gents, into the car, and back to where I had left

## Them and Us

my dog. There she was still guarding the rifle but the pheasants were neatly arranged by the side of the rifle. We were away quickly and I never saw the gamekeeper again.

This story can't harm him. It's many years ago. He will have been dead for years.

CHAPTER THIRTEEN

## FRYSTON WELFARE HALL

Since 1870 when Fryston pit was sunk the village round the colliery site had one way in and one way out. They used to say that in winter when heavy snow fell they were completely isolated, for there is a river running right round the back and snow blocked the only entrance and exit. During the long winter evenings, men believed that a place ought to be built to which men and women could go to meet other men and women. A place well-lit, warm, a place in which to relax. News reached Fryston of a new theatre being built in Leeds, but what did it matter to them, there was no transport to Leeds. Money was tight. Mineworkers were looked upon as a "race apart". Nobody bothered about them. Coal was as cheap as the labour that produced it. Yet if ever a village hall was needed, and needed immediately, it was in this village. These dreams were in men's minds as far back as that. When thoughts become firmly embedded in the mind it becomes an ideal, then it becomes a reality.

Coal had come into its own. Coal from Britain was demanded on all the trade routes of the world. Fryston, and all the Yorkshire pits then in existence, assumed importance. Railways, ships and mills were asking for staggering amounts of the rich steam coals that—from Beeston in Leeds to the East coast and beyond—laid silently beneath the lovely fields, woods and park around Fryston. So men came to get the coal and as they got it they sang the old miners' song:

> There's a ton of dirt from a ton of coal,
> And a gallon of sweat and grime.

## Them and Us

They worked hard and long. When work was finished, because they were young, strong and proud, they walked to neighbouring towns and found mates who could cook, clean and sew. Out of such friendships homes were made, out of such homes children were produced; strong, clean, straight-limbed youngsters who grew and were moulded into great pit traditions.

Youth strives for better things. Because youth is unconquerable better things were demanded. Better conditions of work, better pay, better modes of living. And, a most natural thing in the world under the circumstances, a common meeting place was discussed and a dream was planted in the minds of the men of Fryston.

The dream grew, receded, and grew again for seventy years and by 1950 I was now determined to do something about the dream. The dream had been passed from one generation to another, hopes had risen and been shattered. I had to rekindle that hope and make it a burning desire. Then I had to find ways to create and maintain enthusiasm. Other things necessary were the material things which money and labour could provide. Then we needed vision, ingenuity, organization, planning and bold leadership and this I knew inside me was my job. All these dreams, all these conditions were realized and met in 1951.

During the war and after, we had a very thriving canteen which we slowly developed from selling coffee and biscuits to full meals. From there to pit boots and pit clothes. Then, we were determined that now we had pit-head baths our miners would and should be as well dressed as anybody else. So we started selling suits and trained our canteen manager to measure the miner correctly—so, no more ready-made suits. They now had suits made to measure. We paid cash to the manufacturer and the miners paid by deferred payments so they had the advantage of not having to go shopping. They could pay for their suits so much a week and would pay no more than if they had paid cash. We then started selling radios, radiograms and even television sets on the same terms. We had a lot of money out of course but we had no bad debts. We had

## Fryston Welfare Hall

their money before they did and their weekly payment was decided between them and us. So the small profit we made on each article was quite a large amount of total money with our large sales. We invested this money wisely. Our capital slowly grew. We equipped a sun-ray room and a massage room full of all the latest devices not seen outside of large hospitals.

When the Coal Board took over all canteens, I was serving as a National Director of Welfare, so I knew every move planned. A large number of canteens all over the country were badly in debt and it was quite understandable that if they took over all the debts, they would also take over the few assets of some of the canteens. Even so I was such an ardent private socialist I was determined they wouldn't get their hands on ours. So I called my committees together and told them what was about to happen and also what we could do with our money.

There was an old, deserted, worked-out, desolate quarry that was an eyesore adjoining the village. I interviewed the Area chiefs and asked if we could rent it for one hundred years at a nominal rent.

"What's a nominal rent?" they asked.

"Oh, a shilling a year," I threw over my shoulder.

And a shilling a year was agreed. We approached a brewery company for designs for a Welfare Hall, counted our money and decided what we could afford. All that we needed was courage, determination and enthusiasm.

We had seven thousand pounds. The cheapest sort of hall big enough for us would cost at least fourteen thousand pounds . . . so that is where our optimism was needed. Speed was essential. I borrowed bulldozers and on the very evening of the day we got the land we moved in. The miners were passing when the machines arrived and they gave a real spontaneous cheer when they saw them start. The cynics were also active. "I'll believe we are going to have a Welfare Hall when I see it built; not before," they said. When the same people DID see it . . . they couldn't believe it either.

Incredible things happened at incredible speed. When the big machines arrived the quarry was a mass of old lime kilns,

## Them and Us

tangled undergrowth, years and years of accumulated rubbish. But by nightfall on the first day, there was a beautiful level piece of ground fifty yards long and ten yards wide.

Next day rubble was being led on the site in borrowed lorries, and, after their shift at the pit was finished over eighty miners turned up with picks and shovels and levelled the rubble.

After one and a half days the foundations were laid. Then cement, sand and pebbles arrived.

We borrowed cement mixers from the collieries and local builders, we put out appealing notices for help at the pit gates and organized a week-end blitz.

Miners of all ages appeared at the site; and how they worked. Our tradesmen and our surveyors were there. Levels were taken, pegs driven in, lines drawn and the cement mixers were started.

The cement mixers never stopped until the foundations were complete.

We worked all through the day and at night lit the area with hundreds of miners' lamps. Work continued—as one set of men came on another set went home. It was a triumph of organization.

For my part, I never left the site until the foundations were set. We had neither the money, nor the time, to build a brick or stone building so we bought two ex-Army Nissen huts. One a hundred feet long and the other sixty feet long, we intended building them like a big letter "L", the bottom of the "L" was designed to be for an old people's room.

I never told anyone—except the Union Committee—of the barriers that were in our way, covenants on land, government restrictions, permits, licences, contracts for timber and steel orders, etc.

Every contractor we approached said the place would take months to build, they were bound to respect and adhere to the red tape and procedures which surround any new project.

My theory was that, if I ignored the lot and then pleaded ignorance, I could create delay in any official decision. Also, I felt that if I could get the Welfare Hall built—and opened—it would need a hell of a council—who were miners and elected by miners—to give orders to knock it all down. So my battle-

## Fryston Welfare Hall

cry all the time was: "Let's get it up. Let them talk! We'll talk afterwards."

Many pitmen having a pint of beer at night wondered if they had suddenly gone barmy. Working for nowt? But what was more important, they kept on working.

We went to a dealer in Halifax who sold the type of Nissen huts that we wanted and inspected them on the site.

We purchased the two we wanted, on condition, that they were delivered to Fryston the next day. The dealer agreed and the huts arrived the next day. The dealer's men started to erect the big, steel arch girders, which formed the framework of the hut. They managed to erect two and then they went home. We were all watching them and realized that these arches were nowhere near as difficult to erect as the heavier arch girders we erected in scores every day and every night down the pit.

Here we had far better conditions, so as the contractor's men moved out, we moved in. We had every girder up and joined together in one single day. Next the whole building had to be lined with plasterboard. Permits were needed, or so we were told.

"Send the stuff, we'll send the permits later." We got the plasterboards and all our joiners, fitters, blacksmiths, painters and electricians came up from the pit as their shift ended.

The miners now acted as labourers for the tradesmen. The huts were wired as we built them. As soon as one set of plasterboards went on they were painted. The bar came from the brewery ready-made, and fitted in like a glove.

Among the refugees at Fryston was a Czechoslovak called Francis Drilek. He was an inspired artist and ready to give his art for us. He painted murals on the walls and the vast background to the stage. He also gave puppet shows.

Today, he is a figure of international fame, for he and his wife, Vlasta, are the originators and the operators of the "Pinky and Perky" puppets and are now known as "The Dalibors".

By the end of the first week, we were already printing invitations for the opening ceremony, asking Sir Hubert Houldsworth, Chairman of the National Coal Board, to perform the opening, inviting well-known Trade Union Leaders, local Coun-

## Them and Us

cillors and Magistrates, Police Chiefs, brewery chiefs, and—a master stroke—Ministry officials.

There were so many miners who had helped and many more who were members of the welfare scheme all wanting to come to the opening ceremony that we had to let them ballot for places. By now we knew we would be ready to open fourteen days after starting to level the site! So we arranged a feed and entertainment. Practically everybody we invited accepted our invitation.

Over the entrance of the new Welfare Hall was a proud and conspicuous notice which stated:

> This Hall was built in twelve days by miners, out of monies raised by miners, for themselves and their families, for culture and entertainment.

I had worries enough, I hadn't much time to think about anything else during this period. We wanted the new Welfare Hall to be comfortable. We wanted to be able to relax. In our old people's room we wanted Dunlopillo seating. We wanted rocking chairs and comfortable couches for them. We wanted a reading room with a big projected television screen. But our money had now all gone. We had the site. The Hall was built and paid for.

I asked the brewery if they would lend us the money to pay for these things, then let us have our beer for nothing for a while, so that we could pay the money back that we owed for the furniture.

They agreed, and so the greatest day in the history of our small mining village dawned. The great names arrived. The brewery sent a director to keep a fatherly eye on things and help our very inexperienced steward and his family.

We decided to serve a light Barsac wine with the meal. But the wine bottles went astray and instead bottles of brandy were laid out on the tables. Some men drank the brandy as if it were wine. With the result that towards the end of the dinner the scenes became a little wild. I think that whilst the top men really enjoyed it, they were quite pleased to get away. For our part, we got very excited and carried away with ourselves. By

## Fryston Welfare Hall

nine o'clock we had ceased to take any money at the bar and everybody helped themselves.

There never was and never has been a night just like that. Miners appeared to be still drunk when we opened at dinnertime the next day. Steady, moderate, experienced officials were clamouring to sing on the stage. Respected mine officials were asleep on the graves in the churchyard opposite the hall. Some tried to curl up in children's prams, some miners went home on their hands and knees. But there was no fighting, or quarrelling. Just a real sense of achievement that had to be celebrated.

The first week we sold over seventy barrels of beer. We adopted novel schemes to keep a full house. We had a "Snowball Sweep"—if you were in the club when the draw was made you had £20 extra to come. We made sure we didn't draw the lottery until nearly closing time so everyone had to stay.

Within twelve months we had cleared all our debts and were making money. The Welfare Hall became the real village centre. Our miners and their wives entertained from the stage according to their talents. There are many marvellous musicians and singers in the mining fraternity.

We arranged Sports Nights and got leading sportsmen from all walks of life.

We staged boxing and wrestling inside the club.

We raised money for children's parties, old folks' parties, young people's parties.

But no matter what was the special attraction, the old people's section was always open and admission to any function was always free for our old people. They had newspapers and periodicals delivered daily to their own room.

Young miners sent drinks in to their elders and the old people really appreciated this. The reaction of the old people alone made me feel it had all been worthwhile.

We kept on working. Now we built an outside skating rink —a big youth centre—a bowling green and an old people's rest centre outside in the grounds where they could sit in summer while music from the club was relayed to them.

This work was carried out by our miners and tradesmen all for no charge.

*Them and Us*

Then we started to turn the rest of the huge quarry into a stadium as big as White City in London. This was a real challenge.

I had to adopt all sorts of measures to spur on the men who had given so much of their time and effort for so little reward. We started supplying the workers with a barrel of beer. We got the colliery band to provide "Music while you work". But as we were nearing completion attendances of volunteers gradually dwindled.

It was a climax. So one week-end I put notices out to say that the B.B.C. were going to make a film on the Saturday and Sunday. I got my surveyors to take up their positions on the top of the quarry with their tripods. It looked like the real thing. Everybody worked like mad. Afterwards, the miners kept asking: "When are we going to see the film?" But when I told them that—it was just a lie—they realized that the deception had got the required results and they forgave me.

We were helped, however, by the Press who gave constant reports of our progress and by the B.B.C. who, through Tony Van den Bergh, gave commentaries on what we were achieving. It was through these broadcasts that a sincere and lasting friendship was formed between Tony and myself and since then we have done many broadcasts together. He is the best interviewer I have met. He brings the best out of me with the minimum of questioning. Some interviewers spend so much time telling what they know, that there is little time for the person being interviewed to express his opinion.

The next two years were just as busy. Fryston Colliery was peopled by three villages: Fryston, Fairburn and Brotherton, and these villages, Fairburn and Brotherton, wanted attention to their problems just as much as Fryston.

We built a Welfare Hall for both villages within three months. Fairburn and Brotherton lie about a mile apart opposite Fryston on the eastern bank of the river Aire. Both villages have long histories. Brotherton church was built before 1196 and Brotherton Marshes were scenes of vicious battles during the Wars of the Roses. Skeletons, weapons and armour have

## Fryston Welfare Hall

been unearthed in recent years near to where we built the Welfare Hall.

It was at Brotherton that Queen Margaret, wife of Edward I, gave birth to a son, Thomas de Brotherton. Edward II created Thomas de Brotherton, Duke of Norfolk, Earl Marshal of England; a title still held by descendants. The church carries many evidences of historical association of Henri de Lacy, the Ramsdens, the Tindalls and the Daubes. The church itself was dedicated to Edward the Confessor and inside is an inscription: "Frederick Henry Ramsden, eldest son of Henry James Ramsden, Bart., Captain of the Coldstream Guards, who fell at the battle of Inkerman, 3rd November, 1854, aged twenty-four years. This young officer is buried on the field of battle in the same grave with seven of his brother officers" and another "Julie Daubes, mother of Charles Daubes, vicar of this parish, who with her family in the year 1686 left France, their native country, to avoid the severe persecution against the reformed, died 8th December, 1764, aged seventy-seven years".

So, there they lie; a young man cut off in the prime of life by war and an old woman who had known persecution, but lived to a ripe old age. What is significant about this? What is it to do with the miners? One thing. Suffering.

CHAPTER FOURTEEN

# NATIONALIZATION OF THE COAL MINES

The next date of importance to me was the General Election of 1945. In this election I spoke more often on the platform for the Labour Party than I'd ever done before.

On one occasion I was ordered to take the chair for the Conservative candidate. I had already taken the chair for the Labour candidate the night before in the same hall. The order was forgotten.

When the election results were announced they exceeded our wildest dreams; and certainly all our expectations. Now we had a Labour Government with a working majority for the first time. What would OUR Government do?

We expected so much of them. What we did know was that whatever else they promised they were committed to nationalize the Coal Mines. This to us was important above all else.

"But how would they do it?"

"How would Nationalization work?"

"Would the coal owners be given jobs. If so, would they try as hard to make Nationalization successful when we all knew they were Conservatives and did not believe in Nationalization?"

"How could they try and make a success of something they were fundamentally opposed to?"

These were the questions hotly debated in pits and pubs.

"But, if they did not accept jobs under the Labour Government, who would take over the higher management?"

We had no people with the necessary skills, qualifications and/or experience who could tackle the tremendous task of organizing—under one vast undertaking—a thousand different pits formerly owned by six hundred different companies.

## Nationalization of the Coal Mines

"How were the owners going to be compensated?"
"How were miners going to fare?"
"How were unit and local management going to be treated?"
The miners were jubilant; understandably.
"The pits are ours, no more two sides. Ask and you shall receive," they had been told.

Fifty years of propaganda had stressed how wonderful everything would be once our pits were nationalized.

The great day dawned, the Bill to bring about this long awaited promise was passed and the plans and schemes were made public.

When the pits were handed over there were great celebrations. We had the village band out; the vicar was there and blessed the new N.C.B. flag and the pit; speeches were made from management and Trade Union leaders, pledging utmost co-operation and goodwill. Then the miners gave three cheers for the Labour Government and we set about our new task: To get more coal out; to make Nationalization really work. We all agreed ours—Fryston—was the pit to show how it could work. A Socialist Manager, had already been there over twenty years, knew everybody by name in the pit, coupled with Trade Union leaders, respected and trusted by the men and the manager. What could stop us now?

Plans for the new organization were eagerly awaited and when they came, just as keenly criticized and argued about. We found the coalfields were being split up into Divisions: Scotland, Northumberland and Cumberland, Durham, North Western, North Eastern (Yorkshire), East Midlands (Nottinghamshire and Derbyshire), West Midlands (Staffordshire and Leicestershire), South Western (Wales and Kent) and then subdivided into Areas, with a Divisional Board and Areas in charge of an Area General Manager. The Division had Production Directors, Labour Relations Directors, Marketing, Scientific, Canteen Managers, Surveying and Estates, the lot. The same type of management line was put in at Area and also at National level.

We now had a Board in London, chaired by Lord Hyndley, with all the separate departments managed by a Director-

## Them and Us

General responsible to his senior on the National Coal Board ... same at Division ... same at Area.

Then came the appointments of the various Divisional Chairmen. Now we started getting real shocks. Men we'd never heard of were appointed to the biggest jobs, men who, incidentally, had never heard of—never mind knew—anything about the Coal Industry. Gossip started as to how they had got these positions, but we came to the conclusion that the qualification necessary was that they knew nothing about this great industry.

We had admirals, generals, retired colonels, a discarded Food Minister, landed aristocrats, the lot. The next stage was the vast empire building that took place. Parkinson's Law was here with a vengeance. Men flocked from all over the country to show us how to run our pits and handle our men. This all might sound bitter, but it isn't. I could have been amused by it all if it hadn't been so serious, we were feeling more hurt than angry. Overnight, management status changed, we were no longer the king of our village, the number of officials above the Colliery Manager grew and grew until it was often referred to as the "Heinz Soup set-up" . . . fifty-seven varieties of bosses!

Instead of running our pits as we used to, we found we couldn't make any important decisions. Negotiations were taken over largely by ex-Trade Union leaders, who had lost their jobs for various reasons. Planning was done at Area, approved by Division—or the reverse—then on to London. We had advisers on every subject and every problem. Form creating and form filling at last achieved first place, information on all manner of things was called for. Departments were set up, different branches created for every conceivable operation, but one thing above all others remained, that was that Managers were made to keep one thing in its entirety, that was their responsibility. No one ever shared this.

I have always maintained that no one should be allowed to give orders if he doesn't carry his share of responsibility for the orders so given.

*So now we got going* and Pit Consultative, Area Consultative, Divisional Consultative and National Consultative Committees were set up, soon, I was serving on all of them. Orders were given to each Pit Consultative Committee to fix its colliery tonnage target and any pit that reached the target they had set were then entitled to fly the N.C.B. flag from the pit head for five days.

Now a target to me is something to aim for. I shoot quite a bit with a ·22 rifle and when I am "zero-ing" it—to see if it's shooting accurately—I don't try it out on a barn, a haystack or a big slag heap; I aim at an object about two inches square, something to really aim for.

So when we had to fix a tonnage target, my Consultative Committee and I agreed, that the tonnage we fixed should be a tonnage that we had never yet achieved, but a tonnage we felt *we could* get if we all worked well and things went right. In addition to this we added a thousand tons and this was the target that we decided we would aim for and would eventually achieve.

The first week our output was eight hundred tons more than we had ever had before but it was a few hundred tons below the target we had set. Result—a letter from the Divisional Board wanting to know the reason why we had not got our target, it wasn't a nice letter either.

The pits all around us had fixed their targets on what they were pulling out at the time; and they got letters of congratulation. You can imagine the effect that the letter of condemnation that we received had on our committee members.

All our workers and officials were disappointed because we were one of the few pits not flying the flag of success and we all knew that we were doing better than most pits. But no matter how our output increased we still received letters wanting to know why we hadn't reached our target.

The outcome of this was, we dropped our target to what we knew we could achieve, and from then on we got so many letters of congratulation we could have used them for toilet rolls and still had some to spare. We quickly wore our flag threadbare.

Was this attitude right, either what *they* did or what *we* did?

## Them and Us

This book will pay more attention to the management attitude than to the men's reaction, which is—I hope—understandable because I was a manager and the book is about me. Even so, any book about a man whose life has been spent living and working in the coalfield must be in a way a history of the coalfield as the writer sees it, and I shall dwell a little on the events leading up to and since Nationalization.

The day the mines were bought by the nation from the mine owners was known as 'Vesting Day' and this was 1st January 1947. Twenty years after 'Vesting Day' it is quite easy to forget how big a task confronted the newly formed National Coal Board. It would be easy to overlook and probably forget the unsatisfactory conditions of the coal industry for generations.

The conditions in the coal industry is too easily forgotten by most people. The coal owners—same as everybody else—had in their number those that were good, bad and very bad. Some coal owners had worked out all the best seams. The coal industry had been stricken by depression. It had been starved of capital, unable to find fresh markets and had been practically ruined by unrest. Pits had been on short time for years until the threat of war, in 1937.

The terms "starved of capital" and "industrial unrest" need explaining. The effect on an industry like the mining industry being starved of capital means that there is no money for research, very little investment in modern machinery; that bad working conditions, inadequate ventilation, low roadways have to be tolerated. Low roadways cause inadequate ventilation. The roadways down a pit need to be constantly remade because nature is trying all the time to close the roadways up again. If capital is not available it is impossible to maintain roadways of the necessary size.

If large amounts of fresh air are needed to dilute the gas—which is a natural constituent of coal—then roadways have to be made large enough to carry that ventilation. If this is not done then gas accumulates to an explosive mixture and all that is needed to cause an explosion is a source of ignition.

Lack of capital resulted in apparent reforms in working terms and conditions being avoided by most owners as long as

## Nationalization of the Coal Mines

possible. This resulted in industrial unrest, more accidents and more disasters.

It must not be forgotten that most of the improvements in mining conditions since the turn of the century has been the result of major Acts of Parliament. It needed quite a lot of effort to ban boys and girls working down the pit. It needed legislation to get the working hours improved. It needed legislation to get pit-head baths and welfare facilities.

Therefore, while some owners were enlightened and treated their men reasonably well it must be remembered that Trade Unions were formed and grew in strength to combat the owners whose only thoughts were profit. When seen from this angle what the industry has done since 'Vesting Day' is a major achievement by any standards.

When the Fleck Committee met nine years after 'Vesting Day', it reported that the main structure was right. This was a great testimonial to those who created the structure of the National Coal Board in the early days and one must pay tribute to Lord Hyndley and Sir Arthur Street, in particular, who were the chief architects of the new organization.

Though we were disappointed by some of the results of their efforts, we never failed to realize what a stupendous task they undertook and there is no doubt that the mining industry has been transformed in this last twenty years. It still has plenty of problems, it still has a long way to go, but there is no doubt that new life has been put into the old body, that forces of decline have been taken over by forces of expansion.

One of the best things that happened, as time went on and the new organization began to gain experience, was the study and thought given to the problem of human relations. Even after 'Vesting Day' we were troubled by disputes and stoppages in spite of the carefully thought out conciliation machinery, which should have made all strike action completely unjustified.

Even so, great progress was made for there has been no major strikes in the mining industry since 'Vesting Day'. This is due to many reasons. There has been a more humane approach to labour problems. At first I, along with many other managers, resented the fact that a lot of the labour relations were taken out of our hands. But today taking the broader picture I realize that everybody's labour relations were not as good as the ones we had at Fryston and that labour relations did improve and have continued to improve throughout the mining industry.

There were two important factors about Nationalization:

1 The hostility of the owners and many of higher management.
2 The high hopes and expectations of the mineworkers.

It is now generally accepted that Nationalization is permanent, but that does not stop continued criticism both in political and industrial fields and from within the mining industry itself. Although surely everyone must admit freely that there has been tremendous improvements in terms and conditions of all employed in mining. However, the great hopes and expectations of early exponents of Nationalization have not been entirely fulfilled. There is still an atmosphere of mistrust—though nowhere near as apparent as it used to be—between the men and the bosses. The early advocates of Nationalization always claimed that there would be no longer two sides, everybody would work as a single team. This has not turned out to be so, there are now many sides and quite a few trade unions all representing different sections of the mining community.

But let no one underestimate the tremendous task which did face the new organization and if I, for one, did not like all that was done—or the way it was done—I was astonished by the speed with which it was accomplished.

One thousand pits managed by eight hundred companies were brought into one single organization in a matter of months. Nothing on this scale had ever been planned in British industry before. The Board had not only to develop, they had practically to rebuild the industry and improve its technical and general management. The new Board made many mistakes but there is no wonder. The Board consisted of nine men, all from different walks of life, men who had never worked together before but had now to decide the sort of organization needed

## Nationalization of the Coal Mines

and help to nationalize the industry's assets. They had, with the help of the unions, to establish a system of conciliation which described and prescribed the various stages through which each dispute must pass, and more important, they laid down a time-table for each stage. There had never been a conciliation system anything like this operating in the mining industry before.

The National Union of Mineworkers from the very beginning of nationalization pressed for a five-day week.

The Labour Government had agreed; but there was a great shortage of coal and granting a five-day week posed real supply problems for the Board. This was one of the most difficult decisions the National Coal Board had to make in those early days.

On the one hand, if granted, it would be a great encouragement to the miner and real eminence of "good faith" ... but on the other hand it could lose output so badly needed. The Board made the statement:

"Detailed discussions between the Board and the National Union of Mineworkers began in November. It would take many months to work out the conditions with which the five-day week could be introduced and to make the necessary changes in the coalfields. But the mineworkers set great store by this long awaited reform, and if the Board could make an early announcement about the date when it would be introduced, it would be an earnest of the Board's good intentions. It would encourage the mineworkers to put forth their best efforts and it would give a fillip to recruitment. If the Board delayed they might lose an opportunity of changing the spirit of the industry which might not recur. On the other hand, in 1947, production would be all-important, and costs of production would become more and more important as time went on. The seller's market in the world for British coal and for goods made with it, would not last for ever. The Board weighed all these factors carefully in the balance. They considered what sort of conditions might be attached to the five-day week in order to increase the attendance and improve the daily effort of the mineworkers. They were assured of the full co-operation of the Union in securing the output which the country needed. After consulting the Minister, the Board decided in favour of the early introduction of the five-day week coupled with suitable conditions. By the middle of December, the Board, in agreement with the Union, announced the following time-table. Conditions had to be agreed by the Board and the Union by 1 March 1947, or, failing agreement, referred to arbitration. Then, subject if necessary to the Government's authorization, the date for introducing the five-day week would be 5 May 1947, or, if there was arbitration, four weeks after the arbitrator's award."

Everybody agreed that management at colliery level needed strengthening. Coal was got from the pits, not from London; and the strength or weakness of the industry is directly influenced by the management at colliery level.

When Jim Bowman, an ex-leader of the N.U.M. became Chairman of the National Coal Board, and became Sir James Bowman, he stated: "The pit is the place where we must produce our greatest achievement." He went on to say, "Our colliery managers have *the* most difficult task. The hours they put in have no parallel in any other industry. Look at the size and importance of their jobs, the weight of their responsibilities on the one hand, and the smallness of their supporting staff on the other. There is no industry where so few are doing so much." He concluded his statement by remarking: "This situation will not be eased but will be aggravated, by every advance we make in mechanization and engineering techniques, every advance will add to the colliery manager's responsibilities."

Mr. Shinwell—the old socialist war-horse—was the Minister for Fuel at the time of Nationalization, he knew the tragic history of coalmining. He knew the poor conditions in which miners had been working for generations. No one had spoken more eloquently than he had about the iniquities of the old coal owners.

He grasped the nettle firmly. But it was an extraordinary complex and difficult problem and, even with all his knowledge of the industry and all his sympathy with the miners, he made mistakes . . . mistakes which he himself has always freely

## Nationalization of the Coal Mines

acknowledged. . . . He has stated since, that if he were to do it again he would do it differently. Difficulties are an integral part of the coal industry, but Emmanuel Shinwell said the problems he had met in the industry were less troublesome than the disputes he had to handle between different members of the Board, which finally led to resignations. Years after Mr. Shinwell said he should have done what some of us advocated in the beginning; appoint a small number of capable men to govern and decide questions of policy for the industry and leave functions to be carried on by mining engineers and other trained experts. We found as management at the pits that we had now lost personal contact. We had lost a lot of our authority. We had lost none of our responsibility. We were governed from afar by people we didn't even know.

I, personally, resented the fact that so many jobs and even departments were duplicated. If a job could be done at the pit that's where it should be done. If it's necessary to do it at Area then do it there. If at Division, then at Division. If in London, then let it be carried out in the capital. But for Heavens sake don't let us be doing it at the pit, Area, Division and London all at the same time. I was soon crying out for de-centralization. Appoint big men for big jobs. Give them the job to do inside the framework of national policy but then let them get on with it without so much red tape. And if they can't do it . . . remove them. People at pit level were perfectly willing to co-operate if they knew what they were to co-operate about, but in the early days everything seemed to be hidden by organizational and administration tangles until we didn't know where the hell we were.

People were being given top jobs who didn't know the least thing about the job. Trade Union leaders on the point of retiring from their own industries were appointed to be directors of labour relations at £7,000 per year, with no knowledge whatever of the conditions in the mining industry.

People from outside industries who were given these top jobs had to be trained and given time to settle down and understand what was expected of them in their new positions. The whole machinery of decision became cluttered up while we inside the industry trained them to do their jobs so that in time they could turn round and instruct us how to do our jobs.

If Sir Arthur Street did nothing else, he tried to introduce into the mining industry, civil service traditions and also some civil service nonentities.

I remember at one of the early dinners when we were dining with the Board, sitting next to a director and at the end of the dinner he said to me:

"Your conversation has been really interesting. I shall have to try and visit a pit sometime to find out what it is all about. I never knew there were so many problems."

In 1956 the British Association of Colliery Management was having its national conference at Scarborough and in my presidential address I talked a lot on co-operation and economic issues. The issues involved were not remote from the economic problems which beset the industry, as some people so fondly assumed. My fear was that if the then trends of consumption continued the country would find itself landed with stocks of coal of between forty and fifty million tons by the end of the year. In such a situation when so many adverse winds were blowing against the industry the management union had a vital role to play and I warned the government that it would be wrong to establish the economy of the country on a shaky dependence on oil imports from the Middle East which at any time could be cut off by a Middle East war or a dispute with Arab sheiks.

It has never been part of my union's policy to oppose healthy competition in the fuel field. Secondly, I said, that the livelihood of management, the livelihood of the workmen and the livelihood of the Board is closely bound up with the fortunes of the coalmining industry. This being the case, the need for co-operation between all sections of the industry is of paramount importance.

In that same speech talking on the economic forces I said:

"It is a truism that economic forces do not operate in a vacuum. They operate within political and social climates and within organizational and administrative framework. It is in this sense that life can be seen as a series of actions and reactions. Sometimes the economic forces are favourable, sometimes adverse, but whatever be their character, the best—in the circumstances—is achieved when the economic forces, the political and social climates, the organizational and administrative framework supplement each other to the advantage of the nation. There is nothing original in this view." I warned the government that a peace-time political and social organization has never been found adequate to meet the needs of war. Stagecoach mentalities are not of much use in the nuclear age. These are different ways in which the same idea is being expressed in a different context. I choose to express the idea my way, because it enables me to point out the futility of simply stressing the importance of economic factors. When this happens, one is generally driven to adopt one of two attitudes. Either one buries one's head in the sand and ends up by pretending economic forces are not operating, but if they are, that they can be dispersed by the wave of a magic wand; or, one accepts them as the only motivating force of life and, oblivious to social consequences try to amass facts of creating vacuua in which they can work.

I went on to point out that improving economic trends can at times improve in spite of maladjusted superstructures. Before long mountains of coal were appearing at the pit tops, despite all warnings oil became a real competitor with coal. Therefore, we needed to gear our administrative and organizational sides to provide that elasticity which is so essential for coping with adverse change in circumstances.

Throughout this period I was constantly stressing the need for more and more co-operation between all sides. I didn't want co-operation to be interpreted as a nice cosy cliché to be brought out of its cupboard when anything went wrong and used as a nice soothing balm. I wanted co-operation in a dynamic sense. I didn't want the sort of co-operation which regarded one side of the process as schoolmasters with their subjects to teach, and the other side of the process as schoolboys with their subject to learn.

I was becoming convinced that real co-operation was very difficult inside an undertaking so colossal in administrative

## Them and Us

framework of the National Coal Board. There were disagreements now between the National Coal Board and management. There were many things we were not seeing eye to eye. The National Coal Board were wanting to interfere too much in all operations at all levels. We had a meeting in London with the National Coal Board trying to decide how far de-centralization should go. It was apparent to me and to many others that there were certain things in the industry which must be reserved for national decision.

There must be national negotiation on wages and salaries, national decisions on the allocation of capital, national liaison with the government of the day. It was surprising how in this very large-scale set-up everything tended to sharpen itself into black and white but with no shades of grey.

Throughout the whole of my career as the leader of the management union I have stated that the whole apparatus of decision must not be allowed to be mutilated and crippled by administrative empires established to deal with matters which any competent person should have the freedom to deal with on the spot.

It must be appreciated that this is a serious matter in the coal industry and the levels which really matter are those levels in our pits and area. We were faced with many problems. There was a clear line for subordinates at pit level, to Area, to Division, to London. Big men with big jobs and tremendous responsibility were being by-passed by Lilliputians whose only claim to fame was this direct link with their senior counterpart. This created an air of uncertainty and far too much time was spent looking over one's shoulder wondering who was reporting on who. Some were afraid of doing anything for fear of doing wrong and there was a feeling throughout management of uncertainty.

CHAPTER FIFTEEN

# THE BIRTH OF A MANAGEMENT UNION

Nationalization had not been with us long before management began to realize that because it had no trade union it was neither taking its proper place in conciliation or consultation. They also realized it was high time that the important voice of management should be heard at all levels in the industry. The N.U.M. leaders were now emerging as real giants—"the pits are ours"—"we've access to the Minister", "we're affiliated to the Labour Party", and to colliery managers they would say, "If we don't get what we want, you're for it."

Threats to managers and sheer bullying were now commonplace.

Colliery managers had an association called the National Association of Colliery Managers. This was an association formed to promote the technical advance and knowledge of colliery managers and at the meetings that were held monthly in all parts of Great Britain they talked freely to each other of their experiences under Nationalization. They realized that for the first time in history they had to unite and form a management trade union for their own protection.

The managers were in an industrial and political no-man's land; they were being kicked from pillar to post by people in position below them and above them.

If you had no trouble at your pit you were giving in to the men.

If you had trouble at your pit you were no good at labour relations.

In mining, the biggest single source of dispute has always been the payment made for work done. Now, all orders, re pay

*Them and Us*

and the amounts thereof, were given to the manager from above him.

If he stuck to these orders and carried them out and subsequently had trouble with his men, somebody from the newly formed Labour Relations Department would invariably give way. When this happened the manager looked "the real nigger in the wood pile".

The miners had always looked on the owners as the real culprits but now the owners had gone and the new owners—the National Coal Board—were far away in London. So, all the venom was now turned on the colliery manager.

I have always maintained that if there had to be compromise then the manager should be allowed to do it. After Nationalization if there was anything unpleasant to do or say the manager had to do it. But if there was anything pleasant to do or say, any concession to make, then some big "bug" from Area or Division would come and do it.

So the management of the nationalized coal industry was faced with the problem of how to organize themselves into a union able to protect their interests at all levels.

This was a tremendous task. Men whose only association had been in a professional field now felt the urgent need and necessity at forming a real management trade union. What a task!

Most eligible members were Conservatives. They had never dreamed of being members of a trade union.

How could we form a union?

Would it survive?

Who would lead it?

How would the National Coal Board react to it?

These were just a few of the problems we faced. Meetings were held in Areas all over the country and we were helped greatly by:

National Association of Undermanagers, Institute of Mining Surveyors, National Association of Colliery Managers, Association of Electrical and Mechanical Engineers (Mining). We quickly gained support from all sections of management and professional grades throughout the mining industry. We had

## The Birth of a Management Union

to draw up a charter of our aims and objects; we had to find a suitable name.

Management didn't want to have a title like "Colliery Management Union". They wanted a trade union, but they didn't want to be called one.

Neither did they want to affiliate to the T.U.C.

So in 1947 all the bodies I have mentioned above co-operated to form the first registered trade union established to cater for the needs of those engaged in the management and administration of the coal industry and its ancillary undertakings. It had to have no political or religious affiliations.

As far as I can gather this was the only management union anywhere. I played a very active part in the early days and was quickly appointed the delegate for my own Area on to the Divisional Executive.

Our new union closely followed the organizational pattern of the National Coal Board in that we had Area Committees, Divisional Committees and a National Executive Committee.

Our first president was a former coal owner, named Major Walton Brown, and our first general secretary was a close associate of his named Major Robin Anderson. We established our headquarters at Newcastle in Neville Hall, where Major Walton Brown had his offices.

Now we started to tackle the problems and they were many.

What do we call ourselves? After much discussion we finally settled on The British Association of Colliery Management. Previously we had called ourselves The British Association of Colliery Officials and Staff and in Yorkshire we called ourselves Y.A.C.O.S.—the Yorkshire Association of Colliery Officials and Staff.

When could we arrange meetings convenient for busy men to attend? The National Coal Board were very reluctant to allow their managers time off for Union activities. Nobody below—and few above—had much sympathy with the idea of a colliery management's union.

The miners scorned the idea and their leaders poured ridicule on it. Chairmen of the Divisional Boards who were ex-generals,

*Them and Us*

admirals, aristocrats and ex-cabinet ministers, thought it was ridiculous for management to form a union.

Government ministers were quoted as actually saying, "It's more fitting for a pig to play a piano than for a colliery manager to take part in municipal or trade union affairs."

Another minister was credited with the remark: "Management are vermin and should be treated as such."

Some meetings were held secretly, some members didn't wish it to be known they were members but, credit to them, a great many were completely fearless and outspoken.

In Yorkshire we appointed a miner, called George Tyler, who had been educated at Ruskin College and had had experience as a journalist, as the Union's Divisional Secretary. He was a fearless orator and a good negotiator. When I became president he became the general secretary for the national union on the retirement of Major Anderson.

Lord Hyndley, the Chairman of the National Coal Board, was sympathetic to our ideas when we finally managed to meet him and after many meetings we eventually negotiated an agreement that gave us the right to represent all members of the management structure from undermanager and engineer right up to the directors of the divisional boards.

This was an achievement in itself. Many high officials fancied their careers would suffer if they were members of a trade union.

I had a personal experience which convinced me—if I needed convincing—that a management union was necessary, very early on after Nationalization. I was a speaker for the Labour Party, I was a friend of the Miners' leaders, if my experience could happen how would other managers fare whom the Miners' leaders looked on as their enemies.

The first big deputation after Nationalization at Fryston took place in my office. The Miners' Union side was led by Joseph Hall, president of the Yorkshire miners. Joe was already a veteran, a real fighter, either with his knuckles or with words. He made quite a reputation at inquiries held into various explosions when he represented the miners. Even before Nationalization he was an opponent to be feared. He would

## The Birth of a Management Union

break forth into torrents of abuse against bosses in general and managers in particular. When addressing big miners' meetings he had been known to descend from the platform and personally attack a heckler in the crowd.

Now he had a new sort of power. He was not only eloquent and forceful, he had the complete backing of the miners, knew members of the National Coal Board personally, met them weekly, and had a personal acquaintance with members of the government.

Joe Hall made a point of arriving two hours late for any meeting with colliery managers. On the day he arrived in Fryston village (two hours late) he met a Fryston miner—a real idle fellow—who asked him to go into his coal cellar with him and see the sort of "home coal" that Bullock was sending him.

Although Joe was already two hours late he had plenty of time to go in the man's cellar.

Most miners got a ton of coal free every month delivered to their house. This man had been picking bits of dirt out of every ton he had received for years and stacked it in a corner. He told Joe, however, that this dirt had all come in one load.

"Our Joe" was now fuming. He told the miner: "You wait, my lad. Bullock will be here in half an hour with a lorry and he will shovel every bit of this muck out himself; that will teach him a lesson." And he meant it.

By the time Joe Hall burst into my office, no knocking at the door, in he came—in a real blazing temper—he stamped, slavvered and stormed in front of my superiors and in front of the local union committee, and minutes had to pass before we realized what he was on about. But it was apparent that his venom was directed on me. He told me what had happened, what he had seen and what he had promised the man and then he said:

"I'm giving you five minutes to pick up that telephone, order a lorry to come round here and then you, Jim Bullock, will go and you shovel that muck out yourself, put it in the lorry and see it is carted away."

"And if I don't?"

"Then you'll be thrown out of this office and down the bloody stairs."

"Who'll do it?" I asked.

He thumped his chest like a bull ape and shouted, "Me, I'll do it. Joe Hall."

The atmosphere was tense. There was a deadly silence. Every eye was on we two, facing each other like a couple of ancient gladiators.

Joe did not expect any opposition to his orders. He was a great man, the personal friend of Manny Shinwell, the great Joe Hall!

Then I dropped my bombshell.

"Joe, tha' might have got away with this in any other office in Yorkshire but tha's not getting away with it here because I'm giving thee five minutes to do it. And if tha' doesn't do it tha's going down bloody stairs."

The Area General Manager, as white as a ghost, and looking frightened to death said:

"Don't let's have any trouble, Jim. Get a lorry and send a man."

But Joe was having none of that. He shouted:

"He's sending no man. He's going his b—— self."

"He's talking to and threatening me, not you, so you keep out of it," I said to the Area General Manager. Turning to Joe:

"I'm giving thi five minutes now to do it."

Minutes passed in deadly silence. The big clock ticking away the seconds. I took my coat off, hung it up on the rack, walked across to Joe and said:

"Tha's one minute left."

Suddenly we saw what a marvellous character this man was. He turned round to the union committee and in a voice shaking with sorrow and emotion he exclaimed:

"There, do you see what you've nearly had me do? The best colliery manager in Great Britain. The only bloody Socialist colliery manager we've got and you lot thought—and would have let me—fall out with him."

"Put it there, Jim. Me and thee will never fall out, lad. Sit thissen down and let's get on with meeting. What have we come about?"

And it all finished just as quickly as it had started.

"But," I asked myself, "what if this had happened in the majority of colliery offices with management all half frightened to death?"

This was an experience that took place in one office in front of a few witnesses but imagine what takes place at an enquiry into a mining disaster in front of hundreds of witnesses with the whole glare of publicity and newspapers, radio and even in television interviews.

Fortunately for all concerned the number of mining disasters are diminishing but despite all we do it is still a dangerous undertaking. Things can, and do go wrong. But it is a fact that several factors must be present before there can be an explosion.

First, there must be something that will explode.

Secondly, something must set it off—a source of ignition.

The former is gas and coal dust.

The sources of ignition are numerous: shot-firing, electrical faults, coal cutting machine, picks sparking on rocks, matches being struck, faulty safety lamps and on rare occasions, unauthorized smoking.

When there is a disaster an inquiry is instituted by the Minister of Power and is usually chaired by Her Majesty's Chief Inspector of Mines. Everybody that can contribute to the enquiry are called as witnesses and are subjected to cross examination. Legal representation can be briefed or union officials can cross examine witnesses on behalf of their respective unions.

There has been many really bitter scenes at these enquiries and even at inquests on individuals. The manager is usually cast as "the villain in the piece", he is a lonely tragic figure. "These are my men you've killed," the union leader shouts. But, in truth, they are the manager's men. He knew every one of them personally. He knew their families. He worked with them and they worked for him.

Very often the trades union leader does not know one man

at the colliery for on these enquiries it is the national union officials that represent the union. What do you think the manager's feelings are? He knows his responsibilities. I've seen colliery managers go grey overnight and some have become complete nervous wrecks after these enquiries.

In the witness box he is examined mercilessly by all the different representatives, but at the end of the day it is significant that all the people who are in top positions in the management hierarchy who have been making plans and giving the manager orders have never been in the witness box with the manager. Never been in public view and exposed to this vicious treatment.

This is another reason why I have always maintained that NOBODY should be able to give instructions to a colliery manager if they don't carry the responsibility for those instructions.

The bad feeling directed against generations of coal owners by workmen was now directed on to the heads of the managers. *He* and *not* the National Coal Board was the new enemy. *He* was now the owner. So the bitterness that Nationalization had been going to arrest was still there.

I knew it would take time to change the ideas and suspicions of a century.

After years of suppression and economic bondage, the miners were now important.

They had a voice in the running of their industry for the first time, and they were determined that that voice should be heard—rightly so.

What is more, some of their leaders had suffered hardships and ignominies. They had even been to prison for their principles: Arthur Horner, Abe Moffatt, Alex Moffatt and others. Now they had a chance to get even but the question was who with? The owners had gone. The National Coal Board was a long way off. The members were based in London. So there was only local management on which to vent their newly acquired power.

This was the atmosphere and these were the circumstances that led up to the forming of The British Association of Colliery Management. As a union we were babies compared to the powerful long-established trade unions already united in the T.U.C. But we were the same sort of babies—only not as strong numerically—as these great unions had been a hundred years before. They had formed their unions long ago for self protection and this is just what management were now compelled to do.

So we began our journey. First we had to get members. Then we had to achieve recognition. To elect leaders and to form ourselves into an organization. It needed just as much courage to form a union of management in 1947 as other unions needed in 1900 though it was courage of a different sort.

We had to fight our battles without the strike weapon. We had to remember that we were in charge of—and carried the responsibility for—our collieries, we were expected to set a good example. We didn't wish to become known as a set of 'narks'. Even so we had to be just as determined to pursue our arguments to the end. One of the first things to do was to establish a conciliation agreement that entitled us to be able to go to a High Court judge if we failed to agree with the National Coal Board.

This was a very wise precaution and altogether the union had to go to arbitration fifteen times.

I became one of the leaders of the Association fairly early in the 1950s and by 1956 I became the National President of the union. I felt myself to be fitted for this very important task—probably more so than many other colliery managers. I had been through the whole gamut of mining life. My origin and background were in coalmining. I had suffered the hardships, I had experienced the tragedies both as a workman and a colliery manager.

As a workman I had fought fires. As a manager I had experienced them, organized means of combating them, and, more important found out ways of preventing them.

I was used to public speaking. I was experienced in debates and at my own colliery I had found out what I considered to be some of the basic principles of good management and good labour relations.

## Them and Us

Labour relations are one of the most neglected, but none the less, most essential of all the basic principles of management.

The National Coal Board are doing their best to rectify this neglect by intensive training of their officials. Other industries are following suit. I would make labour relations one of the most important subjects in any curriculum that caters for the training of management in any industry. If I listed some of the things which through a long experience I have found to be necessary for good management I would list them as follows:

1. Keep your word and fulfil your promises.
2. Treat people as you would like to be treated.
3. Use tact: try and avoid saying or writing things that will give offence.
4. Try to be broad minded and fair.
5. Be co-operative, always be willing to help others.
6. Use reason and logic and think before speaking.
7. Don't cheat either with money or time.
8. Be sincere. Don't pretend or act . . . be yourself.
9. Keep calm when things are rough. This inspires confidence in your leadership more than anything.
10. Be willing to learn from the poorest or youngest worker. Listen to them and make them realize that what they say is important.
11. Try to avoid making threats: but if you do threaten make sure you can carry them out.
12. Be firm but still tolerant.

These basic principles go a long way towards attaining the type of leadership so badly or sadly lacking today. Leadership to my mind is the most important of all human activities. It is too difficult to talk about leadership and keep the capital *I* out of it; for leadership is a personal thing. It is the extension of your personality into anothers. It is much more effective to say COME ON than GO ON. Whether you lead ten or ten million men, leadership is the same. It is the blending of persuasion, example and sometimes even compulsion. It is the virtue by which ever since humans first stood on their hind legs,

## The Birth of a Management Union

certain men have been able to pursuade other men to do what they wanted them to do, often with little material reward, often against their inclination and sometimes against reason.

The great test of a leader is how he uses power.

My great difficulty was in convincing men that I meant what I said; that I would be allowed to pay what I promised. I, on my part, had to insist with my superiors that I must be allowed to do this or I should have to resign. This I never had to do. This new experiment in relations techniques was encouraged by a wise and enlightened company and I progressed from there.

In industry after consultation and negotiation has finished and agreement reached, management must try and get the agreements carried out. Sometimes this insistence is called discipline. It's a word that frightens some people. Why?

It can and should correct false impression and relieve fear.

After all you can have discipline, without liberty, but you cannot have liberty without discipline. However, the science of management is not the art of discipline as I stated previously, I am now at an age where I can point out some of the problems I have met and some that I have overcome. I am also old enough to give advice, although, I realize that when one starts to give advice it could mean one may be too old to set a bad example.

Advice however, is seldom welcome and those who need it most, like it least.

The *experience* we older people talk about, could be the name we give to our mistakes. But to be successful in labour relations you should never be ashamed to admit that you have been—or at present are—in the wrong. This admittance only shows that you are now old enough to acknowledge that you are wiser today than you were yesterday.

After a long life spent in management and in the handling of men I have learned that every person is a mixture of various emotions, virtues, vices and weaknesses. It is the way he controls these aspects that decides what he will do—or be—in the future.

Some people I know who have studied hard to qualify have

let their success go to their heads. They become so proud of their knowledge that they only speak to decide; they pronounce judgement without appeal. A consequence of this is that decent men revolt and take the law into their own hands, sit-downs, go-slows, or strikes.

A good leader should be able to act in such a way that the more he knows the more modest he becomes. Even when you are sure, it's better to appear to be doubtful. Tell them *your* ideas. Then listen to *theirs*. It's far better to represent, not *pronounce*. One of the best ways to convince others is to be open to conviction yourself. A leader must be alert and attentive. He must not keep putting things or people, off. He must pursue his objectives constantly and let difficulties animate rather than slacken his efforts.

I don't pretend to have been successful in all these things; but I would have been a much better leader if I had. A leader or manager must never adopt an attitude of patronage. This can be more shocking than downright rudeness. Some people show by their manner that their abilities alone bestow upon them what other people have not even the right to claim.

They appear to be giving protection, not friendship. They give you the impression that you may—rather than you should —sit and have a drink with them. I have met people in very high positions who give advice in a way that insults. They make you feel your own misfortune, point out the difference in their situation and yours; both of which they insinuate are justly merited . . . yours by your folly and theirs by their wisdom. They don't communicate, they dictate their knowledge. Can you wonder why there is so much industrial unrest? They don't give you the benefit of their knowledge and experience . . . they inflict it on you. They try and show you your ignorance by quoting their learning.

These attitudes shock and revolt the pride and vanity which all of us have in our hearts, and certainly can be guaranteed to wipe out any obligation we feel—or any favours we have received—by the way in which the favours have been given.

I remember quoting to one bigwig of the National Coal Board:

## The Birth of a Management Union

Some day when tha's feeling important,
Some day when Thee's ego's in bloom,
Some day when tha's thinking tha's most important
Man in the room....

Go art and get a bucket of water,
Shove thee hand in it up to the wrist.
Pull it art! and the hoil that remains
Is a measure of how much tha'll be missed.

Carry on with thee daily agenda,
Try and do t' best that tha can,
But please ... try to remember:
There's no indispensable man.

I have never accepted the fact that if you can enjoy your occupation you work too hard. As you grow in stature and your experience becomes wider, you begin to look on idleness —if you have any ambition—as a sort of professional suicide. Hard work does not—and should not—forbid pleasure. No man can enjoy either if he doesn't participate in both.

These comments are the outcome of forty years' experience; not just forty years' experience of miners, but with politicians, leaders of industry—National Coal Board members in particular—and trade union presidents and general secretaries throughout Europe.

But they haven't been forty years of serenity or of unbroken success. There have been disappointments and irritations; excitement and unexpected windfalls. I've had moments of intense fear and moments when tension has been broken by the tongue of a "wag". And I have been priviledged to see and know men at their bravest.

CHAPTER SIXTEEN

## COURAGE AND HUMOUR

Every man has his share of cowardice and bravery, humour and stoicism. These characteristics are often deeply hidden and do not appear except in moments of depression, tragedy or danger.

Mining can never be safe, so perhaps the miners' virtues or vices are more often starkly revealed than those of the bowler-hatted commuter, whose greatest danger, is to be caught by the closing tube train doors during the rush hour, or to be knocked down by a passing car.

The miners' bravery is well known. I shall recall some incidents proving this. But what is not so well known is the managerial pattern and behaviour in similar circumstances.

The manager must not only have the same virtues of courage and stoicism as his men . . . but also in moments of great stress and danger supply the example. The manager must have great tact, patience, humour and goodwill to keep the wheels of industry turning. Often the manager has to make decisions, for the good of everybody, which are unpopular. Sometimes he uses methods that are not strictly according to the book of rules. But if his object is *right*—and is proved in practice to be *right*—then the means are proved worthy by the results.

A good example of what I mean can be illustrated by the story of how Fryston pithead baths came to be built. One of the first pithead baths to be built in the coalfield.

In 1931 the Miners' Welfare Fund, financed largely by a small levy from each ton of coal, was to be used to help build pithead baths at every colliery. The Miners' Welfare Committee decided that to avoid any accusation of favouritism they would offer the necessary finance to build pithead baths to each pit in alphabetical order. What the powers—that be—didn't realize was that miners were not at all keen to have pithead baths. So before any plans were made or capital allocated, a ballot was taken at each pit to see if the men wanted pithead baths. If the ballot went against building the baths at any colliery, whose turn it was to have them, then that colliery was relegated to the bottom of the list and maybe would not get another chance for years.

We, the management, and the union committee at Fryston were determined that we wanted pithead baths. The men did not want them. There was an old faith—not superstition—that bathing every day weakened your back and softened your limbs; that you were more likely to catch cold, these fears were very real. I was of a miner's family. I knew all about these fears. I knew the inconvenience of washing at home, particularly to the miners' wives and families.

When I was living at home before I had come to Fryston our bath time was Saturday dinnertime, if we were working on Saturdays; or Friday night if we didn't work Saturday. Our sisters all had to go out, a big zinc bath was placed on the hearth rug in front of the fire, curtains were drawn and the ritual started. Father first, elder brother next and so on until it got to the youngest. As each one got out of the bath another pan of hot water was put into the bath. So, if you were a member of a big family like I was, by the time it was my turn, though the bath was full of hot water, there was at least six inches of solid sludge at the bottom. When I complained about this, my mother would say, "Sit still. Don't move about and then you won't stir the muck up."

My union committee were also members of large families and they agreed with me fully that these were the sort of conditions that we wanted to alter, but which the majority of the men wanted to keep. To allay their fears about bathing weakening their backs I arranged for doctors to come and lecture to our miners on the advantages of constant bathing, to tell them that it wouldn't weaken their backs at all. We all pointed out to them the advantage of leaving the dirt at

## Them and Us

the pit where it belonged, and on leaving their dirty clothes at the pit. "Just fancy," we said, "No more dirty pit clothes, no more dirty pit boots in the house." "You will be able to go to work clean and dressed respectably," we told them. "You will go home clean and tidy." "Ride in a bus without people being afraid to sit near you, or even to sit where you had been sitting, afraid of dirtying their clean clothes." These reasons and many more were repeated to the miners for weeks before our ballot was taken. We fondly thought the result would be a huge "YES". Maybe, the truth about this particular ballot is being told for the first time. When we started counting, nearly every paper was marked *against* pithead baths.

What had we to do? The union committee and I knew that if we lost the ballot it would be years before we had another chance to ballot. A further proof of this assumption was soon to come, for the war came and many pits had no baths at the end of the war. We also knew that once we had installed pithead baths everybody would realize the tremendous benefits from them.

On the day of the ballot I invited the union representatives into my office for a drink. When the union officials knew how the ballot was going they were as disappointed as I was. I filled up their glasses, then went into the next room where the count was taking place and told my secretary and his assistants to keep on counting but to count the "Nays" as "Yays". If I didn't tell them as plainly as this I let them know what I wanted to happen. I went back and joined the union committee and later my secretary came into my office proudly bearing the result—two-thirds majority vote *in favour*—to an inebriated but now jubilant management committee.

Were we right in doing what we did, you answer if you want. Your answer can't hurt me now. A good thing about growing old is that you are practically out of the way of the long arm of vengeance.

It is significant, however, that within weeks of opening the baths the water supply failed one day and the men wouldn't go to work without the baths being open! *That's the answer.*

My Family.

Fryston Colliery Rescue Brigade after winning the annual award for the top rescue team—Lister Addy G.M. *centre*, captain of the team. (I'm looking over Addy's shoulder.)

Here I am speaking at the opening of the Fryston Sports Ground.

Fryston Sports Arena in use.

## Courage and Humour

Cynics could say that I broke the stricter rules of good conduct, I suppose, but I say the result was worth it.

We had a long period at Fryston without strikes or stoppages of any kind and one of our leading newspapers printed a very flattering article about the excellent labour relations at Fryston under the glaring headline: "Never any trouble pit", with a big photograph of me right in the middle of it. The report described in great detail how well we all worked together, how the only reward I hoped for after a twelve or fourteen hour day at the pit was the respectful "Good night, sir", that echoed through the village as I wended my weary way homeward.

All miners in the locality read this article and when our miners went to the local pubs and clubs at the week-end they were greeted with taunts such as: "Here come the no trouble men", or "Here come Bullock's men." Other things were said to them that were not so nice, I won't mention those. But the reaction of our miners was quite typical.

Straightforward, nothing to hide, no beating about the bush on Monday morning a simple request to see me, to inform me that they had decided to stop these taunts, by an outward physical demonstration, of an inward conviction, that they never had been—were not now, and never would be—"bosses' men".

"We've decided to have a one day stoppage. Nowt against you. Just that we are not going to stand this sort of sarcasm."

"All right, I can understand your feelings. But if you are going to have a day's stoppage, do it on a Friday. It will cause the least inconvenience to the pit, to you and to me."

"Right. We thought you'd take it in the right spirit."

So on Friday they didn't come to work, but Friday was pay day. By now all the clerks were in the miners' union. I sent for the clerks and told them the reason for the stoppage—it wasn't a strike—and I suggested that they ought to support the miners by withdrawing *their* labour. This they readily agreed to do, but I asked them not to go home but to go in an inner office and keep out of sight.

By eleven o'clock the pityard and all approaches to it were

## Them and Us

packed with workmen from the day, afternoon and night shifts all coming to draw their wages—but no clerks.

The men and their representatives came to see me and I explained to them very carefully how all the clerks were members of their union, they wanted to support them, they didn't want to leave themselves open to the charge of being a "blackleg", and so on.

"Oh! They needn't strike," the miners said.

"You can't expect them to do anything else, but don't worry I'll get the undermanager—Mr. Mason—and we'll try and give you your checks out and then you'll have to go across to the pay office, wait there until we've given all the checks out and then we'll come across and pay out. Form up in a queue and try to be patient."

What a queue, it stretched for hundreds of yards.

The check boards were huge, circular shelves spinning on a central staft. Each shelf contained hundreds of small metal checks. Every miner had a number and each check had a number on it corresponding to the particular miner. When he received this check he took it across to the wages office, handed it in to the head clerk who then opened the corresponding tin containing the miner's wages and handed him his money in exchange for the check. The clerks who usually gave out the checks could pick them off the boards like lightning and like a typist hits the right keys on her typing machine or the pianist strikes the right notes on the piano instinctively so the clerks knew just where each check was, but we didn't.

We had to spin the boards round and round. A chap would shout out "Number three," the next one might be "Two thousand and one." The undermanager and myself made very slow progress indeed. We were qualified to manage the whole mine but we soon proved to the miners and to ourselves that we were certainly not qualified to give checks out. In an hour only twenty miners had left the window with their checks. By now they were all getting fed-up and the miners asked if they could see the clerks. I had already anticipated this. The clerks were expecting a visit from the miners and they knew what to say. I left them together and the clerks readily agreed to call off

## Courage and Humour

their—supporting action—if the miners they were supporting went back to work. They agreed, the afternoon shift went back, the affair was over, honour was satisfied.

I knew enough about coalfield strikes to know that one day's stoppage could soon lead to another particularly if the weather is good.

The B.B.C's Tony Van den Bergh, was told this story by Fryston miners years later. It was told with appreciative humour and ended with ". . . the manager didn't half make silly buggers out of us". But Tony told me that there was no animosity in the statement whatsoever. As a matter of fact they tell the story themselves many times over a pint of beer.

A law had been passed that made it illegal for any mine owner to pay a man less than a certain amount of money per day, whether he was on contract or not. When a miner is paid so much for every ton of coal he fills his wages were directly dependent on the output he achieved. If he was getting 2s 6d per ton and filled eight tons he would receive £1. On the other hand if he only filled one ton he would only receive 2s 6d.

The Minimum Wage Act was designed to alter this and to make it impossible for men to get less than the agreed day wage. At this time the agreed wage was ten shillings and eightpence per day.

The owners were very fearful that some miners would not try to fill as much coal now that they had a guaranteed ten shillings and eightpence as they did before, so they ordered managers to personally interview every man who did not earn the recognized day wage. During these interviews we had another experience of this in-bred sense of humour.

At this time men worked in teams of six and each one's wages depended on the efforts of all six men.

One set of men had been up to see me—and my senior—week after week. We had stormed, pleaded, threatened and very near prayed with them to alter their ways and they only got their money each week after a lot of argument and considerable inconvenience.

One pay day after a particularly vicious attack from us one

*Them and Us*

of the miners said, "Look here, gaffer, that coal is far too hard for us to carry anybody on our backs, and Jack so-and-so says he's not going to sweat himself to death just for day wage. If he won't try we can't earn any more."

"Right, that's enough," we said. "Here's your money. Where is Jack?"

"He says he's not coming up."

"Oh, he does, does he? Then go down and tell him that he'll get no money at all until he comes up to see us."

They went out and told Jack. In a while Jack came up and we went for him full blast, as one of us tired the other took up the argument and we finished with saying what is to miners a real insult:

"You ought to be downright ashamed of yourself. Every one of your mates is grumbling about you."

Jack didn't seem at all perturbed. He looked at us and said quietly, "How many is all of them?"

"Five. All your mates."

"Oh, well, I don't see why I should worry so much about five men grumbling about me, all bloody pit's grumbling about thee."

We gave him his money. It was sound logic. What else could we do?

Sometimes serious and even dangerous situations bring out hidden sources of humour.

We had a very serious underground fire at Fryston—what is known as a gob fire.

A gob fire is a fire which takes place in the space left behind when the coal seam is taken out. It is known as the waste, the goaf or gob. Much small coal is left lying on the floor and as the roof eventually falls on to the coal that is left the coal gradually heats up and spontaneous combustion takes place and this is known as a gob fire. Gob fires are a real nuisance and can be very dangerous.

On this occasion we decided to use—for the first time—frozen carbon dioxide which was known as cardice to put the fire out. Cardice was delivered down the pit in insulated containers in blocks six inches square and two feet long. Then it had to be handled very carefully by miners all wearing protective clothing. If the cardice touched the naked flesh it would fetch the skin off.

The fire was in an area about two hundred yards long just behind the actual coalface. We plugged each end of the coalface with sand bagged stoppings leaving a passage through the sand bags at one end for the cardice to be thrown in.

The cardice then evaporated to three hundred times its size as pure carbon dioxide gas. This we hoped would put the fire out. At the other end which was already sealed off I had posted officials and men testing for gas with their lamps and carrying canaries to detect any CO—carbon monoxide—or $CO_2$.

We had just finished getting all the cardice in and were putting the final seals on when a young surveyor came running round shouting for Mr. Bullock. He told me I was wanted urgently at the other side as six men were unconscious. I ran as fast as I could, accompanied by my nephew who was the vice-captain of our rescue brigade, pausing only to telephone the pit office and asked them to send for the pit rescue brigade which was stationed at Wakefield.

We met an official coming from the spot where the trouble was and he said that everything was all right; so I asked him to ring up and cancel the call to Wakefield and not to send for them if we were all right. This he did. My nephew and I went round to the other side, however, to see just how things were, to our horror and surprise there *were* six men unconscious. How or why the official concerned had made this tragic mistake I did not know. I told my nephew to bring a canary.

"They are all dead."

I tested for firedamp with my safety lamp and my lamp flared. Then I knew we were in real difficulty.

We started giving the men artificial respiration but as soon as we bent down we started going dizzy and light headed. I quickly realized that the carbon dioxide gas that we had put in had now evaporated and was seeping through cracks in the floor and as the men had come out to rest, this gas—which is heavier than air—lay near the floor and had knocked them out as they lay down to rest.

## Them and Us

"What on earth can we do?" my nephew asked.

It was a low old roadway, no more than four feet high so I said:

"Let's prop them up and get their heads in fresh air."

There were many old props lying about, about three feet long. These were what had been used as temporary supports to hold up the roof. We lifted each man up in turn and put one of these props under his chest and touching the floor at the other end. They would have looked a silly sight on any other occasion, but it was far too serious a situation to be considering what they looked like. The main thing was, their heads were now clear of the deadly gas.

I should think it was the first time that props designed to support the roof were now supporting unconscious men.

The clearer air was now beginning to revive the miners and the first one to come round was a very religious man who I knew very well. He whispered, "Let's thank God for our miraculous deliverance."

I quickly and somewhat harshly replied, "We've nothing to thank God for yet, we are three miles from the pit bottom, quite a way from fresh air, no gas detectors, don't talk, save your energy for walking. As soon as the others come round we'll be moving."

Another man just regaining consciousness heard my words and dreamily murmured, "Let's thank God, there's no bloody wasps!"

What a difference. The men just regaining their senses started to laugh. This made them vomit and they recovered. Quickly we were guiding them to fresh air, bent double trying to keep our heads in fresh air. My nephew leading and me urging from the rear. The result was, all got out safely, a real nasty dangerous situation was considerably eased by one man having a sense of humour and having the wit to express it.

Courage, resolution, sheer grit and strength can be encountered again and again hundreds of feet below the surface.

In all my long experience during which I've seen many

## Courage and Humour

courageous deeds both down the pit and on the surface one stands out alone for sheer bravery backed by physical strength and endurance. One that I've never seen equalled before or since.

On Saturday morning, 3 May 1952, about 6.30 a.m. my telephone—which is always by the side of every colliery manager's bed—rang. A man called Lister Addy was on the telephone at the other end to tell me there had been a mishap in the winding shaft. Lister Addy was the deputy in charge of the pit bottom and haulage, he was also captain of the rescue team. I could tell by the excitement in his voice that this was no ordinary accident. He explained that the cage had set off without a signal, carrying with it an eighteen-year-old boy called Jimmy Winterbottom, and the cage had got stuck in the shaft seventy yards from the pit bottom and four hundred and eighty yards from the surface.

I told him to leave any further explanations, that I would come down straight away. In minutes I was dressed and down at the shaft side. Lister Addy was waiting for me. He, himself, came of a large mining family. He had had two brothers killed down the mine. He was a strong, thick-set man with a face that looked as if it had been hewn out of rock. He was a good fighter, an old-type pit man who believed in authority. His methods of maintaining discipline were somewhat hard but very effective. He now told me in detail what had happened—the onsetter—that's the man in charge of signals at the pit bottom—had been loading a tram containing old railway lines on to the cage. He was assisted in his work by this young man, Jim Winterbottom, who also was a member of an old Fryston mining family. His grandfather who had worked down Fryston colliery all his life was now the watchman at the pit top, one of his uncles was a colliery deputy and his brothers also worked down the pit. Jim Winterbottom was a very willing worker and when they were loading this tram containing rails one of the rails got fast on the side of the cage and Jimmy immediately went into the cage to try and liberate the rail. While he was inside—we never did find the real reason—the cage suddenly set off at its usual speed. As the cage went higher the rail

## Them and Us

which was hanging out of the side of the cage embedded itself in the side of the pit shaft seventy-five yards *up* from the pit bottom.

Now the cage was tightly jammed and young Winterbottom was trapped.

The men in the pit bottom shouted as loud as they could up the shaft to Jimmy and heard a very faint reply. They realized he was at least alive.

A pit shaft has electric cables running right down from the pit top to the pit bottom and long steel ropes called conductors that act as guides for the cages. There are also steel pipes to carry water from pit top to pit bottom and also pipes carrying compressed air to drive underground machinery.

Lister Addy, Freddy Astbury, George Sharp, Ernest Bagnall, all deputies down the pit, had all tried to climb up the cable, the conductor ropes and the pipes but all to no avail. Everything was covered thickly with dust and grease.

By the time I arrived they had all decided that a rescue route from the pit bottom was impossible. After a discussion with these officials I agreed with them. To climb seventy-five yards up a greasy steel cable would defeat a monkey, let alone a man. I knew that eventually whatever decision was reached would be my decision and I should have to carry the responsibility for that decision.

We all agreed that the only way to get to the cage was to lower someone by a rope from another inset above and let him try to liberate the cage and then enable the cage to be lowered carrying young Winterbottom to safety.

Most coalmining shafts have several seams leading off from them at different levels. These different levels are what is known as insets. The nearest inset to the scene of this accident was one hundred and eighty yards above the trapped man. Urgency was the keynote for we didn't know how seriously young Winterbottom was injured.

The question now was—Who would I allow to go?

To their everlasting credit there was no scarcity of volunteers. We had experienced shaftsmen, and tradesmen—some who were on nights—but had immediately come back to the pit when

## Courage and Humour

they heard of the accident. There were blacksmiths who repaired the cage but were they strong enough? It wasn't just a question of skill and courage. If he could get to the cage he would need to be strong enough to free the rail and lift the tram. He had got to have knowledge of first aid and be able to give it to Jimmy Winterbottom.

Without doubt Lister Addy stood out above all the others as the man having all these qualifications.

I'd no need to pick him out, he'd already decided himself that he was the man.

He was the captain of the rescue brigade. It was one of the young men who worked directly under his supervision who was trapped in the cage. It was his *duty*.

We searched for ropes but we had no single ropes strong enough or long enough to reach one hundred and eighty yards. But we had three lengths of rope of sufficient strength, which, knotted together, would lower Addy to the cage.

I told Addy that he must wear a shaftsman's safety harness, this is a leather contraption that fits over his shoulders and through his legs with a steel ring at the back to carry a safety rope. I instructed him that he must wear gloves and carry two spare pairs with him. The harness and gloves were quickly brought. We geared him up, fastened the rope to the ring behind his harness and I realized—and he realized—that the rest would be up to him.

Even in a situation as serious as this Freddy Astbury looked at him and remarked, "I've never seen anything looking more like a bloody ape than thou." But Lister never answered. He understood as well as I did that *his* life would depend now on his skill and strength, on the rope and—more important—on the knots joining the rope. We picked two men with great experience in splicing ropes, Bagnall and Wadsworth, to be responsible for the tying of the knots. We got twelve of the strongest miners and officials we could to control the lowering of Addy and the rope down the shaft.

Lister Addy approached the shaft fully equipped for his journey into the unknown and for the first time he realized to the full what a tremendous task he was about to undertake.

## Them and Us

I shall never forget the look on his face as he saw the awful blackness of the chasm he was about to enter, the chasm into which he would literally have to fling himself to reach the winding rope that I had advised him to cling to and lower himself down the shaft. I felt if he could only straddle the winding rope he would steady himself and that we could take his weight on the rope that was fastened to his harness.

We all knew of course that the winding rope was thick with grease and that this could be a great problem so we provided him with a pair of goggles to keep the grease out of his eyes. As he prepared to jump Lister Addy went higher in my estimation for as I looked at him and he looked back at me I could see the fear in his eyes. He looked so imploringly at me as if to say: "Isn't there any other way?" But he knew, and I knew, there wasn't any other way. To his credit he never voiced his fear but to the other people present he hid it under an air of bravado.

Now was the testing time. Would his nerve fail him?

If it did who else could do it?

What else could we do?

None of these questions needed answering for without any good-byes, no last words of wisdom, no last wishes he sprang to the rope, clutched it with both hands, legs and feet and began that awful descent.

Every word spoken by us was whispered and no unnecessary word was spoken. Lister had shoved the extra pairs of gloves he took inside his shirt, a good job too, for he hadn't gone far before the pair he was wearing was worn completely through. We could hear every word he said very distinctly for the shaft was acting as a telephone and his voice came up loud and clear. He was explaining that the grease from the winding rope was blurring his cap lamp and covering his goggles and even getting in his eyes and up his nose.

He was frightened, there was no doubt about that. This was the first time he had been in the shaft without the comforting walls of the cage surrounding him. Another difficulty arose— he started shouting for more slack rope—but the rope was already slack between him and us and what I had feared had already happened. The rope carrying him was getting twisted round the winding rope. I shouted to him and told him what had happened and asked him to try and twist round the winding rope in the opposite direction to get the rope unravelled. He did this, the rope slackened off suddenly as he liberated it and he dropped an inch or two very quickly. Each time this happened he screamed and yelled: "What the bloody hell are you doing up there? Can't you hold the bloody rope?"

Burly miners were holding the rope and it was wrapped round the body of the last one. When we had played the first length of rope out we had to stop and shout down to Lister Addy to tell him we were now going to tie the next section of rope.

"Be careful," he cried.

He was now having another real difficulty to contend with. We were lowering him down in the downcast shaft and at this depth it was very cold. All the fresh air needed down the pit travelled down this shaft and we needed three hundred thousand cubic feet a minute of fresh air and this was all travelling down a shaft only fourteen feet in diameter so the velocity of the travelling air made him feel colder than ever.

He was now out of sight of course and almost out of shouting distance. He could hear what we were saying much better than we could hear what he was saying for the air current carried our voices further. So seeing that we couldn't see what happened any longer and we couldn't hear what was happening any longer, only Lister Addy knows and can tell what happened next and he described it many times to many people. He had many interviews with newspaper men in my office. Lister's story varied very little no matter how many times he told it. The basic facts remained the same.

*Reynolds News*, then a Sunday newspaper, was doing a series called "The Bravest Men in Britain". One of its journalists interviewed Lister in my presence and the account was published in that newspaper.

Afterwards the Public Relations Branch of the National Coal Board published pamphlets about Lister's heroism and called them "A Mining Man". There were photographs and drawings in this pamphlet that recaptured the drama and the actual occurrence very well.

His feats were the subject of a radio play, "Caged in Darkness", written by Tony Van den Bergh and produced by Alan Burgess, the author of "The Small Woman".

I heard Lister tell what happened so many times that I can practically quote word for word what he said to the newspapermen and to Tony Van den Bergh.

"As I drew nearer the cage that was fast in the shaft I saw it was tilted—leaning over—it was not going to be an easy landing. I had difficulty in keeping a grip with my feet, the winding rope was not straight any more, it was leaning with the cage. My feet slipped off but I still kept sliding downwards, just holding on to the winding rope with my hands. I was really thankful now for the safety rope on my back. My second pair of gloves were worn out and my boots had burned right through at the instep."

We had given him a whistle, to blow a short sharp blast if he wanted us to take the weight on the rope. We heard it blow and we took the weight.

Lister continues: "I changed my gloves, and I thought, I shall have to be careful here if I am going to rescue this lad, and for the first time I began to realize what an awful danger I was in myself. My other pair of gloves I was keeping in reserve fell out of my shirt and dropped down the shaft. I blew two more blasts on my whistle, they gave me slack rope and I started descending again, twisting and re-twisting all the time round the winding rope. I took my goggles off and tried to clean them on my sleeve and get the grease out of my eyes, I peered down.

"Through the darkness I could see the ghostly outlines of the cage, it was getting nearer all the time. Nearer and nearer. I should estimate I was within fifteen feet of the cage when suddenly I was pulled up with a jerk. I blew a long blast on my whistle, this was the pre-arranged signal for 'What's up?' I heard their answer with dismay: 'Tha's got all't rope. We can't githee anymore.'

"'O God!' I said, and I meant it. 'What do I do now?'

"I hung there and I must admit I knew real fear, that fifteen feet which a moment ago had seemed so near now seemed so far away and the longer I hung there wondering what to do the further away it seemed.

"I got my big belt knife out of my pocket. I held on to the winding rope with one hand, knees and feet. I reached up, behind the back of my head, and sawed at the taut rope with my knife. I stopped a moment, suddenly realizing that I was about to cut my last link with my mates in the inset and indeed I was cutting off my only escape route.

"I hesitated a moment longer but I knew I had to get to young Jimmy Winterbottom, so I cut, the rope parted, now indeed I was on my own. I slid down the rest of the cable and landed on the roof of the dangerously tilted cage. I took off my harness, rested a moment and had a look around. The first thing I saw was the new pair of gloves I had dropped, they had landed smack on top of the tilted cage and had not fallen off, my first real bit of luck I thought.

"I took off the pair of gloves I was wearing and realized for the first time that my hands were burned and burned badly. My feet hurt and I saw both my boots were burned through and my feet and calves were burned also."

I will now describe a pit cage. A cage is a huge, boxlike object made of steel, consisting of four separate compartments, each compartment has tramlines laid in the centre and is capable of carrying two trams in each compartment. At each corner of the cage heavy chains are fastened to support the cage on to the winding rope through a huge, heavy capple. They are used for transporting men and materials from the pit top to the pit bottom and from the pit bottom to the pit top. Addy now takes up the story and says:

"I couldn't hear anything from Winterbottom. I called out to him but got no answer. I was very conscious of my own breathing—it sounded louder than I had ever heard it before. On the top of the cage there was a trap door, I opened this and got through to the first compartment which is known as the top deck. I knew the cage had four compartments and I knew —from the man in charge of the cage at the pit bottom—that

## Them and Us

Jimmy Winterbottom was in the second compartment from the top. The only way I could get to him was to climb out of the top compartment and lower myself into the second one.

"There was about a foot of space between the cage and the rounded greasy wall of the shaft. I let my legs dangle and then pressed my back tight against the shaft wall. I knew there was five feet between each deck and a hand-rail in the cage side. I gradually shuffled down and groped for the hand-rail in the next compartment. When I found it I gripped hard and probed with my feet until they found the floor of the next deck. 'Now,' I said and gave a quick twist and I was inside the second deck.

"Looking around I saw the tram held firm by the steel rail that was fastened into the shaft wall, but I couldn't see the lad.

" 'Jim, are you all right?' I asked, but there was no answer. Sorrowfully, I concluded he was dead. I bent down, so that the light from my cap lamp shone under the tram and I could see the sole of Jimmy's boots well towards the other end of the tram. I put my back down, got hold of the tram with my hands and lifted as hard as I could but the tram didn't move. I put my arse to it and lifted with all my strength—what we in mining call a deadlift but I couldn't move it. I said—and again I meant it....

" 'O God, please help me, give me a lift,' and I tried again. This time the tram moved and I heard a quick, sharp intake of breath under the tram and I knew the boy was alive. The tram must have been pressing on his chest.

"I prayed again for the umpteenth time, I was now shouting, 'Oh God, help me.' That's all I said but I lifted the tram and I could now hear Winterbottom gasping. I daren't let go, I held on to the tram and said as quietly as I could, 'Jim. . . .'

" 'What,' the lad said.

" 'It's me, Lister. Tha'll be all right now.'

" 'Thank God, tha's come, Lister,' Winterbottom sighed.

" 'Is it off thee chest?' I asked.

" 'Aye, but get me out, Lister.'

" 'Try and shove thissen forard, Jimmy,' and then Winterbottom slowly shoved himself forward until I could see his feet come from under the tram that I was holding up.

"I took the weight of the tram on my body, freed one arm and got hold of Jim's boot and pulled him forward. I stopped. I realized if I pulled him any further he might panic, we had only two feet of space between the end of the tram and the end of the cage and then a straight drop to the pit bottom. If he wriggled at all, or got the least bit excited he might roll off the sloping cage and drop straight down the shaft.

"'Jim, I'm going to put the tram down again, stop wheer tha is, I can pick it up again. I'm going for a piece of rope.'"

Lister Addy's story now defies imagination. Anyone who didn't know him or who were not there or who read this story could be excused if they thought it was gilded by exaggeration. My reply to this is the deed was so brave, it was of such magnitude that it needed no enlarging. If anyone knew Lister Addy as we knew him he was far too earthy, too matter of fact, too ordinary to fly away on the wings of fancy and imagination.

Every time I heard him tell his story he told it in simple straightforward words, as I have repeated his conversation in this book I have omitted his more lurid and colourful adjectives as it is not my intention to offend any reader who cannot bear to hear or read the everyday expressions of the majority of mining men.

So Lister Addy talked on: "I scrambled back to the roof of the cage again."

He gave no description of the task it was just a simple statement.

"Then I began to climb back up the winding rope to where I had cut the rope that had been used to support me in my descent. The fifteen feet I had to climb to where I had cut the rope was most difficult as I kept slipping back, when I got there —to my joy—the rope was still twisted round the winding rope. I could grip it with one hand and use it to help me climb the winding rope until I reached a point where I had enough rope in my hands for my purpose. Then I cut the rope again and slid back down the winding rope to the top of the cage, carrying my precious fifteen feet of rope with me. Again I struggled into the second compartment. The lad seemed calmer now. 'Come out steady, with your knees bent sideways,' I told him.

"I lifted the tram and the lad shuffled along until he was out but his feet went a little too far forward and hung over the cage side. This brought him up with a jerk, he was very frightened, but I felt calmer now. He was very cold. I dropped the tram, took my pullover off and wrapped it round him. Then for ten minutes we crouched together on the floor of that sloping cage discussing the best means of getting out.

"Our troubles were by no means over but I was with him now. I had my arm around him and it meant a hell of a lot to the lad. He was not trapped under the tram any longer and he had somebody to talk to.

"I tied the rope around my waist, looped it round the hand-rail of the cage, and tied the other end around Jim."

The hand-rail is a rail that travels from one end of the cage to the other on each side of each compartment for men to hold when they are riding up and down the shaft in the cage. Lister talks on:

"Then started what was up to now the most difficult part. Up to now I had only had myself to look after, now I had Jim, also.

"I had to get to the next deck below to get him out of the way while I tried to move the tram to liberate the cage, so I lowered myself head first, over the corner of the second deck, held on to the cage guide cable until I was able to reach the hand bar in the third deck. Then I learned out and coaxed and even threatened the frightened lad until he plucked up enough courage to clamber out and let me help him into the third deck also.

" 'Now look, Jim, stay here, tha's all right. Now I'm going back to try and free the cage.' So once more I climbed back [it was becoming routine now, *my comment*] got hold of the tram, lifted it and let it fall sharply.

"I did this many times, and this jerking eased the rail away from the shaft side and then, to my joy and relief, I felt the cage straighten. I crawled back to the third deck and joined Winterbottom and shouted as hard as I could to the pit bottom:

## Courage and Humour

" 'Can you hear me?'

" 'Yes,' was the reply.

" 'Then listen, get on the 'phone and tell't winding man to lower the cage as slowly as he can.'

"The cage began to move slowly downward."

Now I take up the story again. As soon as we saw the winding rope begin to move we dashed across to the other shaft, into the cage, down to the pit bottom, across to the other shaft to be there to welcome Lister Addy. But alas, when we got there the cage had stuck again, fifteen feet from the bottom! This, however, was child's play to Addy now.

He tied the rope around young Winterbottom and lowered him gently into the arms of his mates waiting in the pit bottom. We rushed young Winterbottom into the office where we had a hot drink waiting for him and ambulance men in attendance. The rope was still round his body.

We were all congratulating him on his miraculous escape when in through the office door burst a hardly human looking apparition. It was Lister Addy all right, but what a Lister! Practically naked, his clothes hanging in tatters, covered from head to foot in thick, black grease. Wet through, hands bleeding, face and arms lacerated.

Did he drop into a chair from exhaustion and accept with due modesty our congratulations? No, he did not.

He stood there, he stamped, he stormed, he cursed me, the pit, his mates, everybody in view and those out of sight as well. It seems we had committed the unpardonable folly of being so overcome with relief at getting the lad alive into our hands, that *nobody* thought about Lister. He'd evidently waited, then shouted, but getting no answer had decided to slide down the conductor rope to the pit bottom. But the rope was so slippery and he was so tired that he couldn't stop himself at the pit bottom but had gone straight down on to the sump boards, full of mud and water. He crawled up by a ladder, came into the office to let us know in no uncertain manner that he was still alive and was back with us. When he had exhausted his vocabulary he had a mug of tea and believe it or not he refused to go home but finished his shift, doing his normal job.

*Them and Us*

When I got out, the grape-vine had been operating efficiently and all approaches to my office were packed with reporters, photographers and villagers. I singled out the lad's mother and thankfully told her that Jim was safe, not badly injured but suffering from shock. To reporters I told them briefly what had happened but asked them to see Lister and let him tell the story.

During these days there was so much going on at Fryston that something about it was so often reported in the Press. One can well understand the editor of a well-known daily saying to his reporters who brought him yet another Fryston story: "Oh! not again. No more of Fryston for a while, let it rest."

Even while the reporter—who told me of this conversation—was in the editor's office the editor's 'phone rang. He picked it up, his eyes sparkled as he listened to the story I've just told of Lister Addy's heroic rescue of Jimmy Winterbottom. The reporter told me that the editor lifted up a second telephone, handed it to him and—by a noiseless invitation to him to listen—the reporter heard words being spoken at dictation speed that wove themselves into an orderly pattern and told the story that any reporter, worthy of his salt, would give his left ear to get.

The editor replaced his telephone.

"Fryston," he said and his eyes supplied the only comment. A few minutes later he added "Fryston!" and "Well, I'll be damned" was a miracle of editorial understatement.

His further comments if unprintable were understandable.

Yes, Lister Addy was one of my men and I was justly proud of him. I was proud when he received the highest award of the Carnegie Hero Trust Fund.

I was prouder still when I accompanied him to Buckingham Palace to receive the highest award for industrial heroism—the George Medal.

The National Coal Board feted him, he was entertained at the Victoria Palace Theatre, went on the stage to meet "The Crazy Gang", was shown round London, attended cocktail parties given in his honour. It was Lister and his wife's first visit to London, and when we arrived at King's Cross Station to come back to Fryston the reporters were there in force, wanting to know what Mrs. Addy thought of London and she simply replied:

"It makes my feet ache."

CHAPTER SEVENTEEN

# NATIONAL PRESIDENT OF MANAGEMENT UNIONS

I was now going through that emotional period which seems to affect many men of various intellectual standards in their late forties and early fifties. It seems to me that this is a real period of danger to one's family life.

You may have reached a position of some importance and still inside you, you begin to realize or dread that you are not quite as virile as you were. You are not as sure of yourself as you might be. You need a sort of mental uplift. You want to prove to yourself that you are as good a man as ever you were and that you really are as good as people think you are.

How does one prove this?

Some work harder than ever and throw themselves heart and soul into their jobs to such an extent that they can become physical and nervous wrecks. Some start drinking and smoking heavily. Some take a keener interest in the opposite sex.

I had always been very fond of the opposite sex but I had a very patient wife. She rarely questioned my activities and as time went on her questions became less and less. I was now away from home more than ever, sometimes abroad on delegations for weeks on end. I was still managing a big pit and when I came back home I had to work all hours that God sent to catch up on the work that had piled up in my absence.

My wife stuck to the chapel, she was not interested in the clubs and welfare halls I had helped to build and gradually it began to dawn on us just how much we had grown apart.

The sharing of problems, the talking over together of my difficulties and hers had finished completely and we both realized somewhat sadly that there wasn't much left of our marriage and it would only be a question of time before she had had as much as she could stand and decided to leave.

I couldn't, didn't and never have blamed her.

I'm still very fond of her and respect her highly, but once she made her decision I knew it was final and I didn't plead. We had spent many happy years together and no one can take away the memories of those happy years from either of us. The greatest tragedy is for the children. I was very fond of them and I believe they were fond of me. In cases like these children seem to be innocent sufferers but my eldest daughter and older son were grown up and could go their respective ways. Marie was happily married, but Diane was still young. I think she caused us greater anxiety than anything else.

But it's better to separate and have done with it than it is for a child to be constantly living in an atmosphere as uncertain as a live volcano. Later, I married again and I have been extremely fortunate. I have had two chances, two wives, both being fine, sympathetic and loyal. Children by my first marriage of whom I could be justly proud and children by my second marriage of whom I am just as proud.

I still see my first family and we can meet and discuss problems without any bitterness. My first wife and I can meet and talk easier than we were able to do twenty years ago. I like to console myself with the old saying: "A man whose youth has no follies, will in his maturity have no powers."

I was now the National President of The British Association of Colliery Management, one of the Vice-Chairmen of the National Consultative Council, joint Chairman of the National Joint Council, a member of the National and Education Training Committee, a National Director of Welfare and a founder member of the National Paraplegic Committee.

I was still devoting a lot of time and attention to work for paraplegics and the seriously disabled in our mining industry but the position was now established, committees had been formed to look after their interests and I felt that my early work had now become consolidated.

These positions gave me the opportunity of not only meeting, but working with, and getting to know the really big men in the coal industry, outside industries, insurance brokers, members of the government and leading industrialists on the Continent.

Looking back on these experiences I know I was able to make a real contribution from the grass roots as it were. Many of the big men were stationed in London far away from the sources of production but I was still near to the pick point for I was still the agent and manager of Fryston Colliery.

Long hours spent away on these duties meant much longer hours spent at work when I was there. The spirit and organization at Fryston Colliery was such that they did as well without me as with me and everybody at the colliery seemed to delight in getting more coal out when I was away.

Circumstances forced on me the art and necessity of delegating responsibility.

The delegation of responsibility is an art and many big men waste hours of other people's time and waste a lot of their own efforts by thinking that they, and they alone, can make correct decisions. If only people would realize that given the chance, many people could, and would, do far better jobs if only they were allowed to get on with it.

Making your subordinates feel important checks frustration, gives encouragement and fosters better co-operation and loyalty.

Loyalty in one's staff is of the greatest importance. I'd sooner have a good hard-working, experienced, loyal man than a brilliant erratic scholar who doesn't know the meaning of loyalty. One should always remember that if one expects loyalty one must be loyal oneself!

One begets the other, it is never one sided.

I found the chief characteristic of these giants of industry, commerce and politics was that "they never worked to the clock". They all worked hard. The majority were men of their word. They had their strengths, they had their weaknesses. In debate, I quickly learned to avoid their strengths and try to exploit their weaknesses.

I had had a long experience of negotiation at all levels but leading a management union I needed every bit of the debating techniques for we were different in many respects from other unions. We had to rely on cold, hard facts, on the sheer logic of our arguments, on the skill in putting our case over. The only force we could use was the vehemence we put into our words to make our points.

We had no strike weapon, we were leading men and negotiating for men who were in high positions, men who were not prepared to throw away all they had achieved by hard work and study, in strike action. We were too responsible for that. We were too closely allied with policy for that.

Even so I've never agreed with the suggestion that all management were part of the National Coal Board. Members of the National Coal Board often claim this when they wanted something out of management, but never admitted it when management wanted something out of them. The Coal Board were the members of the National Coal Board in London, they made the decisions and at this time there was not a lot of real consultation either. We had Consultative Meetings regularly at which we listened to a very able exposition from the Coal Board Chairman as to what they had done, were doing or were about to do but not the sort of consultation that I envisaged.

Consultation to me is for one side to say to the other—this is the problem—this is what we think about it, what do you think about it? Have you any suggestions? Then to listen to these suggestions and discuss them freely and openly.

Also, while negotiating for our members we were constantly reminded that we were men who had no doubt of our own worth, men who had no doubt of their importance to the coal industry. Our members expected and they demanded that we should wring out of the Board some outward visible sign of the oft repeated expression of Board members of our value and capabilities. The Board knew all this, they knew our weaknesses, they knew the limit of our powers and very often they acted accordingly.

It was sufficient for me to even mention a salary claim and an economic blizzard would sweep, not only through the corridors of Hobart House, the headquarters of the National Coal Board, but they would have us believe any increase given to management would start off a string of claims from the workmen, that it would ruin the industry, ruin the export market, upset the balance of payments and even the pound itself might be shaken.

Different men we met used different techniques and we used different techniques with the different men we met.

Lord Hyndley, the first Chairman, was a great administrator and had an equally great assistant in Sir Arthur Street. Sir Arthur practically slept on the job and virtually killed himself in filling the huge task allocated to him.

During that era the Coal Board left most of the negotiations with our union to the Director General of Staff, Mr. Turnbull and his Deputy General of Staff, Mr. Charles Simpson—both of them with no previous knowledge of pits or pit men but very capable men and remarkably quick learners.

Later they brought in Sir Andrew Bryan, who had been the Chief Inspector of Mines. He understood the problems of mine management more than any member of the Board we had met previously but that didn't always work to our advantage. One's opponents can know too much.

During the days of private enterprise most managers and higher officials received a turkey, a bottle of wine and spirits and various other small things at Christmas. Firms that supplied the collieries with their equipment would send small presents to the manager at Christmas. The National Coal Board, however, frowned on this activity and forbade it. In the early days quite a lot of the union's time was spent defending people who for one reason or another had still accepted these gifts. The Coal Board's term for this activity was—bribery and corruption.

So much time seemed to be spent on such trivial things. Bribery and corruption is a very wide term, it can mean so much and so little. I should think that the higher the man, the more influential, the more salary he draws, the bigger the bribe —if it is going to be accepted.

It is no good offering a box of cigars to a man who owns a cigar factory, it is no good offering a board member a motor car at the run down price if he has a new car every year provided by the Board. It is no good offering him first class travel on any transport if all the travel is provided for him, but, say, that some firm said to a man in a very high position: "You look after our business interests while you are with the board and when you retire, or if you leave, you can have a directorship in our company."

Would this be bribery? Or would this be good business?

What is bribery to one, done on a bigger scale can be good business. It depends who does it and what interpretation is placed on the action by the people who matter.

I found out that little men in stature—sometimes with high qualifications—got promoted too quickly and their sense of importance increased out of all proportion to what it should have done. They became a sort of pocket Hitler overnight and set themselves up as little dictators.

One of the union's first tasks was to bring these people down to their proper level and the union did that job well.

It's a funny thing but invariably we found that once we could get to the National Coal Board members themselves we got more satisfaction than we did dealing with people representing the Coal Board much further down the line. We got more satisfaction dealing with the Divisional Boards than we did dealing with Area people.

We were advised by the National Coal Board and by the Minister to wait till the Board had a chance to settle with the miners and the deputies and then submit our claims. The management union was very patient and when we finally went with our first salary claim we expected so much, we achieved so little and the bit we did achieve took us so long.

At the first big meeting the union took quite a strong team of negotiators led by our President, Major Walton Brown. Quite a few of our delegation had never been to the headquarters of the National Coal Board before. They were very much impressed with the size of the place, by the type of people who worked in it and particularly by the way the union's representations were received by National Coal Board members.

Coming home in the train I wrote a bit of doggeral entitled

*Them and Us*

"B.A.C.M. and the Coal Board—Deputation in London". I had this typed out and circulated to many members who had been down on the deputation. Reading it now the only thing I could claim for it is that it describes the situation as it was then very truthfully and the other claim I could make is that no one reading it could accuse me of being a poet.

### B.A.C.M. AND THE COAL BOARD DEPUTATION IN LONDON

*by J. A. Bullock*

Have I told you the story of B.A.C.M.
Of its journeys by car and train
To try and get an agreement
To pay for the skill and the brain.

Of the finest lads in the country
Men who work by night and by day,
For this generous wonderful Coal Board
With no thought of time or pay.

B.A.C.M. said now lads be patient,
The Coal Board's a terrible task,
Let them get all others settled,
Then they'll give us whatever we ask.

Then up spake brave Sir Arthur
"No film star salaries," said he,
"You'll work, and you'll toil, and you'll slave, sir,
And you'll leave your conditions to me."

Hugh Gaitskell said, "Now lads, get cracking,
You're a wonderful crowd of men,
You're patient and wise, and you're cunning,
You tackle absenteeism and then—

"You know we'll always stand by you,
So go have a drink with the men,
Go act as their social leader,
Mother them like on old hen.

## National President of Management Unions

"Without you wonderful officials,
I don't know what mining could do,
If you hadn't stuck to it gamely,
We couldn't have seen the job through."

So down to London went B.A.C.M.,
Full of zeal, hope, and zest,
It's just a matter of asking,
The Coal Board will do all the rest.

So the country lads went to the City,
They came from far and wide.
They came to the mighty building,
They stared with eyes big and wide.

They'd never seen anything like it,
A building like this owned by *them*,
They felt so proud and righteous,
They moved a vote of thanks to old Clem,

For housing our wonderful industry,
In a place so huge and vast,
And for letting us see our employees
Come in wearing tall hats and spats.

Everyone there carried a big umbrella,
And a wonderful case in his hand,
And at this pageant of splendour,
We could only just gaze and stand.

In round-eyed hypnotised wonder
To think that technicians like ours,
Needed thousands and thousands of people
To work millions and millions of hours

To invent all sorts of forms and papers
To make sure we got a square deal
To help run this great undertaking
To stand up to knocks and not squeal,

But let me tell you what happened
When inside the palace we went,

## Them and Us

We felt so shy and timid,
As though they'd ask us for the rent.

We boldly said to a man full of ribbons,
"We're here representing B.A.C.M."
"Oh yes, are you really—my word—
'Pon my honour, what do you want my men?"

"We want to see the Board lad,
Get cracking, let Hyndley know,
That't lads from all the Divisions
Are waiting down here below."

And then the whole system got moving,
My word t'is a fearful sight,
To see this vast organisation,
Spring to life and show its might.

Telephones, Bell boys, and Porters,
They all went off at a trot,
And soon everyone was running,
B.A.C.M. had got rid of the lot.

And nobody came back to tell us
What we were supposed to do,
So we started to wander down't passage,
That's where we met our Waterloo.

We came to the shaft in the basement,
And at once felt quite at home,
A shaft in the centre of Hobart,
No more did we want to roam.

"Why not have a meeting in't Pit Bottom,"
A Welshman was heard to say,
"Nay lad," said a bloke from Yorkshire,
"We see this nearly every day."

Then up dashed a bloke with an eyeglass,
And gave us an icy look.
"Are you the men from B.A.C.M.?
They are waiting, Floor 5, Room 7, sign book."

## National President of Management Unions

Then into the cage piled B.A.C.M.
Like kids going down the first time,
"Shut the gate," said Little Lord Fauntleroy,
And the Scotchman passed him a dime.

And then our troubles started,
As up to the top we flew.
Someone had pressed the wrong button,
How to stop it no one knew.

So back we went to the basement,
The air was sultry and hot,
So we all decided to walk it
And out at the bottom we got.

We finally got to the "Kremlin",
A wonderful room—made you gasp,
There they all sat in their splendour
And now to get down to our task.

Their Chairman read out the hand-out
And gave us their terms point blank,
This caused a breathless silence
And now was the time to be frank!!

The big guns were let loose with fury,
The Major started to stammer and stutter,
But "Reference back" was the only cry
From Turnbull in a mild flutter.

The tempo was quickly increasing,
The representatives all tried hard
To make them see our importance,
But the result was "Leave us your Card."

The Yorkshiremen lapsed into their dialect
To try and get home their points,
But the only result when the days work was done
Was a stiffness in the near vocal joints.

The wonderful feeling of zeal and zest
And the pride on our first arriving,

> Was slowly but surely being quickly dispelled
> With each counter to all our striving.
>
> Needless to say, the meeting closed
> On "Compromise" or "Arbitration",
> So make up your minds what you want us to do
> Do we fight, or submit to frustration?

Despite our lack of success in London our members in the coalfields were passing resolutions that would have done justice to a mass meeting of left-wing agitators ... not one resolution that was carried unanimously was ever accompanied by suggestions as to how the resolutions could be achieved.

After my appointment as President, the first National Coal Board Chairman I met often was Sir Hubert Houldsworth, Q.C., a kind honest man if ever there was one. He pleaded with the men for more output and to work more regularly. He humbled himself to them and nobody did more for the miners than Sir Hubert did while he was in office.

No one had to make the mistake, however, of underestimating Sir Hubert's ability and determination.

Colliery managers were loud in their condemnation at one time about some of the activities of the board and they elected one of their most able men to put their questions and criticism of the Coal Board in general, and Sir Hubert in particular, to Sir Hubert himself.

Sir Hubert came to a crowded meeting and met the managers' representative face to face. The managers' representative did exceptionally well, so much so that we listeners thought that he hadn't left Sir Hubert Houldsworth a leg to stand on; Sir Hubert stood up and literally tore his inquisitor and his arguments shred by shred. He shattered them. Then he shook hands with his vanquished opponent and wished him well.

Another time the Yorkshire branch of our union was called to a meeting in the Danum Hotel at Doncaster, chaired by General Sir Noel Holmes, Divisional Chairman—a chap who liked me about half as much as I liked him—and then the meeting was to be addressed by Sir Hubert Houldsworth.

## National President of Management Unions

Before this assembly we had a private meeting and as I was the spokesman for the Yorkshire branch I was given the task of questioning the Board's action and of voicing our fears, criticisms and complaints. I spoke quite plainly and didn't mince my words.

I could see the general's moustache bristling, his hackles were rising, I knew I had incurred his wrath, but that was nothing unusual and this didn't worry me at all.

Sir Hubert listened very quietly but I knew he was not amused and when I had finished speaking he proceeded to tell me so in no uncertain fashion. So much so that by the time he'd finished speaking I was cast as the real villain of the piece.

General Holmes and Sir Hubert between them frightened our people so much that when we were having coffee after the meeting my own colleagues—who had asked me to say what I'd said—showed a marked reluctance to talk to me—or should I say—be seen talking to me.

There was I stood in a corner like a kid at school "sent to Coventry". But Sir Hubert deliberately sought me out, came across to me, shook hands and said, "Remarkably well put, Jim. It needed courage. Your colleagues evidently thought it wanted saying but when you as their spokesman say these things you must expect me to reply—with spirit."

What a difference. Even the general gave me a frosty smile and my colleagues began to talk to me again.

Such were the beginnings. I had just got to know Sir Hubert really well when he died suddenly; but months before he died Jim Bowman, the ex-miners' leader, had been appointed as his Deputy Chairman and nominated as his successor. How things change even with the mighty! The big men who had been constant visitors to Sir Hubert's office now didn't seem to know the way there but they all knew the way to Jim Bowman's office.

But one man remained loyal to Sir Hubert and that man was Billy Sales, his Labour Director. I'll always admire Bill Sales for that.

He had been with Sir Hubert a long time and it looked to

me more like a father-son relationship, there was certainly real affection between them and they had a remarkably good understanding.

Billy Sales brought a new atmosphere and much needed method into this branch of labour relations and he did a lot of spadework and good work and the industry is still benefiting from his efforts. His was the principal brain behind the first colliery wages structure. So when Jim Bowman's appointment was announced Sir Hubert still had a while to serve but "the king is dead", "Long live the king", runs the cry. By the time Sir Hubert died he appeared to be a lonely man.

Now Jim Bowman was a different type of man altogether. He and I got on very well from the start. He was a pitman, he had been an official for the National Union of Mineworkers for a long time and had become their Vice-President, before he was appointed Chairman of one of the northern divisions of the National Coal Board. He spoke pit language of all types as good and as fluently as any of us.

He had a deputy chairman, now Sir Joseph Latham, then Joe Latham, a very capable finance man. I don't think they always saw eye to eye but they never aired their disagreements in public. One thing was certain very early, however, Bill Sales didn't fit into the new organization and it wasn't long before Bill was asked to take over the chairmanship of the Yorkshire division, known then as the North-East division. General Holmes had retired and Bill took his place.

It was not long before Bill Sales had made his presence felt in Yorkshire. Labour relations took on a totally different aspect and were tremendously improved. Management could discuss their problems with him much easier than with the general. He was a very approachable man. I found the general very unapproachable.

In London Jim Bowman must have felt it very difficult to have to refuse things that his own friends and colleagues, Arthur Horner, the general secretary and Sir William Lawther, National President of the Mineworkers' Union were asking him for.

But he could be firm.

A lighthearted moment with Lord Robens.

The coal belt in a modern mine.

My wife, Jay, and two children Josephine and James, six years ago.

In retirement, in the grounds of my home, Swillington House.

## National President of Management Unions

He was in the chair when the demand for coal slackened off but he would never agree to a policy of closing pits. He stacked the coal he couldn't sell hoping the day would come when it was needed.

We had passed from the period of huge demand and coal at any price; in short, from a seller's market to a buyer's market.

Our salesmen were overnight transformed from eaters of lunches provided by well nigh desperate buyers and consumers, to buyers of lunches and dinners for prospective buyers and reluctant consumers! Oil was here with a vengeance.

Hugh Gaitskell was then our Minister and he called all the union representatives and board representatives together to try and estimate our assets, our drawbacks and our chances for the future. I told him that one of the greatest assets the Coal Board had and they inherited it was the asset of Total Darkness. If anybody could see to the bottom of our deep shafts, two thousand feet deep plus, they would never dare go down. If from the pit bottom the miners could see stretched out before them three to four miles of uphill bad roadway that they had to travel before they even got to their place of work they would never set off.

If they could see twenty tons of coal in a big heap and realize that that was what they had each to fill in one shift they would never start.

If they realized and could see over two thousand feet of solid rock, weighing thousands of tons, supported by props and bars they wouldn't dare stop.

But these comments didn't stop me agreeing about the importance of other assets. We realized that people were wanting a clean fuel, fuel that was easy to handle, fuel you could burn and no ashes to clean out. Oil, electricity and gas filled all these conditions so they were here as real competitors.

Jim Bowman was the first Coal Board Chairman to face these problems. I think he tackled them well. He was a courageous man and dealt with all unions firmly and fairly.

For a long time I had the impression that he didn't care

much for the management union as a whole. He hadn't a great regard for my predecessor, Major W. Brown. It was quite evident that they hadn't always seen eye to eye and this probably distorted Jim's vision.

When I started negotiating I had to fight very hard to get salary increases which we were convinced were justified. Even so, Jim Bowman and I had a high regard for each other and the longer we worked together our trust in each other grew.

Jim Bowman never broke his word once given and his signed photograph looks down very kindly on me from my study walls as I am writing.

When Jim's five years' term was up he had earned his knighthood and is now Sir James Bowman, but I sense that Jim felt that he had had enough.

There was great speculation as to who would succeed him as Chairman of this great industry. Board members, particularly deputy chairmen, divisional chairmen, had their admirers, supporters and advocates.

It was a Conservative government in power, Lord Mills—an industrialist, was our minister so all our "Mr. Know-alls" knew it wouldn't and couldn't be anybody connected with the trade union or with a labour background.

How wrong can you be?

When the appointment was made it was Alf Robens—ex-Labour minister and now Labour M.P. What a setback!

We were all supposed to be in the know. Everybody had secret tips and information.

I can honestly say I had never heard Alf Robens' name mentioned in connection with this job.

We were already beginning to close pits, redundancy was no longer an ugly spectre lurking in the background, it was here, it was a grim reality. An appointment from outside could only make matters worse. Surely, we asked ourselves, haven't we anybody in this vast organization capable of taking on this job?

Jim Bowman had been an ex-blacksmith in the industry and he had done the job well and if he could do it so well surely some of our well-known mining engineers, or finance or administration "wallahs" could do it but no, there it was, after all the different types we had had we now had a politician.

With 'Vesting Day' we'd become rest homes for retired high ranking Service officers. The ever growing pyramid of organization had brought into our industry teams of experts, few of whom had even dirtied their hands with a spade let alone with a pick and shovel at the coalface.

We had accepted this, though not without comment. Then in Jim Bowman, we'd had one of *ourselves* leading the industry; a leader who had done his share, whose face and hands still showed the marks of his calling.

Now with one stroke the clock had not just been put back as far as we could see, it had gone into reverse, for few men who work with their hands have much respect for full-time politicians.

On behalf of the union I wrote to *The Times*—objecting to this appointment.

But it made no difference.

I wrote to the Minister, Lord Mills, but it made no difference.

"I have spoken," said the Minister and spoken he had. "Robens stays," he said, and stayed he did and it's a damned good job for us and this industry that he did.

Within twelve months I had realized that in Alf Robens we had an outstanding man. He stood tall among tall men. He was no push-over. He was nobody's man but his own.

I'm fundamentally honest, so I wrote again to *The Times* saying that although my sentiments were right in my first letter my conclusions were wrong, that we had indeed been fortunate that Lord Mills insisted that Alf Robens was the right man to lead us.

He had brought a breath of fresh air into an industry which was being smothered. He had given confidence where there was doubt. He'd given hope where there was fear and what is more he gave everybody in the industry a new pride in themselves.

How could one man do this? The results speak better than me.

## Them and Us

We had all been here before he came, every one of us, from top to bottom.

After Alf Robens had been here a short while our output soared. Our results improved. New methods, new policies, new ideas were all accepted. We saw him at our pits, in our offices, on our television screens, at our meetings and conferences. We heard him on the radio, we read about him in the Press.

He built no ivory tower to retreat to and stay there. We began to hear more and more about coal and the coal industry.

At long last we again had a feeling of pride to be members of the coal industry. Miners walked with a new assurance. Very shortly Alf Robens became Lord Robens—a peer of the realm —our case was put in the House of Lords. The cutting down of the industry was fought more fiercely than ever before. We had now a chairman who was able and willing to oppose the reduction of output of the industry at all levels. He defied authority above him and he fought against decisions he felt were wrong, but no matter how much he disagreed he supported these decisions once they became law.

He knew all about politicians—he had been one. He understood their devious ways. He was a master in the art of publicity. He gave us a new image.

I found him a good companion. Always assured of one thing; he was as keen as we were to make the industry pay its way, to help it make its real contribution to the nation's difficulties.

Sometimes he appeared to fight a lonely battle. The man at the top is lonely, but Alf Robens made enemies out of powerful friends. He did not do this for himself, but for the sake of the industry he had been *asked* to lead. He worried about the social and moral consequences of pit closures. He fought against the destruction of mining communities. He was tolerant at times; but intolerant of pig-headedness and inefficiency. He could talk a dog's hind leg off! He accepted no case without argument. He could answer any question. If he didn't know the answer, nobody could tell by his answer, that he didn't know the real answer.

## National President of Management Unions

I watched him grow. Oh yes, he is a much bigger man now than he was when he came. He has helped everybody in the mining industry a great deal but they have helped him just as much.

He helped at Aberfan in no small way. He spoke on the radio the same day as the tragedy struck and accepted full responsibility on behalf of the Board. He offered his resignation to the Minister and letters poured into him and the Minister from all four corners of Great Britain, from all the trades unions involved asking him to stay, asking the Minister not to accept his resignation.

Alf Robens is not a fair weather friend either, but he will find he has got a lot of this sort. He has now had his first big strike. Newspapermen have begun finding chinks in his armour. He will survive. Everybody were loud in their praises as output rose from twenty-eight cwts. per person employed to forty-eight cwts. per person employed. But you can't keep making spectacular progress in productivity increases, particularly in the mining industry. There comes a time when your last machine goes in, when you last coalface is manned. You can't keep on improving beyond the capacity to improve. There is only one pint of water in one pint pot and a pint pot won't hold above one pint.

No longer, as good seams become exhausted, can they be replaced by better seams. Most of the best seams were gone before nationalization started. So, results will not improve much more; indeed increased work and still more improvement in techniques of modern machinery will be needed to hold results where they are.

I would say to Lord Robens that he would do well to remember the words of the poet:

> When winds are steady and skies are clear
> Every hand the ship would steer.
> But soon as ever the wild winds blow
> Every hand would go below.

As Chairman of a board you are entitled to credit when things go well and you must expect the reverse when things go

## Them and Us

wrong, but people should be fair in their criticism particularly industrial reporters. By our charter the final decisions on policy are determined by the Government through its minister; and when that policy is decided, the chairman, whether he agrees with it or not has to carry that policy through or resign. The Government felt it was right to reduce the size of the industry. We in the industry thought the Government was wrong but the government's policy has been loyally carried out.

In fairness to the Labour government they have eased the burden of redundancy; they have brought other industries into mining areas and they have given better compensation than has ever been given before.

As far as management are concerned Lord Robens' intense humanity never shone brighter than when we had to arrange compulsory early retirement for our members and agree terms.

There is an old saying "Sympathy without relief, is like mustard without beef". I often wish the public were as concerned with what happens to the men, who an industry has finished with, as they are with what happens to old pit ponies, or lately horses from the Guards regiment.

All old machinery—redundant machinery—is stored and maintained.

Surely! it is not asking too much for human beings to have at least as good treatment and consideration as horses or machinery.

Under Lord Robens' chairmanship the Coal Board had been mindful of the fact that human beings are not dots on a vast landscape; not just numbers on a piece of paper. They are individuals, all with their own personal problems; very often men who have served industry loyally and well for practically a lifetime. All credit to Alf Robens for not forgetting this fact himself or allowing other people to forget it.

I have met many ministers also. The outstanding one to me, until I met Dick Marsh, was Lord Mills; a Tory, I know, but a man of vast knowledge and understanding. He was kind, sympathetic, yet a man of determination. He was a good listener. When he had listened he would comment; when he promised he kept his word. Our political views were poles apart but we were friends until he died.

Ministers come and go, some stay longer than others, but none stay very long. One of the first ministers I ever met was David Grenfell—member for Gower—he was a remarkable character. He was the eldest son of a fairly large family. His father died while they were young and he helped to bring all his family up. In the first Labour government he became the first Minister of Mines and the first who held a first-class certificate of competency. He had taught himself several languages and spoke them fluently—a wonderful character.

In the next Labour government Hugh Gaitskell was our Minister, I was very friendly with him and had a great admiration for him. He didn't stay with us very long. His talents were quickly spotted and it wasn't long before he moved to higher positions.

Later, when I became the leader of the management's union I met ministers more on business than on friendly terms and I was very much impressed with Dick Marsh. I thought—and still think—that he will go a long way in politics, that is if somebody outside politics doesn't recognize his worth and manage to tempt him away.

Ray Gunter came but he didn't stay long enough for us to even get to know him.

Roy Mason came, I have known Roy all his life, I knew he'd be good, but he didn't stay long enough with the power industries to prove me right. He has gone higher and I have faith that he will go higher still.

Through all this period the first management union was outgrowing its childish ailments, it had suffered its growing pains and had emerged mature and strong in its own right, taking its rightful place in consultation and conciliation at all levels.

The mistrust and suspicion with which we were first greeted was replaced by confidence and even comradeship. The miners' leaders—from treating management union as a joke—over the years became increasingly impressed by our sincerity and ability.

*Them and Us*

During this period I met them all and got to know some of them very well.

Miners' leaders that really impressed me were Abe Moffatt, Scotland; Arthur Horner, the general secretary of the National Union of Mineworkers; Alwyn Machin—elected National President—and who died before he could take his seat.

Abe Moffatt was an outstanding character, a man of complete integrity, a man above suspicion, a man of his word. A man who had been to prison for his principles, a Scotsman to his fingertips, generous, hospitable, friendly but what a fighter! The honourable title of Miners' Queen's Counsel was well earned, he was a worthy opponent and a good friend. Every time I go to Scotland, Abe and his wife are people I always try to visit. Mrs. Moffatt worked as a girl on the pit top in Scotland and they are always sure of a real Yorkshire welcome when they come to my house.

Arthur Horner had a brilliant mind and was one of the best debaters I have ever met. He had been a member of the Communist Party a long time but he never let anything interfere with his work for the miners union.

Alwyn Machin died too young and I missed him badly. My respect and love for him was such that my daughter is called Josephine Alwyn after Joseph Alwyn Machin.

When he won the election to be the National President of the mineworkers of Great Britain Laurie Wormald was already the National President of the Colliery Deputies' Union and I was the National President of the British Association of Colliery Management.

Three Yorkshiremen in the three top jobs of three important mining unions, what a chance now for a real new understanding between management and men.

We had already had several talks on how we would tackle labour relations! Sadly it was not to be. Alwyn died on what should have been one of his proudest week-ends, his success in the election had just been announced. He was to be chairman of the Yorkshire Miners' Band Festival in the City Hall at Sheffield with singing guest, Paul Robeson, one of his friends, as the star of the evening. Alwyn was dead, before the concert he had helped to arrange took place. He was sadly missed and his death was a severe blow to the miners.

After nationalization all welfare activities became nationalized also and were controlled by national directors. The National Council consisted of an equal number of Coal Board representatives and Trade Union representatives. I was there as managerial representative. It was funny to listen to some of the arguments that took place in those early days, not only between the Board members and the trade union representatives but between the trade union representatives themselves. Different areas—and counties—in the mining industry of Great Britain had concentrated their welfare activities in many different ways. In Wales they had built picture houses in the valleys. In the Northern areas they had built really good Welfare Institutes. In Lancashire and Yorkshire we concentrated more on convalescent homes.

At one of the early meetings Arthur Horner said, "Now we are nationalized we shall nationalize all our welfare facilities." Everybody agreed, until Arthur went on to explain this meant sharing the Yorkshire and Lancashire convalescent homes. Alwyn Machin looked across the table, "Nay, Arthur, you can't expect Yorkshiremen to go down to Wales to go to the pictures, you can't expect us to go up to Durham to have a drink, but you can rest assured, Arthur, these convalescent homes are ours. They belong to us and we are not losing control of them to anybody."

It reminded me very much of a story that is so often told of the Irishman who after attending a meeting in Manchester on socialism addressed by the famous Kier Hardy, went back to Ireland and told all his friends about the wonderful new doctrine he had heard in England. "You share and share alike, everything," Pat said.

"Does that mean if you had two houses you would give me one?"

"Yes."

"If you had two horses would you give me one?"

"Yes."

"If you had two cows would you give me one?"

## Them and Us

"Yes."

"Two pigs?"

"No fear! I've got two pigs."

Yes there were some great debates around the table between men whom nationalization had brought together.

CHAPTER EIGHTEEN

## LEAVING FRYSTON

Many unions connected with the mining industry—and many other unions—base their headquarters in London. This is done to enable leaders to be near the headquarters of the nationalized industries and to be within easy reach of the Minister responsible for their industry.

Very often union leaders begin to know London for the first time when they have to go and live in London. Living in the big city, far away from the men you represent, can make it very difficult for some people to remember their past; and sometimes their origin. It's not always easy for a national leader to keep in mind the high ideals he had on his election. They gradually get further and further away from the factory, workshop or mine.

They are constantly meeting big men, very often wealthy men, usually well-educated men, men with liberal expense allowances.

To tired, nervous men, sometimes feeling a little out of their depth, probably feeling a slight inferiority complex even, a drink so kindly offered—and if accepted—so generously poured can act as a temporary stimulant, can help to allay any nervousness or any fears but it can so easily become a habit. Many employer's representatives will supply the liquor.

"Let's get to know each other better," they say.

The trade union leader on his own in a strange city, sometimes without even the comfort of his own family around him, with only his own salary—usually small—will find many temptations. Many avenues are open to him, first night at theatres, cocktail parties, visits to night clubs, radio interviews, newspaper articles. Yes, the opportunities gradually appear. He is a

*Them and Us*

strong character if his tastes and desires do not undergo any change whatsoever.

Charles Dickens says: "If the courses change the ends will change."

It is a fact that when you are on a small salary you always feel that another pound or two a week would make all the difference between hardship and comfort. When I was a colliery deputy my salary was three pounds five shillings per week. When I was made overman my salary was five pounds a week —I knew then we should be all right. But we didn't seem any better off.

When I was promoted to undermanager my salary was between eight and ten pounds per week, plus fringe benefits such as free house and free light. Now I was sure we would be better off. But it doesn't work out like that. Your standard of living rises, your expenses increase, you want to be like your opposite number.

When you get in the three or four thousand pounds a year bracket, taxes, cars, bigger houses, more furniture, more entertainment, better education for your children now desired and to be paid for, still seem to keep you where you are, where there is no spare cash. Your standards rise with your income and more often than not exceed it.

Not all men by any means cultivate expensive tastes and habits. I never saw Ernest Jones, one time president of the Miners' Union, take a drink at all. Abe Moffatt and Alwyn Machin were moderate in the extreme, they avoided all the activities I have mentioned previously like the plague.

On the other hand I have seen union leaders with a weakness for drink, have bottles sent into them in the early morning by their opposite number from the employer's side "with my compliments". This isn't friendship, it isn't kindness. It's exploitation of a different kind but just as vicious and just as vile. For "when liquor is in, sense is out".

By 1954 I had become so busy with so many positions at national level that I asked the National Coal Board if I could be released from my position as agent and manager at Fryston Colliery. I felt I could not do justice to the pit, to the men or

## Leaving Fryston

to myself. I was away far too much. It wasn't fair to my other officials and it wasn't fair to me. I was convinced that I could make a greater contribution in national and international affairs than I could ever make locally.

Thirty-four years in one place is a long time, particularly when you start at the bottom and go right through to the top. It took a great deal of thought before I made the final decision. The Board agreed with me and asked me to go away on a six months' management course which would enable me to attend to my national commitments and then, report back to the National Coal Board on other managements' techniques. At the end of this period I could either go back to Fryston or I could take a position at Area level as "Efficiency Engineer" to impart the knowledge I had gained on this course to other managers.

When I announced to my officials and men that I was leaving Fryston they just could not believe it. To them I was part of the valuation. They couldn't visualize Fryston without me. But I knew it had to be.

No one will ever realize what it meant to me to leave the pit —the men and the village—where I had worked among them as a pony driver, miner, shotfirer, deputy, overman, under-manager, manager and agent; where I had seen and helped to turn muckstacks and old quarries into places of beauty. Where welfare halls, cricket and football fields, bowling greens, tennis courts, skating rinks and sports stadiums and youth centres had all been built.

Despite all these things I felt it was easier to get someone to take my place at Fryston than it was to get someone to take over my other duties. I realized I could no longer do both, so the decision was mine and mine alone.

In my experience I had taken part in and organized, many tributes and testimonials to various people for different reasons. Some tributes were made on promotion, some on retirement, some to people leaving to take up other work. I found if you were promoted to a bigger job, at your own place, contributions were bigger and easier to raise. On retirement it depended a lot on how well you were liked and your pecuniary circumstances.

*Them and Us*

If leaving to go somewhere else where the chances were that, locally, nobody would see you again, not much was collected.

In my case I was leaving altogether, I was going out of their sphere but many moving tributes were paid to me by officials, men and villagers. In my study there is a framed certificate drawn on vellum by an art student whose father was a miner. In letters of gold leaf, beautifully printed it says:

> Presented to James Allen Bullock on leaving his position as Agent and Manager of FRYSTON COLLIERY in 1954 for the services he has rendered to the community in general and the colliery in particular and as a mark of the high regard in which he was held by all officials, staff and workmen who served under him and to record for ever their appreciation of his unremitting care for the safety and welfare of all who were associated with him whether at work or at home and with a view to recording the indebtedness of the whole of the Fryston District to his tireless efforts in improving the working conditions and amenities and the social life of all.

Since I left Fryston I often think of that last occasion when I was saying good-bye to a really representative gathering of all our people.

Even now I remember it with emotion. I am not sufficiently skilled in the use of words to describe the atmosphere of that evening when after thirty years we were finally saying good-bye to each other. No words of mine could describe adequately the real sense of sadness, of loss. One of the Fryston trade union leaders said, "We are sad tonight because we have known Jim Bullock in a certain set of circumstances. We have known him a long time. Maybe we have known him too long. We have taken him to be our servant. We have accepted him. We have taken him for granted. We have used him freely. No man seeking help or advice has ever been denied either. We ourselves are to blame", the trade union leader went on, "for cloaking him in a mantle of permanence."

Edrich Sharpe, the undermanager, spoke a very sincere speech, talked about our friendship, presented me with a canteen of cutlery, an illuminated address and said, "That this is a sad and pleasant task." He avoided sentimentality for which I was

## Leaving Fryston

very pleased but he stretched a mental tape measure over the years. He talked of Mr. Bullock the pitman, of "J.B." the manager, of Jimmy Bullock, sportsman, social reformer, fighter, and then I quote "but most of all," said Mr. Sharpe, "I want to pay tribute to Mr. Bullock who has done more, than any man in the past hundred years to change conditions for everybody who worked at Fryston colliery, for everybody who lives in Fryston village so quickly and so efficiently."

My eldest brother spoke on that occasion and through the arches of the years he looked back on my career. I like the words of my brother when he calmly said, "I have watched Jim's progress with great interest."

Yes, this occasion was a terrible wrench for all of us. Twelve months after leaving Fryston I was invited to go back to an Old People's Dinner. It was both inspiring and emotional to experience the reception I had from the old people.

The new manager—Mr. Williams—addressing the gathering said:

"I hope the day will come when the people of Fryston will show me the same affection and respect that tonight they have shown to Mr. Bullock."

When I replied I told Mr. Williams the story of the rich American who came to Britain and let it be known far and wide that the purpose of his visit was to buy the finest turf in Great Britain. He was told that the finest turf was to be found on Lord's Cricket Ground in London. The American went to Lord's and offered the M.C.C. one million dollars for the turf of the Lord's Cricket Ground. He was told the turf was not for sale but he wouldn't be put off and offered two million dollars. Finally he realized that money was not everything and that this turf was not for sale. So he asked, "How do you grow it?"

They sent for the groundsman, explained what the American wanted and the groundsman said, "Get some land, level it, weed it, make sure it is really good soil, cultivate it, get the finest lawn seed you can buy, sow it, roll it, feed it, cut it, roll it, feed it, and cut it for two hundred years and you'll have turf exactly like this."

I turned round to Mr. Williams and said, "There's a moral

## Them and Us

in the story." That was my last public address at any function at Fryston because I told them all that I didn't want to be invited back any more. It was too emotional and I feel certain that anybody who was present at that dinner would understand what I meant.

CHAPTER NINETEEN

# THEN AND NOW

Many people, who know little about mining or mining men, ask me, "What is the difference in the men and the conditions now to what it was in your early days?"

Being born and reared in a miner's family enables me to go much farther back than my own experiences.

In my boyhood the conversation in the home was pits, religion and politics, in that order.

When parents were absent sex was always added to the conversation as it is now. Now sex is talked about much more openly. We discussed it *sotto voce*. We didn't talk about it in front of our sisters; but talk about it we did.

Strange seems to be the things that I was told about sex if judged by present day knowledge.

Masturbation was actually taught to young boys by the older boys. They found willing pupils.

But to come back to the difference in mining conditions, my father remembered small boys working down the pit twelve to fourteen hours a day in conditions that were near slavery.

For well over a hundred years the pits were worked for profit and profit only. Safety was a secondary consideration.

The boss's word was law; no trade unions. Miners lived in tied cottages which meant they couldn't leave the pits without giving up their houses, and these houses had no sanitation and none of the conveniences we have today.

Down the pits there were no steel supports, very small roadways, no electric lamps and the only light available at all was the one carried by the man himself and that in most cases was a candle.

## Them and Us

Miners made their own candles and could tell the time by them.

Roof supports were very flimsy, the cheapest timber being used. Ventilation was very crude and very little of it. Coal dust was never cleaned up so the danger of explosion was always present.

When shot firing started all bore holes had to be drilled by hammer and drill. All the coal was cut by hand pick and then shovelled into little box containers, baskets, or—in some more enlightened mines—into boxes on wheels—which we called tubs. These were then transported by small girls and boys who worked and were treated like animals. They were cheaper than pit ponies.

There was no first aid, no stretchers, no ambulances and no sick rooms.

In 1840, Lord Astley asked for a Commission to inquire into the employment of children of the poorer classes in mines. This was finally agreed and in May 1842 the first report was issued.

This report disclosed for the first time to the public the misery and depravity which existed in coalmines. Even the avowed friends of the working classes had no knowledge that conditions were so despicable.

The report showed that Britain—the most civilized and Christian country in the world—permitted such evils to exist. It is only if details are given and fully described that this generation of the general public and even the present generation of miners can be made to realize just how bad things were then and how much they have improved.

The report stated that many thousands of underground workers were under thirteen years of age, some were sent down the pit between five and six years old and thousands were employed under nine years of age.

To the horror of the public the report made clear that the employment of juveniles was not restricted to boys only, for girls were sent to work in the pits just as young.

In this book I describe my own first experiences underground at the age of thirteen—with a background of mining. To young

## Then and Now

timid children their first descent into the depths of a coalmine must have been *truly* terrifying. Once down the pit their experiences were hardly less horrible. The mines then were wet. The children worked up to their knees in mud in long, low dangerous passages and above all surrounded by the all pervading blackness and stillness that could be felt.

The first job for these young children, was opening and shutting the doors which are necessary to hold back, force, or change the stream of air currents.

If these doors were left open for any length of time gas could accumulate and explosions follow or men could be suffocated.

So these little children had to sit behind these doors listening for the approach of man or beast hauling coal so that they could open the doors and close them immediately the traffic had passed. They had to stay there from the first transport that came in the morning to the last transport that passed at night.

For twelve or fourteen hours each day these children had to sit with their flickering candles as their only companion.

All alone, in the deadly silence, in the damp conditions and they dared not, leave their posts for one moment.

It is easy for adults to fall asleep down a pit, but if these youngsters fell asleep they got "belted" or thrashed by some bullying junior official.

Most mines at that time were full of rats, mice and huge beetles. The rats were so bold that they would eat the lad's food and even run off with his candle!

These youngsters' lives were so full of fear, and acute physical and mental strain, that the effect on young, nervous, sensitive children sometimes produced a condition in their mental make-up approaching idiocy.

Sunday was the only day they saw the sun. They had no leisure hours. They had no holidays. Their meals were eaten with dirty hands in darkness.

When they got home they had little sympathy given to them for even their parents knew no other kind of life and looked on their children's employment as quite ordinary.

As the children grew older they were removed from "trapping" to shoving and pulling the tubs themselves with a harness wrapped round their little bodies attached to whatever conveyance was used for transporting the coal. No distinction whatsoever was made between boys and girls, either in their hours of work or the weight of the mineral to be carried or pulled.

They literally crawled on their hands and knees and were full of sores and bruises from head to foot.

Women also had to do this work and even were forced to fill coal themselves, sometimes, in the last stages of pregnancy.

The roadways were so low that horses couldn't even get there—and of course horses had to be fed.

Some of the shafts had long steps or ladders bolted to the sides of the shaft and coal was loaded into bags from half a hundredweight to a hundredweight and this was carried up the steps nearly always by girls and women. Many of the girls were round about seven years of age. The sacks were strapped to the backs of the children before they climbed these ladders and sometimes the straps broke with disastrous consequences to the bearer and those below on the ladders.

Nobody cared. Labour was cheap. There were no inquiries into accidents or deaths.

Even today water has to be constantly pumped from the pit but now it is done by up-to-date machinery. In those days all water had to be pumped by pumps worked by the hands of these little children.

If any child failed to come to work, another child already there had to carry on working for a double shift—in some cases twenty-four hours.

Some children were made apprentices and copies of these odious agreements are still in existence.

Foremen at the mines bargained for these children, dismissed them when they wanted and just about owned them body and soul.

These conditions were responsible for diseases of heart and lungs in early life and it was a very lucky miner who reached the age of thirty without becoming asthmatic or full of rheumatism.

The chief accidents to the children in those days were falling off the ladders in the shaft, coal or stone falling on them, suffocation by gas, and drowning by sudden inrushes of water.

Regulations have now made all these things impossible.

There was practically no education whatsoever and morals were very low. Can you wonder when males and females worked together practically naked?

Wages were extremely meagre and in many districts the "truck system" was in operation. This meant they were not paid in money but in goods from a shop usually owned by the coalowner; goods that were usually twenty-five per cent dearer than at other shops.

What was the excuse given for this revolting cruelty? The same as it has been throughout history.

That without the employment of child labour the pits could not possibly be worked at a profit.

During the debates for the abolition of child labour down pits, the argument was used that if children were not allowed to go down the mines below the age of ten the vertebrae of their backs would not conform to the position required for future miners. That if they didn't get used to constant bending and stooping they would never be able to be miners when they were adults.

The Earl of Shaftesbury wrote in his diary:

"The Home Office tried to hold the report back, but it came by mistake into the hands of Members and though the Secretary of State succeeded for a long time in preventing the sale of the report he could no longer prevent the publicity which it caused.

"Civilization itself never exhibited such a mass of sin and cruelty. The Government cannot refuse to exclude females and children from coalmines."

So history tells us that in 1841 a commission was formed.

In 1842 the commission reported and despite determined opposition a bill was passed in 1843 which prohibited the labour of females in coalmines. It is a sad fact, however, that young boys were still employed underground for years after this. Women worked on the surface until quite recently, particularly in Scotland.

*Them and Us*

In fact, Helen Moffatt, the wife of my friend, Abe Moffatt, the famous Scottish miners' leader, was working on the surface of the Scottish coalmine until she married Abe—and they are both still living.

It is pleasing to say that the last one hundred years has seen slow but constant changes in mining techniques and conditions; all for the better. Things were still very bad in pits when my father and my elder brothers first went down. It was bad enough when I went down in 1916, even then the roof supports were largely of wood. But at least we had progressed from candles to oil lamps and First Aid was now available.

In 1911 a new 'Coal Mines Act' brought more stringent safety regulations into being than ever there had been before. Higher and better qualifications were needed for colliery officials. More accurate testing for gas. Stricter regulations for shot-firing. Regular hours. Coal dust to be cleaned up and controlled.

Mines Inspectors were given more powers and their numbers were increased.

Miners' Unions were formed and finally they all amalgamated into the great National Union of Mineworkers.

Miners started selecting and financing their own Members of Parliament and by 1932 pithead baths and welfare schemes of all manner and types were being built.

Coalcutting machines eliminated the use of hand picks. Belts conveyed coal that before had been handled by men and horses.

Progress—particularly among the more enlightened big companies—proceeded at a rapid rate.

Then, after the 1939–45 war, came the Labour Government and Nationalization.

Now the terms, conditions and social status of the mineworker took tremendous strides forward and have improved beyond all recognition. No longer is a miner and his family bound to one pit.

He has freedom of choice as to where he or his sons will work.

Villages are no longer isolated.

Transport is more plentiful.

Education is his by right. Scholarships are open to enable him or his family to enter any profession.

It is, however, at the pit itself where the biggest changes have taken place. Mining is no longer a labourer's job. It is, in itself, a profession; a profession needing skilled engineering, for machinery worth hundreds of thousands of pounds is installed throughout the pits.

Picks and shovels are regarded as antiques and reminders of the past.

Pit ponies have disappeared and have been pensioned off into green fields to nibble out their lives in comfort.

Boys no longer go underground under the age of fifteen.

They have ample training under close, personal and expert supervision.

They are not allowed to be alone down the pits until they are fully trained.

Training Officers—themselves highly trained, experienced, men—are appointed at every mine.

Competent Safety Officers with well-trained staff at every mine.

Miners no longer walk miles and miles underground to reach the coalface for modern underground trains take them to and from their work.

When the colliers come out from work they can bathe and feed at the pithead.

Miners are members of the Consultative and Welfare Committees at the pits.

Another big difference, realized far more by older miners than younger miners, is the fact: "It is no longer *so*, because the boss *says so*. It only is *so*, if consultation has taken place and agreement has been reached. Then it is *so*."

The miner has now a shorter working week, longer holidays, much better pay both when he is working and when he is off sick.

Under common law, accidents—both fatal and serious—are far better compensated.

Radar and electronics are now his tools.

Automatic gas testings.

## Them and Us

Mechanical probing of the strata both above and below him all help in geological difficulties.

Safety regulations are rigidly enforced.

All these improvements have happened in my life time and I am proud to say that I have contributed quite a lot to some of them.

Nationalization has made possible developments of all kinds that would have been financially impossible under private ownership.

It must be constantly stressed, however, that no matter what has been done or what will be done, nothing can ever make mining a clean, easy or totally safe job. It is still a battle with the unknown and with nature.

Accidents do and will still occur. Thank God they are getting fewer and fewer.

Accidents always seem to take place in what appears to be the safest pit and in the most unexpected places.

The miner himself is an extremely loyal person. He is hard-working and brave. He respects authority; particularly competent authority.

There is nobody that I would sooner have behind me, in front of me, or at my side in a time of crisis than the British miner.

What a pleasure for a man like me to see the miner walk in with his head held high, with first-class clubs and welfare grounds in which to enjoy his leisure. To see him have the desire and the opportunity to travel abroad.

To see his children going to university and becoming experts in all walks of life.

In recent years the miners have seen pit after pit close. They have witnessed the total number of the mining fraternity reduced by over seven hundred thousand workers. The number of pits closed has been over seven hundred.

Can you wonder that if the collier hears on the radio or on television or reads in his newspaper that someone or other in high places says, "that if he does this or doesn't do that, it will result in loss of trade and more pit closures", that he replies, "for years we have had no strikes, we have had no go-slows, we have co-operated in everything we have been asked to do, we have accepted and operated and made successful new techniques. We have even given up our homes and our own environment and moved to far distant coalfields and still we have witnessed our numbers being reduced and our pits closed."

"No," the miner says. "Threats don't worry us. If you want to close the pits close them. But as for me I am going to demand a wage commensurate with my skills, with my efforts and the ever present day to day risks at my job."

I don't blame him, do you?

CHAPTER TWENTY

## NEW HOME: NEW LIFE

When I left Fryston colliery I had to find another house. It has always been an agreement between the owners and management and with the National Coal Board and management that the manager of a colliery lives in "the manager's house" belonging to that colliery. A new manager at Fryston had been appointed, it was essential that he lived on the spot. Therefore, I had to vacate "The house on the hill" as soon as possible.

Houses were not easy to get. I wanted a detached house with a garden and a place to keep my dogs. I needed room to breathe. I wanted room to expand and above all I wanted somewhere where I could knock down and rebuild, and re-construct.

For years I had been the big man, deciding, and then doing, at one village pit. I was a big fish in a small pond. When I went to Area I found I was a *little* fish in a *big* pond, what a change; at Fryston I had a big office, beautifully furnished. I had a personal secretary with assistant secretary and all the other assistants that a big job carries.

At Area I'd to start a new department, I had to try my interpretation of Parkinson's law. First and foremost, however, I had to find somewhere to live.

Eventually I found a very old cottage for sale called "The Mount" at Swillington. Back home with a vengeance, for this was the next village to Bowers Row where I had been brought up as a boy. Swillington House was the home of the Lowther family who had built the only school I had attended, who were the ex-royalty owners of the first coalmine where I worked.

There were peculiarities about this cottage that appealed to

## New Home: New Life

me. It was owned by a very old widow—whose husband used to be the local colliery engineer. She proudly admitted, when we went to see her that her house was haunted by a friendly spirit. In addition she said she had three old hens, to me, they looked as old as I was. A condition of sale was that I must do nothing to hinder the activities of the spirit nor must I kill the hens.

On promising both of these clauses she agreed to sell the house. We got it very cheap. Very few people wanted to buy a ghost with a house, so she went out and we moved in. It was surrounded by owls and inhabited by bats. It was a weird place.

We stayed at "The Mount" for five years and during that time we completely redesigned it. The old washhouse we lined all round with polished half-round wooden bars. We built inglenook fireplaces with corner seats. We re-christened the old washhouse "The Dive". We built an old-fashioned bar. We placed a firebox in the centre of the room and built a chimney straight through the roof which left an open fire over which we placed a spit where we could cook anything. It looked like an old log cabin. It was the scene of some marvellous get-togethers, twenty-first birthday parties, sing-songs, dart matches and sheer booze-ups. We built extensions to the kitchen. We built a porch of very old stone. We bricked doorways up and moved doors to different places. We built new garages, a fine balcony and conservatory. When we had finished it was really nice.

During this period we had ample evidence as to why it was known as "the haunted house". There certainly was "a presence". Whatever he, or she, or it was, we called it "Harry". Harry was very useful, if we had friends visit us and we wished them to stay he was an interesting topic of conversation and sometimes he gave them a demonstration. If people came who we didn't care for very much we could make their blood curdle with stories of Harry's exploits. They didn't stay very long.

At this time we were breeding Labrador and St. Bernard dogs, we kept them outside, but if there is one thing they liked more than anything else it was to be allowed in the house.

## Them and Us

When Harry was busy they just wanted to get out of the house as quickly as possible and if they were out they wouldn't come in. They reacted to "the presence" much quicker than us. Their hair used to stand up on their backs. Dogs' hair only stands up with excitement, anger or fear. Our dogs would whimper and howl. No matter what you did you could not persuade them to go upstairs, normally they were delighted to do so.

Upstairs was where most of the ghostly activities took place. I'm sure dogs are more sensitive than humans. Our dogs certainly heard things before we did. I placed a tape recorder upstairs to see if it would pick up sounds that they could hear and we couldn't. It only seemed to pick up the sounds we could hear, of footsteps going upstairs and across the bedroom floors. The sounds of doors opening and closing.

There was one small bedroom at the back of the house which we decided would make an ideal nursery. My wife and I were born optimists and we hoped to fill it. We lined the bedroom with rubber tiles, floor and sides, installed ceiling heaters. We never found any explanation, but we never got the temperature in that room above forty degrees fahrenheit, neither in summer or winter.

Jay, my wife, was absolutely marvellous during this period. She not only kept on working at her own job—medical social worker—but she helped in the reconstruction and was a real help to me in all my activities. She acted as chauffeur, adviser, and confidante.

One night Jay and I were both in London and we had arranged for one of my elder sisters—Lydia—to stay to look after our animals. We left her our telephone number and at 10.30 p.m. she rang us in London to say she couldn't stay a moment longer in the house. Clocks were striking that didn't strike; she heard the sounds of doors closing where there were no doors. She apologized for her lack of courage and told us she had telephoned for her son to take her away. She never came again to "The Mount".

While we were at "The Mount" we heard indistinct voices often and distinct voices occasionally; both when we were on our own and when we had visitors. Neither of us were spiri-

## New Home: New Life

tualistically inclined or superstitious but there was something in that house that neither of us could explain. Whatever it was it was friendly and fortunately we were not of the nervous kind.

While we were at "The Mount" my wife had a lovely baby girl, we called her Josephine Alwyn, after my good friend Joseph Alwyn Machin the miners' leader. Owing to the coldness of the nursery built with such loving care for her she never occupied it.

A member of the Society of Psychic Research came to visit us and asked if he could investigate the happenings which they had known for years were taking place at "The Mount". The old lady would not allow them in. We immediately told him we didn't want Harry disturbing either. He then told us a wonderful story of a Spanish ambassador who had rented "The Mount" one summer, centuries ago. While there his daughter fell in love with a farm labourer. Her father banished her to Spain and on the voyage she jumped overboard and her spirit came back to the house where she had known real happiness. She used to go out of a door in the outside wall of what we tried to make into a nursery and down a flight of stone steps outside. I said there is no outside door and no stone steps. Later we found there had been a door and there were traces of where steps had been but it had all been bricked and plastered over. We didn't want any investigation or exorcizing. We were quite happy to keep our promise to the old lady. The hens disappeared so we did not destroy them either.

We were both fond of riding and stabled our horse in the old ruined stables at Swillington House. Years before while at Fryston I'd blown up the ruins of the great mansion itself and used the stone in the building of Fryston Welfare Hall and grounds. The ornaments and gates were taken to our welfare ground at Fryston by dozens of voluntary helpers. Marvellous statues, two beautiful stags, were taken from the grounds to beautify the adjacent colliery—Mount Pleasant.

It was very quiet in Swillington Park. The grounds had been neglected so long they had reverted back to nature. Once over the park wall there was no sign of human habitation. The

## Them and Us

stables had no windows, roof, sanitation or light but they had good solid walls made of York stone.

We were fascinated by the old stables. We talked about the possibilities of making a house out of these stables and of buying the ground surrounding the stables until we literally talked ourselves into approaching the National Coal Board to see if we could buy them.

Billy Sales was the chairman of the Yorkshire Division of the Board at this time and he came down to inspect the premises. He looked at me, shook his head very sadly and said, "Jim! I wouldn't give this to my worst enemy, never mind sell it to my friend." But he did. When we bought it we began to realize what a stupendous task we had now given ourselves.

But we had to sell "The Mount" to get enough capital to finance our new venture. This was not easy. Locals knew its history and money was scarce. Most of our prospective purchasers wished to borrow money from the local council. The council wondered why they wanted to borrow such a lot of money to buy such a small cottage.

As a result they had to come and inspect "The Mount". When they arrived they couldn't recognize what they saw as the place they had in their records and on their maps. Now I was in real trouble again. Who had authorized the alterations? Where had I had permission to erect a garage? Had I asked permission to turn a washhouse into a party room? Oh, dear! The ways of the transgressors are hard.

Eventually we did sell it to a nice young couple—Mr. and Mrs. Oxtoby. We had to get out as quickly as possible so that they could get in and we came down to Swillington House and occupied it just as it was without roof, without any lighting, very little water and no sanitation. Fortunately for us it was a lovely summer and we practically camped out. This was in 1959.

During the period of removal my wife presented me with a son and we called him James Allen, after me. He has never known any other home except this one.

My respect for my wife really increased. Here we were with a set of stables without a roof, two young children, one only

## New Home: New Life

a fortnight old, sleeping on camp beds, cooking on a primus stove, the whole stables full of rubble, cement, sand and timber. I was away from home quite a lot, she had all this to contend with and never grumbled. She started work again at her old job six weeks after James was born.

We hadn't been down here long before the new occupiers of "The Mount" came to ask us if we had ever seen anything unusual at "The Mount". We could truthfully say we had not *seen* anything . . . but they had. We calmed their fears and I understand that "Harry" has now left for other fields.

For four months we went upstairs by ladder and then across planks to sleep. Upstairs there were two big barns but very little roof. Downstairs there were beautiful standings for hunting horses, complete with mangers, but there was no place for us to eat.

My friends asked, "Why on earth do you want to live in a stable? Buying a place like this you are either an idiot or a genius."

But we always saw the possibilities. Again there was the dream, the vision of what it could be like. Neither my wife or I had any illusion about the work involved but we had faith in our own ability.

We had plans for the reconstruction drawn up by an architect friend of ours. He had drawn the plans for the welfare halls that I had built at Fryston, so he had experience of my methods and my ways. He would only help us now on condition that all plans were submitted to, and passed by the local council. Also he said that in future he would deal with my wife when plans were to be discussed and not me. I agreed to this. The plans were submitted. The plans were passed. Here was where I intended to stay. I wanted no mistakes this time. We made a five-year plan. First we would complete a bedroom, then a kitchen, after that a bathroom, then a livingroom. No luxury building until the essentials were built.

What an Herculean but enjoyable task it has been. We have realized what good friends we have had. We have received so much help from such a variety of people. One of my nephews—

## Them and Us

Dick Milner—was a first-class builder and craftsman. He spent every minute of his spare time here. Another nephew—Freddy Bullock—a forester, helped us with the planting of Christmas trees and laying out the grounds. Miners from Fryston came at week-ends and worked as if they were on contract.

My old friend Freddy Astbury, and his two sons, never missed a week-end for two or three years and worked as hard as if the place belonged to them. But of all the people who helped my wife made the greatest contribution. She not only kept working at her own job—helping to provide much needed capital—but she did the cooking for many and varied people. She put up with dirt and dust and inconveniences that would have daunted most women. She looked after both our young children and one bedroom even took on the appearance of home.

My daughter, Diane, from my previous marriage, was about to be married and we arranged for the wedding reception to be held here. Another good example of the relationship that existed between the two families.

When the caterer came to view the place a fortnight before the wedding, we showed him the room where the reception was going to be held. It was still complete with six horse standings and mangers, a brick floor and was a dirty whitewashed building, covered from top to bottom in spiders' webs.

He looked at us as if we were raving mad. I said, "Don't you worry, it will be ready all right." The nearness of the wedding spurred us on. My wife and I, Dick Milner and Freddy Astbury took a week of our holidays and we worked eighteen hours a day. On the day before the wedding the caterer came again, the room was ready, all the walls were covered with rhododendrons and all the bits and pieces that were not finished were hidden by huge banks of flowers. The whole place looked as though it had been lived in for years.

The reception was held and people from all over the country, my old friends and new friends, from all walks of life, mixed with Diane's friends to make a really memorable occasion.

When people ask me:

## New Home: New Life

"Why on earth do you want to live in a stable?" I simply state: "If a stable was good enough for Jesus to be born in, then a stable is good enough for me to live in."

When a family has a country seat for hundreds of years, each different generation seems to leave its mark. While the great house itself may not change much the estate does. So it was with the Lowthers of Swillington. They were part of the great Lonsdale family. The interests of the various members can be traced through the centuries by the mementoes they have left behind.

The southern border of the Lowther estate was the river Aire, in which was a horseshoe bend which ran right into the estate. One of the Lowther family straightened the river Aire and left the horseshoe as a fishing stream. Another Lowther made a cockpit inside the huge horseshoe where cockfighting was carried on for years. Yet another used the material dug from making a new river course to make a walled garden. He had walls built sixteen feet high, all hollow with fires at each corner. He designed ascentional ventilation, so that the smoke rising through the walls kept away any frost. Huge greenhouses were built all the way round the garden. Another member of the family was a great traveller and brought back to Swillington Park all sorts of trees and shrubs. Many are still here today and we preserve them jealously. Indeed, I have tried to plant two of every sort of tree that grows here. People might think it is rather foolish to set trees at my age, but if the Lowthers had thought that, we should not be enjoying the beauty of the trees we now enjoy.

Another example of the changes in power of these old families is illustrated by the following. We have a nice little wood called the "New Forest"—these trees had to be set and allowed to grow to a height that would hide a new pithead from view from the mansion. The coal owners were not allowed to erect the pithead buildings until the forest was high enough to hide them. One of my friends, who died recently, was chairman of a big engineering company in Leeds. He told me a wonderful story of some of the things that happened in the inner circles of these famous families. He had the story from his grandfather.

## Them and Us

It has a particular interest for me because it tells of how the beautiful Lowther stables that I converted to my present home came to be built.

There were three well known big landowning families living at Temple Newsam, Swillington and Methley. They used to meet in each others houses for gambling sessions. There was no post or telephones then and either messages went by grooms on horseback or signalling was done from the towers of one residence to another. During one of the sessions a quarrel took place between the owners of Methley Hall and Swillington. The Methley owner said his stables were better than the Lowther mansions. Lowther replied saying, "I'll build better stables than your mansion." When he got home he had plans drawn up and the work commenced on this wonderful building. York stone was used, similar to the stone of Selby Abbey, and the stables were built in Georgian style and constructed in a way that would withstand the ravages of time and last for centuries.

Another member of the family built an "Ice House" which was the early type of refrigerator. This is still in perfect condition today.

When we bought the place it had all deteriorated very badly but nearly all the surrounding mansions were being knocked down and we visited all we could and bought big fireplaces, cupboards and huge tables that were either sold cheap or were destroyed. They were cheap because very few modern rooms were big enough to house such articles. It does seem a pity that so called progress is seeing the elimination of these beautiful buildings and lovely pieces of furniture. We feel happy that we have been able to save at least a few of these lovely relics from the scrap heap.

There is one tree in particular that is still in its full beauty that has real sentimental importance, it is a huge copper beech over two hundred years old. It is still known as Lady Lowther's tree. When I was a boy, the women—including my mother—used to be brought from the mining village once a year in wagonettes. They had tea on the grass under the beech tree. Boys and girls from the village school came up on that day

## New Home: New Life

and carried sandwiches and tea for the women. To many this was the only afternoon out they had in the whole year. My mother used to look forward to it so much that I often wish she was still alive. Now, she could sit there as often as she wished.

The colliery where the statues and stone ornaments were taken and installed is now nearly finished and I have already applied to the National Coal Board to see if I can have them back to where they rightly belong. I've found ornaments from here in all sorts of unexpected places and up to now I have been able to get them back.

My nephew, Freddy Bullock, is now head forester in Lincoln and he is still helping us to set Norwegian spruce trees on land we have reclaimed. We are hoping to set three or four thousand of these trees every year on land that our pigs have cleaned.

The rebuilding of the stables into a dwelling house and the reclaiming of land from scrub and swamp have been a major operation, for so few of us to tackle with such small capital resources. Enthusiasm and endeavour have had to be used to make up for the lack of labour and money.

My two children, Josephine and James, although still very young help as much as they can and each have their own responsibilities. Josephine intends to be a veterinary surgeon and she is responsible for keeping hens, to provide the family with eggs. She has a flock of Muscovy ducks. She shows marked skill in handling our sows and at week-ends she looks after the baby pigs. We have bought James a small sit-down mower—he'd ride on this all day—and he keeps all our lawns well trimmed. He likes building and for a small boy he does really well, laying bricks and plastering walls.

For the first seven years we were down here my wife kept on working and the money she earned along with the money presented to me by the union on my retirement was spent on purchasing the lake and the swamps so we could develop all the land surrounding the house.

I was doing a bit of broadcasting and every penny we could spare we were using to pay for development.

*Them and Us*

We are quite proud of our achievement and can say with the poet:

> Happy the man whose wish and care
> A few paternal acres bound.
> Content to breath his native air
> In his own ground.
>
> Whose herds with milk, whose field with bread,
> Whose flocks supply him with attire.
> Whose trees in summer yield him shade,
> In winter fire.

This poem really does express our feelings. Yes, the last ten years have been very busy. We have worked very hard indeed but it has been very rewarding work. We have something tangible to show for our efforts. We have recovered valuable land from swamp. We have set out plantations on scrubland. We have made ruined stables into a beautiful home. We have been able to entertain many visitors from all walks of life and many of my old friends from Fryston come down to see me.

CHAPTER TWENTY-ONE

# THE UNIONS

The last ten years has seen the union I led grow stronger and become consolidated. Leading officials of our union have made visits to Europe and behind the Iron Curtain.

These overseas visits can be of very real value to trade union leaders. You can see and hear things about conditions and terms of employment. You learn about their history and this can only enlarge your knowledge of men and their work.

Different countries, different opinions. The Polish miners, for instance held us responsible for the 1939 war.

On that visit our interpreter was a Polish miner who had learned his English while working down the pit in Pontefract during the war. As a result he spoke really broad Yorkshire; the dialect of our County's mining men.

The rest of our delegation which came from different parts of England, couldn't understand a word he said. So they had to give their questions to me so that I could put them to him on their behalf. Then I had to explain his answers back again.

The Poles proved excellent hosts and we were free to go down their mines and into their factories, colleges, hospitals, research centres and convalescent homes.

The dinners were real tests of endurance, very different from official dinners at home. Toasts were drunk with great gusto and enthusiasm by anybody at any time before, during or after dinner. At one big feast in Warsaw, I gave up counting—or was unable to count—after thirty toasts. Towards midnight I solemnly moved: "Freddie Trueman coupled with the name of Leeds United." Everybody drunk it with the utmost enthusiasm.

We also saw a German concentration camp where over a

million Jews had been murdered. The place had been kept intact, just as it was when the Russians surprised the Germans and captured it in full operation. Our guides were former inmates of the camp. Did they hate the Germans!

As we went round the camp we noticed we were being followed by a party of Germans. I asked: "If you hate them so much, why are your guides making such a fuss over them?"

"Those are East Germans," replied our guide. "They weren't responsible for what happened here. It was the West Germans who did all this."

We visited a famous salt mine in the centre of Poland, used by the Germans as a bomb-proof factory.

To me, as a mining engineer, the method of roof support used to hold excavations large enough to take a full size tennis court and gymnasium was really amazing. There was an underground cathedral with pulpit, pews and altar, all in solid salt. All round this underground cathedral there were carvings depicting the whole life of Jesus from his birth to his crucifixion. All done by members of the same family, generation after generation had worked there for years.

It was interesting to me—in a Communist state—to see the reverence always shown by our guides and by the Polish leaders when they were in a cathedral. They always genuflected and made the sign of the cross before the statues of Jesus or the Virgin Mary.

New towns and villages were being built all over Poland and all had a Catholic church included in the planning. The leaders openly admitted that it had to be done to keep the people quiet.

We were repeatedly assured and indeed witnessed the equality among the sexes. We were told there was no prostitution in Poland, but it was suggested by one of our guides that a possible explanation could be that the ladies found sex so enjoyable that they couldn't conscientiously charge for it.

It is difficult when you cannot understand a word of the language. In a broadcast I gave in Poland, I said I had noticed an absence of make-up on the faces of the Polish women and that the children were remarkably well dressed. The man who

## The Unions

was interpreting the broadcast said, "Mr. Bullock says Polish women are so beautiful and are so well fed that they don't need make-up but English women have to use make-up to hide the ravages of hunger. British children are nowhere near as well dressed and well fed as Polish children."

The Polish miners work very hard. Women still work at the surface of the mines and for eight hours a day, six days a week.

Their system of pay is different to ours. They have a small weekly wage and then a share-out based on productivity at the end of the month. All officials and workpeople share in this.

Many incentives are given for good work such as better flats, washing machines, television sets and better and longer holidays.

It is significant, however, that if their performances slacken the incentives are withdrawn.

The pithead buildings are all under one roof and are like a huge market-place.

Doctors, dentists, opticians, masseurs, are all housed round the shafts in modern surgeries. Trades Union officials have their offices equal to and next door to the managers.

The Polish mineworker seems very amenable to discipline.

We visited a very gassy pit and when shot firing took place all the underground workers were brought to the surface and went back only when it was all over. This was a safety measure, but I cannot imagine English miners doing this; particularly, going back down the pits if the sun happened to be shining.

Police can fine on the spot for motoring or minor offences.

They certainly gave our driver a going-over because he nearly ran over a young miner.

"Forty years of work left in him. He fills four thousand tons a year. If you had killed him Poland would have lost one hundred and sixty thousand tons of export coal."

By the time the police had finished with our driver he looked —and felt—as if he had wrecked the whole Polish economy.

While visiting Germany it struck me very forcibly that countries who had lost the war and been completely devastated by it should be now in a much better position than those who

## Them and Us

were supposed to have been the victors. Their factories and mines had been rebuilt. The people were all working harder and the whole nation seemed to be more prosperous than we were.

At a dinner given in our honour by the German mine owners, I was talking about the British sense of humour and said I had never once heard a German tell a joke. The Chairman replying to my speech said he would correct Mr. Bullock's impression and told the story of two German miners, named Hans and Fritz, who lived on the top floor of a new twenty-five storey block of flats.

The lift serving all the floors closed down at midnight. Hans and Fritz had been out drinking, got very merry, and arrived at the foot of the lift at nearly 1 a.m. The lift was closed down for the night. They pondered a bit and Hans said, "I'll tell you what we'll do—we'll climb one flight of stairs, sit down, and I'll tell you a funny story—then we'll climb another flight of stairs, sit down, and you can tell me a funny story."

Fritz thought this a good idea and so the long climb started and it didn't seem so bad after all. When they got next to the top floor they were both breathing very heavily and Hans said, "I've saved the funniest story until the last."

"Good," Fritz said. "Let's be hearing it and get to bed."

Hans' story was very brief: "I've forgotten the key."

So it seems the Germans have a sense of humour after all.

Of all the countries in Europe I have visited I felt by far the most at home in Holland. The Dutch are so much like us in every way. Nearly every person, man, woman or child I met could speak English. What is more, they liked us and were not ashamed to let us know they liked us.

The Poles blamed us for the war.

The Germans resented the destruction of their cities.

The French were a little snooty and superior.

But the Dutch knew that the British armies had liberated their country. It was our airmen who fell at Arnhem. It was British soldiers who were so well behaved in their country. The Dutch will never forget it.

I made friends in Holland who are friends today.

## The Unions

The Dutch people have had a greater upheaval in their mining industry than we have had. North Sea Gas there—is a reality. They have tackled their displaced labour problems in a way that is an example to the world. They are a clean, tidy race with Catholics and Protestants living amicably together.

Through this travelling—and because of it—my knowledge and experience have grown. Our union has never had a strike, it has had no go-slows, no refusing to co-operate and progress in terms and conditions of employment have constantly improved.

It is an acknowledged fact in most circles that management in publicly owned industries do not receive salaries commensurate with their responsibilities, nor do they compare favourably with some sections of privately owned companies. No government should allow a situation to develop where only those unions with the opportunity, or desire to strike, should be receiving salary increases above the "norm" laid down by the government.

It is all wrong that anybody who works in a vital industry, an industry on which our exports depend, or one that could paralyse our lines of communication, or bring transport to chaos, should be able to hold the country to ransom, and then get increases that are denied to people who are doing work that is just as important, but not as vital to our export market.

This causes even the most level headed and law abiding citizens to become frustrated and to do things completely out of character—such as schoolteachers. It is fundamentally wrong for any employer or government to exploit the loyalty of huge, hard-working sections of our community. These are not idle words. I have heard people in positions, who ought to know better, say, "Oh, well, they won't go out on strike, let them wait a bit."

If any government wants a Prices and Incomes Policy to really work they must not only *be* fair but *seen* to be fair to all sections of the community, management and men.

The union leader of an important union, who has the strike weapon at his disposal, is not of necessity any better or even as good as his counterpart who leads another union, but owing to the circumstances under which they both operate the leader with the strike weapon at his disposal can get better increases than his counterpart.

Good leadership of a union should be rewarded by fair play from the government and the employer. In an ideal society advantage would not be taken by either side of strengths or weaknesses. I have constantly pleaded, and worked hard to achieve, a plan to train all management in "labour relations" but this should not apply to management only. Trade union leaders should have training. While experience is a great teacher experience is not the only training for trades union leaders. The should not be appointed to top jobs without being fitted to carry the responsibility and the power.

Probably the subject they should try and specialize in should be management relations.

Many union leaders in the past have developed from "narks" often from those who have no desire to work hard at a monotonous job, and have no desire to study hard or to achieve higher positions. Trades union leadership, same as the managerial class, are alike in the fact that you can get good ones; some not so good; and some who never ought to be in these positions at all.

While I was negotiator for management I used every avenue I could conceive. I shouted, threatened, pleaded, exploited the "more in sorrow than in anger" technique, I called on the experience I gained as a young man from listening to the old miners' leaders' negotiators and the coal owners' representatives.

In addition, however, the officials of the management union when negotiating, tried to use sound common sense based on the righteousness of our case. Even so, we never got all we wanted but we did bring order and reason into things instead of chaos. We did negotiate a salary grading structure so designed that we could negotiate for all our members at once instead of many different groups.

We persuaded our members to share things they had such as free coal, and also to share things that were bad, such as redundancy. We persuaded them to accept the transfer of management from Scotland and Wales or any Area where redund-

## The Unions

ancy was bad, knowing full well that any person so moved could delay the promotion prospects of the individual who had agreed to the move.

One is delighted to be able to say that men who had no previous experience, of the oft stated principles, of the brotherhood of trades unionism, could and did act in such a way.

It has been a real privilege to me to have been unanimously elected year after year to be their national leader. During that period I have often had to ask them to do and accept unpopular things which we as leaders felt would be for their ultimate good and for the good of the industry. Never once did they refuse.

People who have not much knowledge of industry have the idea that it must be an easy task leading a management union. They forget that most members of management are capable of thinking for themselves. They know the facts as well as anyone else. They are qualified, intelligent people. They do not accept: "That it is so because I say so." It only "is so" if they can see and agree that the facts are in line with the decision.

In our union we have had continuity of leadership for over twenty years. We have only had two presidents and only two general secretaries. This I think is a good thing. You get accustomed to each other's style. You can plan ahead and most important you have to take responsibility for your own decisions.

How different this is from Ministers of the Crown, for in my period as national president I have had to work with at least ten ministers and at one period we had three different ministers in twelve months.

It is difficult to get a good understanding or even a working basis with ministers when they change as quickly as this. We got on with them all fairly well but we got on better with some than with others.

What different types you meet. With some you can hardly get a word in, they are so busy trying to impress you with what they know. Some hardly speak at all, they are "the good listener type", and the best of leaders get tired of talking to themselves.

Some puff at their pipes, look very wise and you know that

at the end of the day they are going to say, "Leave it with me, I'll think about it." You often wonder if they will.

Some agree with every word you say. But! Some don't agree with anything you say.

The best are those that listen, then answer, and give some sound logical explanation for their answer. They will explain the government policy and decisions.

Experience teaches you to sort them out, even mysterious politicians cannot hide their weaknesses for long and their strengths become apparent.

I know it is necessary for ministers to occupy different posts to gain experience but I would like it to become possible for a minister to stay in one post long enough to enable him to convince the people he has to meet that he does understand the basic problems of the industry for which he has been given ministerial responsibility.

CHAPTER TWENTY-TWO

# RETIREMENT

In 1968, I reached the age of sixty-five and the time had come for me to retire. The industry and the management union were going through a very difficult period. The industry had just been re-organized, Divisions had been abolished. The number of Areas reduced, pits were closing and redundancy was very serious.

It was a real compliment and testimonial to me when our national conference asked me to stay on as president for another year. I am glad that I accepted their invitation but I wouldn't have stayed any longer for many reasons.

A different generation was growing up.

New modern techniques were being introduced.

Much younger men were now in responsible posts.

Most of my contemporaries were retired.

It was now time for me to do what I had always wanted to do to get out while I was still fit and capable. I wanted our members, in general, and the conference in particular, to remember me as a man in full possession of his faculties, able to conduct his own arguments, to stand on his own two feet. I never had wanted to carry on in office until I was an object of pity and was re-elected out of sentiment and sympathy. Above all I wanted to devote more time to my family. My wife had been very patient for many years. She had carried the responsibility of our small farm on her shoulders for long periods. Very often she had been in this lonely place with just the two children for company. I wanted to enjoy my children's companionship. I wanted to exploit to the full the good fortune that I had had, in that I have had two families and now

## Them and Us

I wanted the opportunity to avoid making any of the mistakes that I might have made with my first children.

I wanted to be able to go to bed, sleep soundly, with no fear of the telephone ringing in the middle of the night. I wanted to spend some time shooting, developing the land I had bought, setting more trees, rearing my pigs and sheep. I wanted time to sit down quietly and think, there is so little time amid the stress and strain of modern life to sit quietly and think. This alone is worth retiring for.

So my last conference came and during it, and before it, I went through a period that is both pleasant and sad. So many committees to attend for the last time.

So many annual functions to attend for the last time.

These sad occasions can be humorous if you have a sense of humour. The British coal industry is one of the biggest industries in the world, but even so it has only one chairman.

The chairman of the National Coal Board also chairs most of its committees and is the leader of most of its social functions. So from April 1968 to May 1969 practically every time Lord Robens and I met we were saying good-bye. I felt quite concerned about the strain I thought it would place on his command of words or suitable phrases. I needn't have worried, he rose to every occasion. He said good-bye to me fourteen times and, as far as I can remember, he never repeated himself once. Marvellous! I still don't know how he managed it. He is sincere enough, and I'm conceited enough, to believe that he meant all he said.

On the last occasion we met he came to Yorkshire to make a presentation to me on behalf of all the Yorkshire Colliery Management and he came to my home and saw just what we had done and what we were planning for the future. He understood what we had achieved and he understood it in terms of bricks and mortar, of sand and cement. When he was an M.P. he had a pig farm of his own, so he knew the work involved.

I have looked on him for a long time as a personal friend. We've had our disagreements, but I was always sure of one thing, he had the good of the industry at heart, and if every-

## Retirement

body had worked as hard and as skilfully as he has done the coal industry would be in a better position than it is in today.

On the night of my presentation in Doncaster the big ballroom at the Danum Hotel was crowded with men and women from all over this vast coalfield who had come to say farewell and wish me a long and happy retirement—I hope their wishes come true.

Lord Robens made a speech that suited the occasion. I enclose extracts from it, he said:

"It's no mean achievement to rise from pony driver to the president of the coal industry's management union. That's what Jim has done. I have known him a long time. When I first came in contact with him he had just written a long letter to *The Times* objecting to my appointment. It was not a letter denegrating me but a powerful plea for promotion inside the industry and I agreed with his sentiments. Jim would have made a success in anything he undertook. This afternoon I have seen what he has done at his own place. I've done a bit of this reconstruction work but what I had seen this afternoon staggered me. I looked on it in terms of cement and sand, in physical effort and I was amazed.

"Jim Bullock never missed an opportunity, when he invited me as a guest to any of his functions or when he came as a guest to one of mine, of nailing me to my chair while he did a bit of negotiating. In the scores of these sort of functions which we attended together, if ever I sat next to him—which I invariably did—I knew the meal wasn't going to be as good as all that. He always seizes every opportunity of putting some difficult case for the people he represents. I always felt it would be churlish of me if I didn't respond. I like him and admire him.

"I'll just end my remarks by paying my tribute to your president, who sits as president for the last time. For years he has led you all with great skill. There will never be another Jim Bullock, whoever succeeds him. His approach, his methods, his tactics are essentially his own, and some people don't like his methods or his style, others enjoy his refreshing candour with which he approaches any task. I belong to the latter. I support

## Them and Us

Jim Bullock. I like his invigorating straightforwardness. He talks and argues hard, but he is from a hard industry and he represents the mining industry. It is an industry which produces men who fearlessly speak their minds and do not engage in double talk. Shakespeare said: 'It is not in mortals to command success, but we will do more, deserve it.' Jim has not commanded success, he has deserved it. In his success has been the steadily improving situation of management in mining and upon the foundations which he has laid, so securely and so well, people coming after him will find they can build an edifice much more easily than if he had founded it, and left it, on sinking sand."

Lord Robens then turned round to me and said:

"Jim, I pay you my personal tribute. You have done a magnificent job for your members and for the whole of the mining industry. I have felt proud and privileged to have worked with and alongside you, and to argue with you, but there has never been any doubt that we had one common objective—the success of the great mining industry in which we occupy so much of our time and in which we have such tremendous faith and confidence."

Since that evening I have received presentations from many of our branches and many of our members from all over the country, pipes, tankards, plaques, but none has pleased me better than a really beautiful illuminated address presented to me on behalf of all the union and which reads as follows:

"James Allen Bullock who was a founder member of the British Association of Colliery Management from its inception in 1947 until his retirement in May, 1969. We are indebted to him for his wise counsel, competence and advice over this period and for these qualities he has earned the respect and admiration of us all. He has served as an executive officer, as chairman of the Yorkshire branch of the Association and of the National Executive Committee. From May, 1956 to May, 1969, he was the National President of the Association. In this capacity his outstanding qualities of leadership won our respect and admiration. He was a great negotiator, a wise counsellor and a shrewd adviser.

# Retirement

"This address is designed to record for posterity the acknowledgement by the members, of his outstanding and distinguished services to the British Association of Colliery Management in particular, to the mining industry of the United Kingdom in general."

These sort of tributes are happy reminders of the days that are gone. Many people have wondered how I would take to the leisure of retirement after having been busy for so long. To them I would say, "Don't worry, the only worry I have is there are not enough hours in the day to enable me to do all I want to do."

I have no problems with my retirement for I am busy all day long with writing, broadcasting occasionally, reading, helping my two small children with their homework, which I find is becoming more and more difficult each term. Josephine is quite happy at Wakefield Girls' High School, James is just as happy at Silcoates School for Boys. Both of them are getting more and more interested in this place every day.

My first family are now all grown up and happily married. Marie has two girls and a boy, and Diane has two girls. Jane, my eldest grand-daughter gives me cause for great pride, she went to Normanton Grammar School, was the head girl there, in her examinations she took twelve "O" levels, took her "A" levels and is now at London University studying to be a barrister. My other grand-daughter, Marney—these are Marie's children, is also going to Normanton Grammar School and doing quite well. Both my daughters presented me with sons-in-law that if I could have chosen them myself I wouldn't have chosen anyone different.

My wife, Jay, is now in full charge of the farm and I give her the benefit of my advice which sometimes she accepts and sometimes she doesn't.

Turning from mining engineer, trade union leader, to be a farmer is not easy. I don't believe there is such a thing as a gentleman farmer today and if there is I certainly couldn't be one but I do know enough about farming to know that we are all working as hard as ever we did for returns—in terms of finance—less than we both earned when we were "working".

## Them and Us

The satisfaction we receive, however, far outweighs monetary things.

It is a wonderful thing to walk round your own grounds, in your own time and to have so many pleasant and rewarding thoughts, to be surrounded by one's family, to have visits from one's friends.

Wise old David Grenfell once said to me:

"When you get to be seventy, if you have enough friends, to count them on the fingers of one hand you are a very, very lucky man." I have that number of friends so I am lucky.

As I walk round my own land and occasionally see a pheasant feeding, or a wild duck flying my mind goes back to my poaching escapades. A year or two ago I decided to rear my own pheasants. The experience I gained through this venture was sufficiently costly for me to determine that I would never poach another bird again as long as I lived. We bought twenty bantam hens to sit two hundred and forty pheasant eggs. We bought twenty coups and runs. When the pheasants started hatching they suffered from every disease the mortal mind could conceive. Our place—having been neglected so long—was over-run with all manner of vermin. The young pheasants were killed by rats, stoats and weasels. They were carried off by crows and hawks. They were killed by cats and finally out of over two hundred hatched we reared about seven. I honestly believe it is cheaper to breed children than it is for an inexperienced man to breed pheasants.

My son, James, has certainly inherited my love of shooting and as he develops I think he will have more ability, though I am trying to persuade him to give up seeing if he can shoot straight with his air gun by trying his gun out on our barn windows.

In a long experience one sees death, its heartache and its suffering—sometimes even bringing relief from misery—in many different ways.

A mine manager sees more various forms of death than most people.

One asks oneself: "Can there ever be a right time to die?"

# Retirement

If a child dies we say, "Just at the outset of life, what a waste."

If a teenager dies we say, "Just when he had begun his higher school career or had started work. What a pity."

If death takes place in their twenties we say, "Just got married. Just buying their house. What a shame."

If in their thirties or forties, we say, "His family growing up around him. Just when he is needed most he is taken away. Isn't life unfair?"

If in his fifties we say, "What a thing to happen, his family grown up, his grandchildren around him, his house is paid for, he was just beginning to reap the benefits of all his efforts."

If in his sixties we say, "Fancy, worked hard all his life and then on the very eve of his retirement, which he was looking forward to so much, he dies. He has paid for his pension and never lived to draw it. How awful."

Even when he is over seventy if his wife is still living we say, "What a pity, think of his wife, they were so happy together."

So it goes on. You never seem to be able to die at the right time.

People's reactions to death are as many and varied as the manner of death. If a young man dies you will hear it said by those who have no family connection or particular friendship for him, "Ah well, he didn't live to suffer pain." If he died quickly they say, "It's the best way, he didn't know anything about it and nobody will ever know what suffering he has missed."

If death comes in middle life the same sort of person will say, "At least he has seen his family grown up and he will not have to endure old age."

If death comes after long illness: "What a happy release."

If the person dies when he is drawing his pension: "He's had a good innings. What else can you expect?"

It all depends on how closely you are connected and on your point of view.

I have seen death in many forms. I have been there when it has happened suddenly. I have been there when it has happened to imprisoned men slowly. I have been at the death-bed. I have heard miners cry: "Don't let me die." "O God, help me." Some curse, some ask the question very seriously: "I am not going to die, am I?"

One night I was taking the chair at a concert in the local village and during the performance a note was passed to me—telling me that one of my deputies was entombed behind a huge fall of rock in the Flockton Seam.

A manager never broadcasts things like this for fear of causing panic, so I asked one of our local people to take the chair, went quietly out of the room, tapping one or two miners on their shoulders as I passed and beckoning them to follow me.

Outside I told them what had happened. Typical of miners, without any comment, they went straight to the pithead baths, changed into their pit clothes, and we were all at the scene of the accident in less than half an hour.

The fall had occurred at the entrance to a thin seam, only two feet six inches high, and one hundred and fifty yards long. The fall at the entrance to the seam had been followed by another fall of stone at the exit from the seam and the deputy was alone, in between the two falls.

Nobody could hear anything, but other men in the seam knew the deputy was trapped and they had sent for me.

On this particular coalface, we had pipes carrying compressed air for use on the face.

These pipes had been dismantled ready to be rebuilt for use on the next day.

I shouted down the pipe which, fortunately, was long enough to go through the fall of stone and to my delight I heard the deputy reply. His first question was: "Is Mr. Bullock there?"

"Yes," I replied.

"Thank God. The water is rising and I am completely trapped. Please Mr. Bullock get me out."

"How deep is the water?" I asked.

"Over a foot, and its rising," came the reply.

"Keep still, we'll get you out." I said this much more optimistically than I felt.

I again experienced the awful responsibility that a manager feels in times like these and the real sterling courage and strength of miners.

We couldn't possibly shift the whole heap of rock, we hadn't time, the imprisoned man would certainly have drowned.

So I told the men we would make a hole just large enough for a man to lie flat, pass dirt back under his body to the next man, and we would form a human chain. One man at the front digging, the next man holding on to his ankles and so on.

This is a real hazardous undertaking. One false move and the whole heap of dirt would have collapsed on the men attempting rescue.

Every man there knew this but they never hesitated. They knew the danger but they also knew that a man's life depended on their efforts.

Without a word being spoken, unaided by any machinery, just strength, courage, and the skill of our calling, enabled us to tunnel through to the trapped man.

When he saw the first glimmer of light he literally screamed with relief.

This was the real danger. Would he panic? Would he rush towards us? Would he disturb the stone we had yet to move and cause all of us to be buried?

I talked to him like a son though he was a much older man than myself. I talked to him firmly too, but I shall never forget the grip of his hands as I stretched out my hands to his. There was no fear of him letting go. It was like a drowning man clutching a straw.

Everybody then pulled quietly backwards, all holding on to each other's ankles, all except the deputy who was coming out head first. When we got him safely out, what was his attitude? Had he prayed? For if ever a man had faced death in the face, he had.

He told me later that he hadn't given up hope until he realized the water was rising and then all he hoped for was that somebody would get me, as he knew I would get him out somehow.

I asked him: "Did you think about God?"

*Them and Us*

"I didn't," he said. "I thought I would like to write a note to the wife but I had nothing to write on."

The miners who helped in his rescue reacted typically:

"What! Have we come out of a concert to dig for a b—— deputy?" But their handshakes with the deputy said far more than any words could have done.

When we got out of the pit the concert was over, so we went to my office and had a drink. Not one miner said to me, "Are you going to recommend me for a medal?" It never entered their heads.

Some deaths, however, made more impression on me than others.

First, when I was eight, and my eldest brother got killed down the pit, I was affected more by the suffering and sadness of my father and mother and of his widow than any personal loss on my part. The gap it left in his children's life, the hardships his family endured in those days were much worse then than now but the effects of other people affected me more than his death did.

Later, in my youth, I was present at the death of my mother. This was the biggest personal tragedy I had experienced to date. It is the different attitude of the person dying that makes it interesting—in sudden death there are no attitudes.

During an illness, when the person knows they are dying, however, it is a totally different thing.

My mother knew she was dying, she was a Christian, and she died like one. Faith in her beliefs were with her until the end.

She died softly murmuring the twenty-third psalm, "Even though I walk through the valley of the shadow of death, Thou art with me," etc. etc.

Then weakly she looked at each of us and told us not to weep, she was only going before us.

My father accepted her death like a true Christian. "Thank God for allowing us to have known her, to have loved her and to have been loved by her for so long."

But, to my young man's inquiring mind I couldn't help but ask myself: "Why should this happen? My father is so much

## Retirement

older than she. She is so much kinder to us. He has been expecting death ever since I was born. Why, oh why, should my mother die before him?"

Many years later my father—a Christian most of his life, a man who had seen scores of people across the river, a man who said there was nothing to fear in death—now lay on his death-bed, but what a difference.

There was none of the quiet peace and serenity like my mother's passing, no murmuring by him of the twenty-third psalm, no saying as I had heard him before: "I am coming, Lord, coming now to Thee." And I reminded him: "There is one thing, Dad, *you know* where *you* are going. You've always taught us to have no fear of death."

To my complete astonishment he replied, "It's all reight, for thee. It's not thee that's dying, it's me. Nobody has been back to tell us."

This shattered me and again added to my puzzlement about the beliefs we had been taught and the mystery of eternal life.

There were no doubts in the minds of my sisters, however; nothing disturbs their faith. My eldest sister, herself a grandmother, and over sixty, said, "Let's all kneel down and ask God's help and blessing for we are all orphans now."

I don't scoff or ridicule this kind of faith, it just never ceases to amaze me. But these experiences often made me wonder what would be my attitude if I came face to face with death.

One of the differences between humans and animals is, that every human being knows that the surest thing in life is death, and that some day we shall have to face it one way or another.

Always I had a secret hope that when the time came for me to die I would at least be given an opportunity to think about it, to have the mental capacity to put my house in order —and to make my peace with things in general.

Since I started writing this book this opportunity has been given. For one morning last summer I was working like mad mixing cement and sand to build a pigsty, when a violent pain, such as I had never had before, struck me in my chest, I collapsed. The doctor was sent for and I heard him tell my wife that I had had a coronary thrombosis, that I must be sent to hospital straight away and that he feared the worst.

Within minutes I was in the heart ward of Pontefract Infirmary surrounded by doctors and nurses. I don't know what they did for me but the terrible searing pain went and left me feeling very weak. I had no pain, I was completely and utterly relaxed and for the first time in my life I was experiencing perfect and absolute peace of mind and body. Surely, I said to myself, "This is death; and if it is, it is wonderful."

Whether it rained, whether the harvest was ruined, whether the sows farrowed, never entered my mind.

No visions of my past life, sins, successes, failures, good deeds or bad deeds came floating through my mind. No thought of the future, no thoughts of eternity, no thoughts of religion, no thoughts of those who had gone before and strangely no thoughts of those that remained, just this lovely feeling of tiredness and absolute serenity of mind.

Later that night my family came to see me and as a special favour the sister on the ward let my wife bring in my young daughter and son. I was ill all right but not too ill to realize the real anguish and sorrow in their faces. Their gentle question: "You'll be coming home soon, Daddy, won't you?" will live with me as long as I live. They were too young to pretend. I knew they meant it and it made all the difference to my mental outlook. They didn't ask to be born and I realized that at their age they really needed me. This is a great thing when you are growing old: to feel you are still needed. It makes all the difference and my desire to live and get well was much stronger after they left my bedside.

I quickly felt better, but I was kept in hospital until the staff had finished all their exhaustive tests.

It was with great relief that my own doctor came down a week or two later and told me that although I had all the signs and symptoms of a coronary, I had not had one. I was all right, but I had to treat what I had had as a warning. I had to cut down on smoking, I had to cut down on the amount of work I tried to do and to regulate all the things that could be harmful.

# Retirement

So, I also, have faced death, for there is no doubt they thought I was dying... and so did I.

My reaction was such that I don't dread it any more, I have no more fear of the unknown—although I have great fear of pain—but I know now what my attitude to death is.

Retirement can present real problems to people who have always been active. Inactivity and boredom can be great killers.

To have been an important person, a person in authority, to have been a useful citizen, a good worker, and now suddenly to feel you are in danger of becoming a vegetable, not needed any more except on odd occasions, is too much for some people to bear. Time drags, friends die, travelling becomes difficult and loneliness creeps in.

Personally I think it is a mistake to retire to some strange seaside town where you are unknown, and where you have no friends. One might do this to fulfil a young man's dream that you had when you enjoyed sea bathing, running on the sands, and visiting amusement arcades. When you retire these pastimes have not the same attraction. The best thing to do is to get some interest, to give yourself something to live for, even if you have no family, but have a small garden, you could buy and sell unusual trees or plants and shrubs. Then, if you are anything like me, you'll want to live out of sheer curiosity to see what sort of stuff you've bought.

Yes! it's been an exciting, full life. I have seen many records made and many records broken. There has been many achievements and I have made many mistakes.

But there is one thing that, if it isn't a record, can't be far from being a record. That is, one hundred and ten years elapsed between the birth of my *father* and the birth of my *son*, James!

My chief desire now is to live long enough to see my young family grow up.

I'd also like to live long enough to see what does eventually happen to the mining industry.

I've no burning desire to be young again. I've enjoyed my life. I want to keep on being healthy enough, to continue to enjoy it.

## Them and Us

A fitting verse to end this book is one that I read the other day, a verse that I am sure my wife would agree with, as would also Mr. Tyler, the general secretary of our union and a close colleague for many years—

> In all thy humours whether grave or mellow
> Tha's been such a touchy, testy, pleasant fellow.
> Thou has so much wit and mirth and spleen about thee
> There's been no living with thee or without thee.

# THE LAST WORD
## by
## LORD ROBENS

This has been the story of a man's life. A man who exchanged the promotion his natural abilities and professional skill could have brought him in the ordinary flow of events, in order to devote himself to the service of his Coal Board colleagues in the management team. Had he remained in Management he would undoubtedly have reached the top of the tree. He combined the absolute essentials in modern Management, his own mining engineering qualifications obtained the hard way and a unique ability to deal with people. It did not matter to Jim Bullock whether it was Eton or Oxford he was talking to or the fifteen-year-old without any "O" Levels straight from school. He knew how to handle both and everyone in between. There will never be another Jim Bullock, he was as much hewn out of the solid earth as the mineral he spent a lifetime in winning. He could never be anything but himself. Blunt, frank, fresh as a daisy with an immense streak of good humour that flashed out like the gleams of gold in the gold prospector's pan, he was never humble but nevertheless always respectful.

In all my dealings with him, and we were on Christian name terms, he never took advantage of the friendly familiarity that existed between us. He was a character. He was a rough diamond, literally enjoying his strong Yorkshire accent and idioms. He was forceful and could be righteously indignant, but never to the point of quarrelsomeness. His members never knew, and indeed they will never know, how much he achieved for them by these endearing qualities. He was a trade union leader who could really deliver the goods and he was able to do this because he never made a promise or gave an undertaking that he could not carry out.

## Them and Us

As he recalls he was opposed to my appointment because he believed that after a decade of nationalization the industry should have produced its own Chairman from within its own ranks. This was not opposition to me as a person, indeed upon our first meeting he made this quite clear with characteristic candour. The principle that he ennunciated was quite right in my view, and my pleasure and his instinctive judgment were consummated when, upon my own retirement as Chairman of the National Coal Board, the subsequent appointment of Chairman was indeed from the industry. In 1960 those who were in the position to make these decisions evidently thought otherwise. Perhaps they considered that the time was not yet ripe in the changing situation of the industry and the traumatic experience that was just beginning and lasted for another decade, to do other than bring in someone from outside. However, the choice fell upon me and so my first encounter with Jim Bullock was via his letter to *The Times* objecting to my appointment.

It was hardly a good start, but, typical of the man, within twelve months he had written to *The Times* again, and on this occasion said that whilst his sentiments were right his conclusions were wrong. He didn't leave this retraction only with a single letter to *The Times*. On more than one occasion at meetings of his members at which I was present, he not only repeated his new-found conviction, but used to spell out in clear and unmistakable terms why he had changed his mind. It was all very simple to him. "We have the same Management," he used to say, "we have the same men, we have the same pits, the only change we have is the Chairman. What else could explain the metamorphosis on our industry but the advent of Robens," all this said with the vehemence of an Oxford Grouper in the '30s, and his members loved it. Their Jim—the man who spoke his mind even if it meant going back on an equally forceful declaration long before.

He was a great orator, forceful and eloquent, always translating his facts in a logical sequence that brought the thinking of his hearers on to the same wavelength as his own and hence to the same conclusion.

His trade union leadership was not just confined to making

demands for wages and improved conditions for his members, which he did with great vigour and clarity of argument, but he was ready at the drop of a hat to discuss very constructively, the problems of the industry and possible solutions. On these occasions I never felt that I was dealing with a trade union leader but rather with a man who could easily have been a Board member with all the responsibility of Board membership. Not only were we in for massive pit closures year after year, which affected highly qualified Mining Engineers and the other specialisms associated with coal mining, but in addition we were completely reorganizing the whole structure of the apparatus of Management. This alone meant a considerable slimming in addition to the jobs that were disappearing with the closure of every mine. The closure of 400 mines meant the disappearance of a similar number of colliery managers and all their supporting mining Management staff.

This exercise, therefore, was one that called for considerable skill and thought and without the ready, willing and indeed eager co-operation of Jim Bullock, the change could never have been accomplished in the smooth way the operation was finally concluded.

From five levels of senior Management we eliminated two, the Divisional Board and Group Managers disappeared. Thirty-eight Area General Managers gave way to seventeen Area Directors. The large pits that began to emerge, that is pits producing a million tons of coal a year employing 2,000 men or more, required a newer kind of Management than the previously small pits had needed. The speed of mechanization brought completely new problems both of Geology and Management in their turn. Jim Bullock knew and understood all this. He was a practical person himself and his pragmatic approach to these new Management problems made him a tower of strength to both his union membership and the industry. These were the hard testing times for men with responsibility and he showed his sterling worth and quality of character, by refusing to seek refuge, as he might well have done, by saying that these were the Board's problems to solve and that his sole responsibility was merely to safeguard his members' interests. The fact that he took the appropriate view, taking care of his members' interest certainly, but actively sharing and helping in solving the industry's problems, showed the sincerity of the man, his devotion to the industry and courage in facing unpopular decisions.

These qualities and attitudes in trade union officials are, unfortunately, becoming increasingly rare in the newer generation of professional union officials, which is much to be regretted. The philosophy of demanding "What the lads want", irrespective of the consequences is becoming very much the order of the day. But of course it is much easier to be led from below, it requires no original thinking, but it is the negation of real leadership.

No, Jim Bullock was a leader of men in the true sense of the word. He was unique and often travelling in my car I have heard him broadcasting on some experience of his or another, and it could have been Jim sat beside me chatting away, as large as life. All his stories however were interrupted by his own laughter just before he came to the funny bits. By the time he reached the "denouement" you found yourself already laughing because his own laughter was so infectious.

Now he has retired to Swillington Hall, which with loving care and a fantastic amount of hard work, he is gradually restoring. There'll always be a cup of tea, a smoke and a friendly chat full of reminiscences of events and people that have packed his life, for all his old friends who chance to call.

I have a shrewd suspicion that as he sits them in his own cosy study, surrounded by a whole picture gallery of his friends, toasting his slippered feet before a good coal fire, puffing slowly on his pipe, his quiet inward satisfaction is, that the pony boy and his family occupy the old colliery owners ancestral palace. That quiet smile will be playing around his lips for a long time yet. Bless him.